Sober with God

Sober with God

Recovery of the Body, Redemption of the Soul

Joseph Antonio Liao

Book Stack PUBLISHING

Sober with God

Published by Book Stack Publishing OPC
Marikina Heights, Marikina City
1800 Philippines

Some of the names in this book have been changed to protect the privacy of the individuals involved.

Disclaimer: Although the publisher and the author have made every effort to ensure that the information in this book was correct at press time and while this publication is designed to provide accurate information in regard to the subject matter covered, the publisher and the author assume no responsibility for errors, inaccuracies, omissions, or any other inconsistencies herein and hereby disclaim any liability to any party for any loss, damage, or disruption caused by errors or omissions, whether such errors or omissions result from negligence, accident, or any other cause.

© Copyright 2020 by Book Stack Publishing OPC
All rights reserved.

For email inquiries and orders: bookstackopc@gmail.com

Editing by Arla Fontamillas
Cover design by Clarquin Aguilar
Interior design by Jonathan and Mercedita Balignasay

ISBN 978-621-96282-0-4

Printed in the Philippines

Foreword

Joseph Liao, author of Sober with God, has written a book of inspiration and hope coming from the dark years of his struggles with addiction and alcoholism. Hitting "rock bottom", the pains and unrest of his body and soul ceased when he met God as the highest power. After many relapses and unsuccessful attempts to gain recovery, the Lord ultimately destroyed the vile strongholds of addiction in his life.

This book was not written based solely on the theoretical frameworks and standards of medical science, but mostly on the fruitful labor of his experiential learning with the Almighty God. Each grain of truth, harnessed on every page of the book, is timely and relevant. Sober with God provides answers to anyone who desperately seeks absolute deliverance from the realm of self-indulging illusion and deception of drugs.

Indeed, there is no other way to long, lasting freedom for lost souls, except by the sovereign power of God, through our Lord Jesus Christ.

ALFREDO P. CASTRO JR.
—*Pastor*, Jesus Christ the Gospel of
    Salvation Christian Ministry
—*Former Director*, Marikina
    Rehabilitation Center
—*Accredited Rehabilitation Practitioner*,
    Dept. of Health PH

Contents

Introduction

O n that momentous day in 2008, the neighborhood felt calm and holy, despite the constant shrieks of the children playing in the streets. I sat in the living room as the dusky glow from the setting sun bathed the house in gentle light.

Angie, my wife, bedridden with disabilities, was the only other person home. She peered at me, anxiety etched on her face, and I knew she was probably wondering if everything was all right.

I glanced at the wall clock and realized that over thirty-six hours had passed since I last ate any food or drank even a drop of water. My limbs felt feeble, but my mind and senses were keen. Besides the peculiar feelings, a sense of astonishment and tranquility quelled the pangs of hunger and thirst.

If I can endure the fast, I can also survive without drugs.

I was on a complete fast—an offering of repentance to God and a plea for divine healing. For the last two weeks, I had submitted myself to an indefinite, extended fast, with random breaks for small amounts of food and water.

Clutching a Holy Bible and a dated *Our Daily Bread* devotional in my hands, I prayed and meditated on God's Word and presence. The Lord convicted me of sin and disbelief, yet He saw me as worthy of His kingdom.

Amazingly, the drug cravings and the expected withdrawal pains had disappeared. I had always found it extremely difficult to stop taking drugs because of physical distress. The anxiety and depression that had besieged me for decades also faded away.

Since starting the fast, my insomnia vanished, and the food tasted better. For 25 years, I took a tranquilizer before meals to muster a good appetite and a strong sedative to make me sleep at night.

The Devil has fallen!

Not a single pill, or a drop of alcohol, or a puff of methamphetamine passed into my body. To live free and clean of any addictive substance for two weeks was a miracle. With God's help, I have remained sober up to the present time.

The Scriptures underscore the sacred power of prayer and fasting to bring about divine healing. God has instructed His people to fast for absolution and deliverance from extreme satanic bondage such as insanity, demonic possession, mental illness, drunkenness, and addiction.

Today, Christians and believers of various faiths fast for repentance, cleansing, spiritual awakening, and rejuvenation. Fasting also promotes physical and psychological well-being. Modern medical science also attests to the physiological benefits of fasting. It has been proven effective in the treatment and management of cancer, liver disease, cardiovascular diseases, depression, and other mental health disorders.

I was a polydrug user—addicted to methamphetamine ("meth" or "shabu") and benzodiazepines, a group of medication that includes sedatives, tranquilizers, and antidepressants. Alcoholism also consumed me in my earlier professional life. Just like many addicts, I took a variety of drugs to enhance my total psychoactive experience and to produce an increased psychotropic (mind-altering) effect. I took "uppers" to be "high" and combined them with "downers" to induce calm, which prevented me from going over the edge.

In the drug world, the constant up-and-down intoxication is also called "living on a roller coaster." My favorite "downers" were diazepam and midazolam. The pills provided relief for my anxiety, depression, restlessness, and insomnia; meanwhile, meth supplied me with euphoria.

My dependency on drugs, coupled with alcoholism, sent me to the hospital roughly nine times and to a drug rehabilitation facility twice. However, these interventions failed to bring lasting recovery.

Drugs and alcohol are two of the most popular but dangerous substances people use to escape from the miseries in life or to have some plain fun. Like fast food, a pill, a shot of brandy, or a line of cocaine is easily within reach. Ancient organic substances, including alcohol, tobacco, cocaine, marijuana, and opium remain widespread in most parts of the world. New synthetic narcotics such as Ecstasy attract young users because of their novel psychotropic effects.

Drug dependency is a global crisis; every home is a target or a victim. According to the *World Drug Report* 2020 of the United Nations Office on Drugs and Crime (UNODC), approximately 269 million people used at least one drug in 2017. In a World Health Organization (WHO) report published in May 2020, it was found that tobacco kills over eight million people yearly. In addition, the WHO 2018 Global Status Report attributed three million deaths or 5% of all global deaths in 2016 to alcohol. The Philippines' Department of Health reported that there are about four million drug dependents in the country (Mindanao Summit Report, Nov. 2017). From 2018, eye-popping caches of meth and cocaine are frequently flashed on newspapers and TV screens. Despite the government's intensive efforts in curbing drug addiction—mainly through supply reduction and relentless drug arrests, raids, and seizures—the menace persists.

The costs of addiction are high. Drugs shatter family and social lives, compromise upright values, and disrupt education and work. Addicts become vulnerable to AIDS, tuberculosis, hepatitis, and other deadly diseases. Addiction also causes or exacerbates mental illness.

Many people don't possess sufficient and accurate knowledge of the scourge of addiction. Ask a person on the street to define drug dependency, and he probably will not utter a quick reply. Yet, it is highly probable that this problem exists in his home. It's a serious topic, often a dark one, for many people. They refuse to probe deeper into the aspects of addiction because it reminds them of their helplessness and the havoc their families experience because of their addiction.

When addiction strikes, the family is stunned. Rather than taking the right steps, the family members panic, rationalize, and conceal that a crisis exists. Many are more concerned with the social stigma that comes with drug abuse. They ask: *What will our neighbors and friends think?* On the other hand, the addict quickly justifies that it is not her fault that she fell into the destructive habit. She shrugs and proclaims: *The whole world is unfair and full of pain.*

Despite society's innovative legislation surrounding legalization and decriminalization to curb drug dependence, we still wrestle with how to rescue lost souls caught up with harmful substances. We question why our child gets hooked on street drugs and turns into a bum, despite our love and support.

This book demonstrates how God rescues addicts and alcoholics from the besetting tyranny of drug addiction and guides them toward lasting sobriety, recovery, and redemption. It relies on the Holy Bible as its foremost authority and resource, giving utmost care in the faithful adherence to scriptural doctrines. Data from authoritative sources, personal experiences, observations, and testimonies are referenced to substantiate the truth: we are up against an Unseen Enemy.

The essence, understanding, and conquest of substance compulsion are comparable and applicable to other forms of addictions—gambling, digital obsession, food, and other behavioral bondage. If we sneak into the psyche of a person under enslavement, we will find Satan.

My narratives in this book depict how common vulnerabilities, dysfunctional life circumstances, tragedies, and attachments to the cares of this world can make a person faithless and separated from God.

From the 1980s to the 1990s, I was vice president and a principal shareholder of our family firm (Fema Group), one of the top

3000 firms in the Philippines for two decades. Tragedies in the family and business pushed me deep into drugs and alcohol. I fell from the pinnacle of wealth and success to the depths of defeat and despair. Our company closed in 2000, and my wife was paralyzed in 2002 due to a massive stroke. These extreme emotional aches and traumas almost cost me my sanity. In 2017, she also contracted stage-four breast cancer. My beloved Angie passed away in May 2020.

Under bondage for thirty-six years, I experienced and witnessed Satan's relentless and cunning attacks to compel me into his fold. After many unsuccessful treatments and incarcerations, Jesus finally intervened in my life. Despite the family tragedies and loss of valuable relationships, material possessions, and social stature, I have found hope and a new life in Christ. He wiped out my addictions and transformed me into a new creation. He alone drove out evil from the deep recesses of my soul.

The defining motive that moved me to give up taking drugs is the trembling fear that I would eternally rot in hell if I remained a doper. The tremendous guilt and anguish I have inflicted upon myself, my family, and others also became unbearable.

Since 2002, it has been a privilege to share the Scriptures with residents of the Marikina Rehabilitation Center (MRC). Ministering to people in recovery, along with their families in their homes, is also an eye-opener for me on how deep addiction harms the household.

Beyond the diverse secular and professional diagnoses of addiction, it is a revelation that evil lurks in the minds and souls of these drug dependents. As long as Satan is in control of the life of the addicts, drug dependency is chronic and difficult to vanquish.

The ultimate message of this book is that recovery from substance abuse is also about the redemption of the addict from his fallen and sinful state. The road to sobriety is lined with perilous traps and sharp spikes that an addict must surmount to gain true freedom. There's no easy way out. Satan does not just give up.

Yet, with God as our Helper and beacon, addicts can regain control and put order back in their messed-up lives. Maintaining sobriety with a sound mind is a primary goal. Many former addicts who remain drug-free for a long time may still show behavioral abnormalities because genuine sobriety is not achieved. Divine healing assures full recovery of the body and redemption of the soul.

This book is primarily intended for drug dependents, alcoholics, people in recovery, and their families who are held bondage by addictive substances. Many descriptive passages and testimonies in this book attest to the severe and arduous battle with addiction. Positive traits and habits are illustrated, including ways to overcome common barriers that hinder recovery.

This book also emphasizes the constructive roles of families and institutions in providing proper recovery measures and support. Rehabs, churches, support groups, public officials, and lawmakers can also gain added insights and knowledge from this book. Every individual, home, community, or nation is a target of or prey to the drug contagion.

This book is also a great resource, especially during this pandemic. When traditional methods of recovery may not be ideal in rehab, where social distancing and other preventive measures can't be fully implemented, God heals in the confines of our homes.

The COVID-19 pandemic has shown us our utter helplessness on things unseen. Once again, like the Israelites, our faith and reliance on God are being tested as we face death, starvation, and the reality of a radically new way of life. Despite the virus, the drug menace remains.

Ultimately, drug abuse is a spiritual concern—a battle between good and evil. Ephesians 6:12 says, "For our struggle is not against flesh and blood, but against the rulers, against the authorities, against the powers of this dark world and against the spiritual forces of evil in the heavenly realms."

We live in treacherous times. Humanity departs from how God wants us to conduct our lives. We adore false gods, celebrities, rock stars, jobs, pleasures, and possessions. Lord Mammon escalates his onslaught upon humankind, as money and all things unholy replace God as the object of man's treasures and desires.

Worshiping drugs is a slice of what humanity does in pursuit of Satan. The incessant desires of the flesh eclipse the obedience to God. Many people seldom go to Sunday church services, spend quality time with their families, or volunteer in city orphanages. Instead, they prefer to shop and linger in fancy malls, play wild digital games, bask in social media all day long, or get smashed with alcohol and mind-altering substances.

This book will help bring weary and desperate drug users and alcoholics on their knees to worship God as Creator and Divine Healer. God created man to praise and exalt Him. We must offer ourselves to God as an act of love and worship, not sacrifice our bodies to Satan in exchange for instant gratification. I hope and pray that the Lord will fill our homes, which have been trampled by many years of grief and desecration, with serenity, love, and healing.

Addiction as Idolatry

*For you have spent enough time in the past doing
what pagans choose to do—living in debauchery,
lust, drunkenness, orgies, carousing and detestable
idolatry.*
—1 Peter 4:3

Early one morning in 2001, I wandered around the house with a single thought burning in my mind. The disconnected power lines sucked the life out of our home. In the gloomy half-light, I could see the few scattered pieces of furniture—an end table, chairs, a lamp—strewn through the living room and the hallway. Most of the appliances were gone.

Angie reclined silently in bed on the second floor because of her disabilities. All of our three children were out of the house.

Restless and jittery, I headed outside toward my favorite spot—a round patch of rough concrete in the middle of our yard. Wild, green shrubs surrounded the lawn, and a tall Narra tree stood majestically in a corner against the sunny sky.

I paced in circles. My nerves snaked through my pores, crawling in and out of my skin. A painful knot also twisted in my gut.

I've got to get that meth fix. Now! But I have no money.

The intense cravings awakened my crafty, criminal mind. A sinister force compelled me to the living room. I grabbed an oriental vase from on top of my wife's china cabinet—*this is adequate for a drug swap.* I also swiped the wall clock beside the stairway—*it could also suffice as cab fare to the meth house.*

Driven by a desperate need to get high, I hurriedly hailed a taxi. The drug dens were about fifteen minutes away in a busy underbelly of Quezon City. They sporadically dotted a congested compound where most residents were poor.

Upon arrival at the meth zone, I begged the cab driver to accept the wall clock as taxi fare. "I'm sorry, but I have no money," I said. With a grim face, he reluctantly nodded, took the clock, and sped away.

The drug-infested district teemed with users, pushers, runners, and other shady characters darting in different directions. As a regular buyer, I became familiar with the place and knew the dealers and runners by name. Many would swarm all over me whenever I arrived.

Rickety, tiny houses lined the narrow, winding streets inside the compound. Many indigents operated the meth dens in a discrete, but busy manner. Sometimes, the whole family, including young children, was actively involved in the business. As a hidden street bazaar, one could shop around and bargain for drugs. Young children, senior citizens, pregnant mothers, and odd characters milled around and waited for their turns at the day's favorite spot. Addicted police officers always got exclusive use of the place. The preferred den offered the best buy—that is, it is the lowest price, of the best quality, or the most quantity.

Drug characters and wary bystanders lurked in the pathway entrance waiting for new or familiar faces to show up. Like seasoned salespeople, young underlings of pushers competed with one another and swarmed over any arriving, prospective buyer. These charlatans also possessed an uncanny sense of discernment on whether a prospect had ample money for drugs. Congenial and persuasive, they rambled their pitches and pulled the arms of customers to patronize their turf.

Sellers, dealers, runners, or other users often joined or sneaked uninvited into a drug session, took free hits, and gave a friendly rapport. This exasperating practice would often slash the meth purchased by a buyer. However, the dealer would sometimes add free portions if he felt happy or generous. A code of reciprocity prevailed in the dens in which a buyer who shared his drug could have the favor returned the next time he came around. Over time, regular users became comfortable with their circle of dealers and user-friends.

Frauds were common occurrences in these dens, including bizarre, disappointing, infuriating, and scary incidents. A dealer or runner would sometimes vanish in the busy compounds after receiving advance payment for takeout meth. The buyer would curse or scream in frustration after waiting for nothing or for the drug to arrive six hours later. These tricksters often pooled cash payments from several buyers, purchased meth in bulk at a discount, and earned extra cash or portions of meth. They also passed fake meth (made of alum) that looked similar to the real stuff.

A handgun could sometimes be seen tucked in the waist of the dealer in a drug deal. In one session, I saw a firearm on top of a table, alongside worn-out glass pipes, used aluminum strips, and cheap lighters.

One horrifying incident that will stay imprinted on my mind forever was the time I witnessed the accidental death of an infant in the drug lair. A drug-crazed, gun-wielding man intruded our meth session on the ground floor of the den. The stranger pointed the weapon at me and asked, "Is he the one?" He fired the gun, but a companion of the gun-wielder deflected his arm upward toward the ceiling. The stray bullet accidentally hit a baby on the second floor. I panicked and bolted out of the room, pushed past hanging clothes and empty wooden crates, and out into the crowded streets. The high from meth instantly vanished. Instead, a pang of trembling guilt consumed me because a baby had died in my place.

I never knew the culprit or learned the exact circumstances of the incident. However, this horrific episode didn't frighten me enough to stop taking meth. I even went back to the same spot.

Let us get back to my main story. I approached my favorite dealer, uttered a quick hello, and offered the vase in exchange for drugs. After some crude haggling, he agreed and gave me a small sachet of the prohibited substance. I didn't mind the cheap valuation of the vase; it had to go for my needed drug fix. I was more concerned that my wife would notice that it was missing.

Drug dealers seldom entertained swap deals, but typically yielded to regular clients. Sometimes, they would request a favorite comic book, a video, or anything that speaks to their fancy in exchange for drugs.

My hands trembled as I poured the meth into a thin, long, rectangular strip of aluminum foil. I heated the drug with a lighter, puffed its grayish smoke, and wallowed in its strong, initial kick of exhilaration.

The time to leave had come, and I hailed another cab for home. On arrival, I excused myself from the driver and dashed toward the house. Again, I grabbed another wall clock, ran back to the cab, and handed it to the driver as cab fare. After I flashed a stern "take-it-or-leave-it" stare, the poor cabbie relented.

Home at last. The daunting and exhausting part of the day was done.

Soaring on meth, I wandered in a repertoire of useless thoughts and activities. Surfing the internet on peculiar subjects such as astronomy or clandestine espionage was my favorite past time. I once clicked on the CIA website, took their online character test, and passed. The site responded I was competent enough for covert operations. I knew, however, that my application couldn't be completed because I'm not an American citizen.

After more hours of meaningless meanderings, the euphoria wore off. Again, my nerves flared up, and that familiar aching knot formed in my gut. I also felt edgy with the pestering withdrawal pains.

It is time for my benzodiazepines.

I took a few tablets of diazepam to soothe my rattled body and make the ache in my stomach go away. For three decades, I always stocked a ready supply of tranquilizers and took an average of eight (50-mg.) pills per day.

My body could endure a day without meth or alcohol, but running out of pills was unthinkable. The gnawing and excruciating withdrawal aches, which surface after twelve hours from the last intake of pills, were dreadful.

After several hours, the calming effect of the tranquilizers dissipated. Once again, my cravings for more meth appeared. I prepared and smoked another line of the drug from the extra stash I brought home from the drug lair. With a renewed high, I again pandered in a pointless, digital journey on the computer.

To cap the day, I took a strong sedative (midazolam) to knock me off to sleep. In sum, I consumed three types of drugs in twenty-four hours. Another typical day in the life of an addict had passed.

Thirty-Six Years of Bondage

Then your heart will become proud and you will forget the Lord your God, who brought you out of Egypt, out of the land of slavery.
—Deuteronomy 8:14

I started using drugs at the age of nine. My grade school classmates and I found out that speed (amphetamines) and memory pills were helpful when we were preparing for exams. The stimulating effects sharpened our minds during tests, but also caused sleepless nights. These first experiences with amphetamines marked the beginning of my long struggle with drugs and alcohol.

In high school, my friends and I often spent nights at a classmate's house under the guise of studying. Once the parents were asleep, we would take pills and drink alcohol.

Flower power, Woodstock, the peace sign, and psychedelic substances swept the whole world—but especially North America—in the 1960s and 1970s. Many students, myself included, sported waist-long hair and other hippie-like fashions of the time. We idolized rock stars and emulated their perverted manners and lingo. Listening and gyrating to the blaring rock music of the Rolling Stones and Black Sabbath, while strung out on pot, was our favorite pastime. I used to get goosebumps whenever Jimmy Page walloped his lead guitar performing "Stairway to Heaven."

We had access to an array of illicit substances available in the nooks and alleys of Manila. Marijuana was inexpensive and popular with students. We also used LSD, amphetamines, tranquilizers, barbiturates, hashish, and heroin. During parties, we inhaled anesthetics dispensed from a spray glass bottle. To test its intensity, we often bashed our heads against a wall. The numbness also doused our shyness, allowing us to approach girls for a dance easily.

Over-the-counter medicines, such as cough syrup, were also easy to obtain and could induce mind-altering effects. Narcotic laws were lax. Government authorities, including pharmacy assistants, were uninformed about the addictive properties of the latest products.

LSD was very popular. The song "Lucy in the Sky with Diamonds" by the Beatles is often considered about a drug trip—the title itself is thought to be a nod to the acronym "LSD." This substance induces amazing, but frightening colored hallucinations. During my first trip, the effects made me see roads rising from the ground and small butterflies transforming into huge ones. Once, my friends and I went to a mountainside vacation house for an LSD trip. Some of us had to stay sober so we could restrain others from walking off the cliff if they had a bad trip. I had one friend who was institutionalized in a mental hospital after experiencing the harmful effects of the drug.

Our adventurous spirit led us into a countless number of unforgettable and reckless experiences while loaded with narcotics and alcohol. Despite our despicable behavior, we excelled in class and held key positions across school organizations and interschool associations. At my high school graduation, I climbed the stage to receive an honors medal while high on pot.

After high school, our peer group broke up because we all went to different universities. In college, I continued using drugs, and my dependency became destructive. Disorientation, lack of focus, and an impaired memory affected my studies. Once, I threw up beside the school guardhouse in broad daylight because I consumed too much cough syrup. For the first time in my life, I failed some of my subjects, and I experienced panic attacks in class.

Going to school became torture. I was not used to being a mediocre student. Depression and a sense of worthlessness drove me deeper into using other illicit substances. Surprisingly, I hurdled college with a liberal arts degree. Many of my memories from that time, however, remain hazy—including memories about things I learned in class.

After college, I landed a job as a scriptwriter at the National Media Production Center, a government-owned media outfit. After six months, I quit the job and joined my father in our family business. Because I was the eldest son, Dad told me I should succeed him someday as president. Following Chinese business tradition, I started in the lowest ranks and worked my way up the corporate ladder.

I married Angie in 1981, and God blessed us with two sons, Arvin and Aries, and a daughter named Janine. I drew so much joy and comfort from my family. We lived in luxury and had all the trappings of a coveted lifestyle.

However, hedonism and extravagance became the paradigm of our everyday living. We even had four telephone lines inside the house. I used to pick up takeout food after work, despite the knowledge that adequate food was at the dinner table at home. Seeing that dinner was just not good enough, I would finally call for a food delivery service. We abhorred any discomfort. Whenever power disruptions occurred in the neighborhood, we often checked-in into five-star hotels.

We attended church on Sundays, but my presence was devoid of sanctity and worship. I often stood outside smoking cigarettes during the service while looking at girls or thinking about more money.

From the 1980s to the 1990s, I was a director and vice president of our family corporation, engaged in international trade, distribution, and support of office and retail systems. Beneath the success and wealth, however, I became an alcoholic and a benzodiazepine addict.

These substances couldn't seriously hurt me.

I was wrong. I caught a dangerous liver disease and spiraled down into a chasm of drunkenness and bondage. I wanted to believe that drinking alcohol was an essential and customary practice for socialization and doing business. Drinking and girls were nightly escapades with friends, local clients, foreign visitors, and business partners. I gambled in casinos and pandered in promiscuity. Because of my depraved lifestyle, I frequently came home late and spent less time with my wife and children.

This is the life I had dreamed of—full of pleasure and worldly delight.

I knew I became a full-blown alcoholic when I started to drink before breakfast. My hands always trembled, and my body would break out into a cold sweat (delirium tremens) if alcohol was not running in my veins. Whenever these maladies showed up, I would reach for a shot of whiskey as an instant remedy. While driving, a bottle of liquor was often tucked under the front seat of my car, which I could effortlessly pull out for a needed swig. In the office, another bottle of whiskey was also accessible in the bottom drawer of my desk.

After seeing blood in my urine, and the added family pressure that I should seek help, I consulted a psychiatrist. "You are committing slow suicide," he retorted. The doctor diagnosed me as an alcoholic and prescribed anti-anxiety medication and antidepressants to curb my alcoholism.

The medicines successfully wiped out my cravings for alcohol and eased the pains of withdrawal. As a bonus, these pills produced slight euphoria—a fantastic buzz in the head. I felt good and worked better because the annoying hangovers and cravings for alcohol disappeared. My family was pleased because I often went home early after work.

I could settle and be happy with these pills for the rest of my life!

However, these medications soon became a nightmare and another source of dependency. Without them, I could not function and work properly. The pills substituted my addiction to alcohol. A pillbox was always tucked in my pocket so I could quickly reach them at any time. If I missed a dose, my nerves would go haywire, and a painful, squeezing knot would form inside my belly.

I realized the difficulty and hesitation that doctors contend with in prescribing these medications to ward off alcoholism. Like alcohol, benzodiazepines are just as addictive. Most of the time, I exceeded my maximum daily dosage and popped these tablets like candies. My physician always scolded me for the abuse and prescribed substitute pills of different brands, types, shapes, and colors. However, my addiction remained. Despite my protests, he also scaled down my prescription.

To ensure my desired supply of pills, I approached several doctors on rotation, claiming I had insomnia. Physicians were sympathetic to people who can't sleep. I also tricked pharmacies by faking prescriptions. As a registered nurse, my wife had a MIMS (Monthly Index of Medical Specialties) pharmacy book. It enumerated all the medications in the market, including dosages, use, and effects. Over time, I tried most of the medicines listed under the sedatives and tranquilizers group. These unlawful acts had also saved me a considerable amount of money that could have gone to the physicians' fees.

My family preferred the tranquilizers over liquor because the pills resulted in less trouble in our lives. I survived for two years without alcohol, but I soon relapsed and mixed them with pills—a dangerous combination.

Finally, my wife admitted me to a hospital basement (my first treatment) at the Makati Medical Center for alcoholism and addiction to pills. The doctors gave me controlled doses of benzodiazepines to ease the withdrawal pains. I found it strange to be confined to a treatment facility and have my addiction sustained with reduced amounts of pills. I felt I was just on a vacation break.

After three weeks, my attending physician discharged me from the hospital with a firm order that I should stop drinking liquor. For maintenance medication, he again prescribed anti-anxiety pills and antidepressants so I could be sober with controlled and minimized addiction. I surmised the doctor thought it would be better if I remained as a "functional" pill addict than be a drunkard, further damaging my liver and causing more trouble to other people.

Though I was no longer using illicit drugs, my drinking habits became worse. My father often admonished me whenever my drinking made me miss work. However, I always redeemed myself by clinching big deals for the company. Scratching his head, my helpless father often felt perplexed and disgusted because he had a paradoxical son.

Despite my apparent depravity, people still looked at me with respect and high regard. They blindly saw a successful man in a suit. However, behind the wealth and success, a vile spirit strangled my soul.

Between 1985 and 2001, I was admitted around eleven times to several hospitals and drug rehabilitation centers for alcoholism and drug addiction. I failed to achieve lasting recovery and sobriety from these interventions.

The Altar of Meth and Pills

Put to death, therefore, whatever belongs to your earthly nature: Sexual immorality, impurity, lust, evil desires, and greed, which is idolatry.
—Colossians 3:5

At the foot of Mount Sinai, the Israelites became restless, waiting for their leader Moses who went up to the mountain to meet with

God. Driven by desperate anxiety and their ever-wavering faith in God, they looked for another deity to worship. They chorused, "Come, make us gods who will go before us. As for this fellow Moses who brought us up out of Egypt, we don't know what has happened to him" (Exodus 32:1[b]). Led by Aaron, they gathered and melted all their gold earrings, and formed a golden calf (vv.2-4). They built an altar in front of the idol and "sacrificed burnt offerings and presented fellowship offerings" and celebrated with feasting and drinking, indulging in pagan revelry" (v.6).

The story of the golden calf is one of the greatest scandals in the desert experience of God's chosen people. King Jeroboam also built two golden calves at Bethel and Dan (1 Kings 12: 25-33). Despite God's love, as evidenced by their deliverance from the tyranny of Egypt, the Israelites often doubted His sovereign love and supremacy.

The idol reveals man's innate need to worship and its tendency to stray away from revering the true God. Today idolatry still pervades as a multitude of people continue to adore false gods: money, possessions, pleasure, and drugs.

> *Whatever your heart clings to and confides in, that is really your God, your functional savior.*
> **—Martin Luther, Augustinian monk**

Under bondage for thirty-six years, I lived in a world where reality could be temporarily changed with mind-altering substances. I always thought that life would be a bore without dope and alcohol. From 1999 to 2007, meth and pills controlled my life. This lifetime mistake had led me to a dark abyss of depravity and self-imposed suffering.

I endured the daily and grinding pursuit of drugs—aimless and incessant scrambling to raise money, endless waiting, constant scouring for a good source, and just wasting time on drug tripping. The euphoria and tranquility from the drug hits were worth the agony and exhaustion of the hunt for these substances. The meth and pills served as my escape from a depressed and humdrum life.

With military precision, I planned and carried out humiliating and horrifying schemes to feed my addiction. I pawned and sold things to friends and strangers and peddled used pots and pans to neighbors. A nearby junk shop became my regular and instant source of cash. I sold copper wires, steel gates, and other metal taken from the house. The overwhelming drug cravings anesthetized all the guilt and shame I developed because of my actions.

I have often felt I have forsaken my family. Two of my three children dropped out of school due to financial difficulties. Our electricity and water lines were disconnected for about two years because of the unpaid bills. We lit candles at night and used mosquito nets inside our modern bedrooms.

I fetched water at two pesos per five-gallon container from a neighbor outside the subdivision. Since the source was about 250 feet away, I had to use a cart and parade back and forth in full view of my rich neighbors. It took several trips to fill all the drinking jugs in the kitchen and water buckets in the bathrooms on the ground and second floors.

Despite the adversities and addiction, I mustered the strength to take care of Angie and my family by ensuring that food, at the very least, was served at the dinner table. Something good was still inside of me.

Every time I felt a wave of guilt coming on, I would rush to the drug den or my home stash, drowning my troubles in the pleasure of drugs. They always had a quick and effective way of washing every negative thought away.

I was hesitant to admit that drugs were essential in my life. Pride and denial prevented me from confessing I was addicted to meth and downers. I couldn't accept the truth that my life was miserable because of drugs.

Edward Welch, author of *Addictions: A Banquet in the Grave,* wrote: "Addiction is a bondage to the rule of a substance, activity, or state of mind, which then becomes the center of life, defending itself from the truth so that even bad consequences don't bring repentance, and leading to further estrangement from God."[1]

Raising cash to buy drugs was my number one daily priority—every day, every hour. Each moment seemed to be drug-related. Without a job, I learned to be extra resourceful and skillful in both manipulation and deception to satisfy both my bad habits and the needs of my household. Getting back to work was hard because of depression and phobia. Guilt and denial consumed me. I couldn't move on.

If I had any money, I used it to first purchase (with no prescription) some tranquilizer pills at a nearby pharmacy. Next, I would rush to the drug den to buy and smoke meth and purchase extra portions for later use at home. The tranquilizers neutralized the panicky effect of meth and produced the needed guts to deal with the loud and menacing drug dealers and runners.

This daily routine left me with little or no time to help clean the house, wash dishes, bond with my family, read a book, or even take good care of myself. Nutrition was trifling as eating was often a chore, not a joy. One thing I had positively gained, however, was plenty of physical exercise from the constant and grueling hunt for money and drugs. God, prayer, and other spiritual matters were always set aside. I was guilty of idolatry.

> *[Manasseh] erected altars to Baal and made an Asherah pole, as Ahab king of Israel had done. He bowed down to all the starry hosts and worshiped them.*
> **—2 Kings 21:3[b]**

The grim, odd, and amusing accounts of addicts desperately trying to raise money for drugs are numerous and diverse. Drug dependents can muster enormous strength and go to extreme lengths to get meth, pot, or other substances to satisfy their cravings.

The WHO defines addiction as the "repeated use of a psychoactive substance or substances, to the extent that the user (referred to as an addict) is periodically or chronically intoxicated, shows a compulsion to take the preferred substance (or substances), has great difficulty in voluntarily ceasing or modifying substance use, and exhibits determination to obtain psychoactive substances *by almost any means*" (italics mine).[2]

At the MRC, one resident sold their refrigerator from the second floor of his home to buy meth. He carefully lowered the appliance with a rope, through the terrace, so his family wouldn't notice. Another fellow claimed he sold his blood at a hospital in downtown Manila to raise money for drugs. I also learned he did this despicable act more than once. Edgar Allan Poe, the famous American poet and writer, escaped reality by using alcohol and opium. He wrote:

> *I have absolutely no pleasure in the stimulants in which I sometimes so madly indulge. In the pursuit of pleasure, I have periled life, reputation, and reason. It has been the desperate attempt to escape from torturing memories, from a sense of insupportable loneliness and a dread of some strange impending doom.*[3]

I also suffered from paranoia—a common, deep-seated psychological disorder experienced by meth users. Many residents of the MRC also claim that they often looked behind their backs, particularly when they were high on meth. They felt sure somebody was following or pursuing them when they were out on the streets. They also believed a police officer was always waiting outside the meth house, ready to grab them the moment they get out. After a meth session, I used to take a chain of quick commuter rides to evade these imagined people. Like in spy movies, I had to "lose my tail."

Likewise, I encountered recurring bouts of megalomania (self-delusion). Despite my miserable situation, I still felt I was a special person—superior to everybody else. Some MRC residents believe they gained superpowers or extrasensory perception.

A few declared they had acquired a "third eye." Others reported they were "appointed descendants of a supreme being." They also heard voices or suffered thoughts of condemnation. These dysfunctional behaviors, however, ordinarily disappear the moment an addict stops taking the substances.

Unfortunately, former users may still exhibit these abnormalities long after they've stopped using drugs. Depending on the severity of impairment, the repair of damaged brain cells due to heavy substance use may take many years.

Reverting to sobriety after a lengthy period of addiction is perplexing and traumatic. Addicts detest the sobering reality of suffering and imperfections. Adjusting back to reality is a radical shift that requires patience, courage, and perseverance—and this means experiencing again real-life pains and difficulties.

> *For we also once were foolish ourselves, disobedient, deceived, enslaved to various lusts and pleasures, spending our life in malice and envy, hateful, hating one another.*
> **—Titus 3:3, *NASB***

God created man to worship Him. "And now, Israel, what does the Lord your God ask of you but to fear the Lord your God, to walk in obedience to him, to love him, to serve the Lord your God with all your heart and with all your soul" (Deuteronomy 10:12). Without godly adoration, people succumb to idolatrous atrocities. If a person is not exalting God, he is worshiping someone else and many things—money, power, job, ideology, possessions, himself, drugs, or the Unseen Enemy.

If a person is not exalting God, he is worshiping someone else and many things—money, power, job, ideology, possessions, himself, drugs, or the Unseen Enemy.

Drug dependents worship Satan by indulging in addictive substances, vile revelry, and promiscuity. Drug dens, packed with strung-out drug worshippers, reflect the present-day kingdom of Baal. Addiction is an idol. Barbara Brown Taylor wrote, "The simplest definition of an addiction is anything we use to fill the empty place inside of us that belongs to God alone."[4]

Addicts, alcoholics, and sinners are headed toward doom. The loss of a job does not justify a person from committing theft so that he can provide for his family. In like manner, drug dependents are not vindicated from the use of drugs because of any personal ill or social injustice. Aside from losing faith, addicts are also steered to other sins: hedonism, lying, stealing, manipulation, and adultery.

In Galatians 5:19-21 (*GW*), it says:

> *Now, the effects of the corrupt nature are obvious: illicit sex, perversion, promiscuity, idolatry, drug use, hatred, rivalry, jealousy, angry outbursts, selfish ambition, conflict, factions, envy, drunkenness, wild partying, and similar things. I have told you in the past and I am telling you again that people who do these kinds of things will not inherit God's kingdom.*

Other major faiths express similar repugnance regarding intoxication and drug addiction. In Islam, Allah Almighty states in the Noble Quran 5:90: "You who believe! Indeed, intoxicants, gambling, [sacrificing on] stone alters [to other than Allah], and divining arrows are but defilement from the work of Satan, so avoid it that you may be successful." Muslims strictly stay away from intoxicating liquor and addictive substances—an affirmation that humans can live and lead fulfilling lives without drugs and alcohol.

Likewise, Buddhists detest worldly pleasure, drugs included. The Dhammapada (Sayings of the Buddha) verse 216 states: "From craving arises sorrow and from craving arises fear. If a man is free from craving, he is free from fear and sorrow." A research paper entitled *Buddhism and Addictions* by P. Groves and R. Farmer reads, "From a Buddhist perspective, addictive behavior may be seen as a false refuge and a source of attachment which unwittingly, but inevitably, leads to suffering."[5]

> *Consider it pure joy, my brothers, and sisters, whenever you face trials of many kinds, because you know that the testing of your faith produces perseverance. Let perseverance finish its work so that you may be mature and complete, not lacking anything*
> **—James 1:2-4**

A significant vulnerability that causes a person to use drugs is the difficulty he experiences when faced with troubles in life. Death of a loved one, poverty, job loss, separation of a spouse, rejection, and depression are common gateways to addiction. Ask the street children in Manila why they sniff cheap household glue or solvent. "It takes away hunger" is a quick and frequent reply.

Life is never easy. Jesus said, "I have told you these things, so that in me you may have peace. In this world you will have trouble. But take heart! I have overcome the world" (Matthew 16:33). Maya Angelou, an American poet and civil rights activist, wrote, "You may not control all the events that happen to you, but you can decide not to be reduced by them."[6]

To legitimize their bad habits, addicts internalize and proclaim these real or perceived reasons as excuses for taking dope. Instinctively, they also pass the blame for their plight to their parents, society, or the government. It's tough to pry open the real feelings and mindset of a doper.

Addicts lack focus and cannot properly carry out even basic mundane tasks. Sweeping the floor, taking a needed bath, and doing other household chores and routines are often neglected. The quest and use of drugs take much of their time. They are practically left with no time for the most important aspects of life: God, family, and work.

Dr. Marvin Seppala, Chief Medical Officer of the Hazelden Betty Ford Foundation, revealed that drug use alters brain chemistry in its reward and pleasure centers. He said, "This can affect alcoholics and addicts to the point their brains re-prioritize what's most important, such as eating and survival. It's almost unfathomable that the survival instinct could be superseded by something else."[7]

Having faith is the least or none of their concerns. Mustering true contentment is an aversion or extreme difficulty. Since becoming high, drunk, or stoned is their constant daily mission, God is often set aside, or worse, forsaken. Many addicts also doubt the existence of heaven and hell. If divine judgment comes, they believe God would spare them from eternal damnation because they think they are worthy of salvation. They also wryly assume that the end of the world is still remote. They believe they have all the time to reform and repent later in life.

> *A junkie spends half his life waiting.*
> **—William S. Burroughs, writer and visual artist**

Drug dependents spend an enormous amount of time looking for money and waiting for their favorite dealer to show up with their drugs. They also scour distant places for a good source of meth. An addict cannot rely on one dealer alone for his daily fix as all pushers recurrently run out of supply. Sometimes, ongoing police surveillance also hinders dealers from selling these illegal substances.

The punishing pursuit of drugs often takes a whole day to complete. Oddly, addicts find this debilitating and time-consuming struggle worthy once they snort a line of cocaine, pop a pill, or shoot their veins full of heroin.

Addicts learn and master patience, persistence, and salesmanship in drug-related matters and transactions. Also, they become adept at badgering and convincing friends and strangers for a loan. Like highly trained salespeople, addicts can quickly sell their used shoes, motorbikes, cell phones, and other stuff, even at ridiculous, giveaway prices. In extreme cases, they beg or resort to crime.

In the Philippines, police figures show that 17 percent of murder and homicide cases in 2016 were drug-related.[8] Also, in the

United States, drugs and alcohol are associated with about 85% of offenses leading to imprisonment.[9]

Despite this wretchedness, addicts *know* the costs and dreary consequences of their actions. However, the pleasure of taking drugs often overshadows the expected dangers. An addict is like a skydiver who experiences fear from jumping out of an airplane but is later compensated with exhilaration when the parachute opens. The greater danger from drug use usually creates more excitement—a notable reason why incarceration or lethal sanction doesn't effectively deter substance abuse.

> *Addicts know the costs and dreary consequences of their actions. However, the pleasure of taking drugs often overshadows the expected dangers.*

Every day, addicts are trapped in a successive vortex of craving, tolerance, and withdrawal. They also seek at least the same satisfactory level of high they've got used to. Charlotte Kasl, author of *Many Roads, One Journey*, wrote: "Ultimately, the withdrawal symptoms exceed the body's physical tolerance for the substance, which means the addicted person lives in a constant state of withdrawal."[10]

The addicted cigarette smoker exhibits this syndrome. A nicotine addict often erroneously proclaims that smoking relieves tension and stress. Usually, these physical disturbances and irritations come from nicotine withdrawal and cravings, which can start just 30 minutes after the last cigarette.[11] Under these conditions, the smoker feels relieved at the moment he lights up another cigarette. The same symptoms also manifest in drug addiction and alcoholism.

There is no shortcut to recovery. The bumpy road to sobriety also entails the sustained love and support of the family, the church, and other support groups such as AA (Alcoholics Anonymous) or NA (Narcotics Anonymous). However, after-care efforts are commonly deficient, misunderstood, or ignored. In the Philippines, there is a shortage of support mechanisms available to recovering addicts. Social stigma is also attached to a person who goes to these sessions.

The Costs of Addiction

Because you are called an outcast, Zion for whom no one cares.
—Jeremiah 30:17[b]

In biblical times, leprosy was a dreaded disease. Apart from being physically afflicted from this deadly infectious ailment, the lepers were ostracized by the community. Leviticus 13:45-46 says: "Anyone with such a defiling disease must wear torn clothes, let their hair be unkempt, cover the lower part of their face and cry out, 'Unclean! Unclean!' As long as they have the disease, they remain unclean. They must live alone; they must live outside the camp." The lepers suffered physical and spiritual condemnation.

Like the lepers, drug addicts struggle with faith and suffering as they bear the rejection of society. As social outcasts, they also wrestle with sin and experience the burning shame and isolation brought about by substance abuse. Caught up in a fantasy world, they spend most of their time in bars, drug dens, street corners, or in the locked rooms of their homes. Comparable to leprosy, addiction worsens if left untreated. The scourge of substance dependency also affects the whole family.

Addiction devastates the mind, body, and spirit. It removes our love and faith in God and other people. Sin, faith, and disease are related. Pain, brokenness, illness, and death are significant and common consequences of addiction and sin. Jesus Christ preached the relationship between suffering, faith, sin, and divine healing on the streets of Jerusalem when He healed the sick. Mark 2:5 reads: "When Jesus saw their faith, he said to the paralyzed man, 'Son, your sins are forgiven.'"

*There is a way that appears to be right, but in the end,
it leads to death.*
—Proverbs 14:12

Despite the proven dangers of addictive substances to individuals and society, generations remain stalwarts in the use of drugs and alcohol. Death, disease, family separation, and job loss are some of the common consequences of substance dependency.

Robin Williams, a popular actor, and comedian, openly spoke about his bondage to cocaine and alcohol. In 2006, after completing an alcohol treatment program, he told *Good Morning America* that the chronic disease of addiction is "not caused by anything, it's just there. It waits. It lays in wait for the time when you think, 'It's fine now, I'm OK.' Then, the next thing you know, it's not OK."[12] He later committed suicide.

People aren't scared of death as the ultimate result of substance abuse. Addiction is a scourge and a *lingering pandemic*. Today, tobacco is the biggest killer in the world. According to the *Fact Sheet* (updated July 2019) of the WHO, out of the one billion smokers worldwide, more than eight million are killed yearly. More than seven million of those deaths are the result of direct tobacco use, while more than 1.2 million are the result of non-smokers being exposed to secondhand smoke.[13]

There are approximately 600 ingredients in cigarettes. When burned, they create over 7,000 chemicals. At least sixty-nine chemicals are known to cause cancer, and many are poisonous.[14] *The British Medical Journal* reports that a smoker cuts 11 minutes of his life for every cigarette consumed.[15]

Alcohol is the second deadliest popular substance. The Global Status Report (2018) of the WHO indicates that more than 3 million deaths, or around 5 percent of all global deaths in 2016, were attributed to alcohol consumption.[16] According to James R. Milam, Ph.D., and Katherine Ketcham in their book, *Under the Influence: A Guide to the Myths and Realities of Alcoholism*:

*Most alcoholics will die 10 to 12 years earlier than
their non-alcoholic friends. Most will never receive
treatment for their primary disease of alcoholism.
Their death certificates will typically state "heart
failure," "accident victim," "suicide," or "respiratory
failure" as the cause of death. The chances are that
no one—physician, social worker, family member, or
alcoholic—will diagnose the cause of the problem as
addiction to alcohol.*[17]

Drug overdose is also an epidemic. According to the Centers for Disease Prevention and Control (CDC) of the U.S.: In 2018, 67,367 people died from drug overdoses, making it a leading cause of injury-related death in the United States. Nearly seventy percent of those deaths involved a prescription or illicit opioid.[18]

Pop icon Michael Jackson died because of the substance *propofol* and a host of other medications;[19] rock star Prince died of an overdose of *fentanyl* (50-100 times more potent than morphine).[20] According to the World Drug Report (2019), around 585,000 people are estimated to have died as a result of drug use in 2017.[21]

The Substance Abuse Mental Health Services Administration of the United States (SAMSHA) reported that alcohol and substance abuse are second risk factors for suicide next to depression and other mood disorders. Alcoholics and drug addicts are six times more likely to kill themselves.[22]

The health consequences of substance abuse, particularly people who inject drugs, are staggering. The UNODC disclosed that in 2017, from around 11.3 million users worldwide who inject drugs, approximately 1.4 million are living with HIV.[23] Tuberculosis is also one of the leading causes of death among drug users with HIV.[24] More than half of 585,000 reported deaths from drug use were the result of untreated hepatitis C leading to liver cancer and cirrhosis; almost one-third were attributed to drug use disorders.[25]

Behind many murders, rapes, robberies, human trafficking, and other serious crimes are illegal drugs and alcohol. These substances are also common denominators and precursors of many other social ills such as prostitution, gang violence, rebellion, and terrorism.

According to the UNODC report in 2015, data from 17 countries estimate that 37 percent of homicide perpetrators were under the influence of a psychoactive substance, in most cases alcohol, when committing the offense.[26]

Addicts and alcoholics land in jail because of criminal offenses. In the Philippines, thousands are locked up in prisons for drug use or possession for personal consumption. In a report by CNN, sixty percent of over 4,000 inmates incarcerated at a Quezon City jail in the Philippines were admitted for drug offenses. This jail was built in 1953 to house only 800 people. Many prisoners could be released, but they can't afford the bail, which can be as little as 4,000 to 6,000 pesos ($86 to $129).[27] Possession of drugs can send a person to jail from twelve to twenty years if caught with less than five grams of marijuana, cocaine, or meth.[28]

Drug offenders also face death. According to the Drug Policy Alliance, China executes between 2,000 and 15,000 people yearly for various drug offenses.[29] In many countries, drug possession is punishable by death if the quantity reaches the prescribed levels. Addicts do not mind the high costs of addiction. People also remain stubborn about the apparent dangers of substance abuse. Instead, they continue to revere drugs and heed the enticement of the Unseen Enemy.

Under God's Wrath

They have become filled with every kind of wickedness, evil, greed and depravity. They are full of envy, murder, strife, deceit and malice. They are gossips, slanderers, God-haters, insolent, arrogant and boastful; they invent ways of doing evil; they disobey their parents; they have no understanding, no fidelity, no love, no mercy.
—Romans 1:29-31

In the ninth century B.C.E., a Phoenician princess named Jezebel married Ahab, the king of the northern kingdom of Israel. The Phoenicians worshiped a multitude of gods and goddesses, including Baal, the head of fertility and agricultural god of the Canaanites. When she arrived in Israel, she brought with her pagan practices and Ahab was influenced to build an altar to Baal (1 Kings 16:31[b]). Idol worship propagated throughout the land. Two pagan temples were built, one at Samaria with its 450 priests, and the other at Jezreel with its 400 priests. Jezebel expelled the true prophets of Jehovah from the land.

She became the first female religious persecutor in history. As the most wicked woman in the Bible, Jezebel advanced sexual immorality and the eating of food sacrificed to idols (Revelation 2:20). She practiced sorcery (2 Kings 9:22) and killed the Lord's prophets (1 Kings 18:4[a]). Because she conspired to take Naboth's vineyard, she deceptively led Naboth to be accused of "cursing God and the King," which led to his death by stoning (1 Kings 21 5-14). In worshiping Baal, child sacrifice also perpetuated during these times (2 Kings 17:16-18).

The accounts of Jezebel reveal her evil influence of many kinds over people and nations. Idolatry, envy, murder, deception, promiscuity, and seduction marked her reign as queen of Israel.

Today, the spirit of Jezebel continues to reign in our lives. Idolatry, lust for power, greed, abortion, addiction, and other wicked sins and practices invade the family home and rule the social and political landscape across nations.

Paganism is also on the rise. After 1,000 years of the Nordic Age in Iceland, a temple will be completed where people can worship the Norse gods Odin and Thor. At Stonehenge, England, many modern-day pagans gather yearly to celebrate the Winter Solstice by greeting the rising sun like the ancient pagans.

Present-day drug addicts are like infidels who forsake God and worship pleasure. Heathenism also mirrors the contemporary curse of drug addiction to nations. Romans 1:18 (*ESV*) reads: "For the wrath of God is revealed from heaven against all ungodliness and unrighteousness of men, who by their unrighteousness suppress the truth." God's punishment is also unveiled when an individual suffers from chronic addiction. He could have been delivered to Satan for his idolatrous nature at an earlier time. Rehab, detox centers, AA, and NA do not work for him. First Corinthians 5:5 says: "Hand this man over to Satan for the destruction of the flesh, so that his spirit may be saved on the day of the Lord."

Even if the addict had repented for his sins, punishment might still follow. David confessed and sought forgiveness from the Lord after he committed adultery and murder involving Bathsheba and her husband, Uriah. The prophet Nathan told David, "The Lord has taken away your sin. You are not going to die. But because by doing this you have shown utter contempt for the Lord, the son born to you will die" (2 Samuel 12:12-14). Forgiveness from God does not always revoke the natural consequences of our sins.

Nations suffer the toll of God's anger because of spiritual decay. The Opium Scourge in China affected millions of lives in the 1700s. Western countries, mainly Britain, exported opium to China to obtain silk, tea, and other goods high on demand back home. Used for centuries as a medicine, the Chinese abused opium, which ultimately produced millions of addicts by the 1830s. Despite being outlawed with the corresponding arrests and executions, opium continued to proliferate in the country.[30]

Today the scourge of addiction spreads across countries, producing increasing millions of addicts as drugs and alcohol replace God as the center of their lives. Drug kingpins, smugglers, traffickers, dealers, and users, altogether comprise the modern-day Canaanites, known in the Old Testament for their idolatry and wickedness.

Addiction breeds spiritual harlotry. Drug dependents are ready and willing to sacrifice their souls to the Devil and lead a dark, abysmal life in exchange for drugs.

Addiction breeds spiritual harlotry. Drug dependents are ready and willing to sacrifice their souls to the Devil and lead a dark, abysmal life in exchange for drugs. Addiction remains because the wrath of God is not removed.

In biblical history, God repeatedly unleashed severe or catastrophic punishment on the Israelites who practiced idolatry. The destruction of Sodom and Gomorrah demonstrated how God released His wrath because of the people's debauchery (Genesis 19:24-25). If a man or woman were found guilty, he or she would be stoned to death at the city gates (Deuteronomy 17:5). Likewise, the mass killing of people and livestock in idolatrous towns was commanded by God (Deuteronomy 13:15).

The stubbornness of the Israelites brought the ire of God. They idolized golden calves, disobeyed God, and often complained about many things. Because of their transgressions, God brought down from the heavens plagues, sickness, death, and other catastrophes.

The COVID-19 pandemic is possibly a clear illustration of God's wrath to a large part of a defiant and ungrateful humanity. Despite the blessings in our lives, we remain dissatisfied, stubborn, and disobedient to our Creator.

The Lord demands we worship only Him. He detests our reverence to money, possessions, and drugs. Perhaps, if cocaine, marijuana, and heroin were prevalent in Old Testament times, addicts would be brought to the city gates and, literally, stoned.

> *Or do you not know that wrongdoers will not inherit the kingdom of God? Do not be deceived: Neither the sexually immoral nor idolaters nor adulterers nor men who have sex with men nor thieves nor the greedy nor drunkards nor slanderers nor swindlers will inherit the kingdom of God.*
> **—1 Corinthians 6:9-10**

Sacrifice is an intrinsic part of worship. Our forefathers worshiped God by offering goats, bulls, sheep, or other animals as a burnt offering. God told Moses, "Make an altar of earth for me and sacrifice on it your burnt offerings and fellowship offerings, your sheep and goats and your cattle. Wherever I cause my name to be honored, I will come to you and bless you" (Exodus 20:24).

On the other hand, the pagans offered food and their offspring as burnt sacrifices to idols. Leviticus 18:21 says: "Do not give any of your children to be sacrificed to Molek [foreign deity], for you must not profane the name of your God. I am the Lord." Manasseh, the evil king of Judah, "sacrificed his children in the fire in the Valley of Ben Hinnom, practiced divination and witchcraft, sought omens, and consulted mediums and spiritists" (2 Chronicles 33:6[a]). Today, addicts and alcoholics worship Satan by practicing black arts, sacrificing their health, families, jobs, and their sanity in exchange for drugs.

Our minds and bodies are God's abode; we are made in His image (Genesis 1:27). "Do you not know that your bodies are temples of the Holy Spirit, who is in you, whom you have received from God? You are not your own" (1 Corinthians 6:19). Drug addicts, alcoholics, and cigarette smokers defile their bodies and deny they are God's temple. Instead, they affirm and exercise their self-sovereignty—the right to do whatever they please with their bodies. They don't walk by the spirit but feed the desires of their flesh.

Edward Welch, author of *Addictions: A Banquet in the Grave,* added:

> *Drugs and sex are the modern golden calves erected by addicts to find meaning, power, and pleasure apart from God. Addicts often believe they have found life, but any payoff they experience is short-lived and deceptive. They are blinded by the fact that they are having a banquet in the grave. They are truly out of control, victims of their own lust.*[31]

Vanquishing addiction as idols of the users' hearts and minds is an enormous adversity. Addicts who seek the elusive path toward wholeness and redemption face roadblocks as they grapple through their bondage.

God is our Great Healer. Following Christ denies Satan's dominion over our lives. A.W. Tozer wrote, "Our pursuit of God is successful because He is forever seeking to manifest Himself to us."[32] We must depart from Satan and obliterate his altar of addictions by seeking the grace of God.

Addiction as Satan's Deception

The Sting of Drugs and Alcohol

Let us eat and drink, for tomorrow we die.
—1 Corinthians 15:32[a]

ALEX: "I CAN'T LIVE WITHOUT DRUGS AND ALCOHOL."

Alex is a middle-aged alcoholic and doper. He was one of the harshest and extreme cases we had ever encountered in our church drug ministry. A tall man with a large frame, he exuded a scary demeanor with an unshaven face and husky voice.

His family rejected him and he was forced to live alone because of substance abuse. An intelligent and educated person, Alex worked for two years in the United States as a medical assistant. But he turned into an addict, drunkard, and a homeless street bum. After a brush with the law, he went back to the Philippines and entered rehab countless times. He was often expelled from these facilities because he turns violent whenever his demands for benzodiazepines were denied. He insisted on taking pills to counter his drug cravings and to achieve a sense of euphoria.

Despite his family's admonition, his brother gives him a weekly allowance, which he withdraws from money centers, for food and lodging. He is homeless by choice because he always squanders his rent money for more alcohol and drugs.

Alex got used to the rain and the sheer difficulty of sleeping on the streets. He often pronounces, "My main reason for drinking is to escape from the guilt and depression of being left alone and abandoned by my family."

He voluntarily joined our drug ministry, hoping to break free from his bondage. "I want to get well," he repeatedly mumbled. Alex initially agreed to submit to our home care rules. He also had a terrible cough. After some prodding, he eventually went to the clinic, where the physician diagnosed him with tuberculosis. The doctor emphasized that he should stop drinking to completely heal from it.

Despite the visible extreme drug cravings, he managed to stay sober for two weeks. With his brother's consent, Alex agreed that we keep and handle his money. We also rented a room where he could regularly have a bath and a proper place to sleep. He functioned better and took his medicines for tuberculosis.

We evangelized and tried to lead Alex to Christ. He diligently attended church services and participated in Bible studies. However, his cravings for alcohol soon escalated. We asked him to fast, but he refused. He later asked for loose change purportedly to buy candy and snacks. Instead, we discovered he was saving the money to buy cheap gin. He also stopped taking his medication for tuberculosis and demanded more cash. "This is my money. You have no right...!" he shouted. Alex relapsed and became disobedient and troublesome. We were forced to let him go.

Back in his old ways, he again roams in our neighborhood—sick, addicted, and oppressed. He explained, "Most of the time, I believe God exists, but I can't imagine living without alcohol and drugs." Alex's case is but one of the heartbreaking examples of how Satan deceives users that they can't be happy in life without drugs and alcohol.

> *Do not gaze at wine when it is red, when it sparkles in the cup, when it goes down smoothly! In the end, it bites like a snake and poisons like a viper. Your eyes*

will see strange sights, and your mind will imagine
confusing things. You will be like one sleeping on the
high seas, lying on top of the rigging. "They hit me,"
you will say, "but I'm not hurt! They beat me, but I
don't feel it! When will I wake up so I can find another
drink?"
— Proverbs 23:31-35

King Solomon's verses epitomized man's struggle with the lure and bite of alcohol in the early biblical period. Today, the battle with alcoholism continues to rage. Winston Churchill, former Prime Minister of the UK, led the country towards victory over Germany during World War II. Known as a notorious whiskey drinker, he also took barbiturates and amphetamines. Meanwhile, Academy Award winner Anthony Hopkins conquered alcoholism when he found God. He once said, "It was like being possessed by a demon, an addiction, and I couldn't stop. And millions of people around are like that."[1]

Galatians 5:19-21 says:

The acts of the flesh are obvious: sexual immorality,
impurity, and debauchery; idolatry and witchcraft;
hatred, discord, jealousy, fits of rage, selfish ambition,
dissensions, factions and envy; drunkenness, orgies,
and the like. I warn you, as I did before, that those
who live like this will not inherit the kingdom of God.

Alcohol and drug abuse are two of the most common avenues of demon-possession. The Old Testament Greek word for sorcery and witchcraft is *pharmakeia*, which is the modern translation of the word *pharmacy*. Addicts concoct modern-day elixirs and potions through polydrug use to achieve a mixture of ecstatic but atrocious sensations. Demons, drugs, and alcohol are related.

Alcohol has beset humankind since ancient times. In the Old Testament, Noah became intoxicated with wine and was found naked in his tent (Genesis 9:20-23). Lot got his two daughters pregnant when he was drunk. And because he was under the influence of alcohol, he didn't know what happened (Genesis 19:30-37).

The Scriptures admonish that drunkenness is sinful and thwarts a holy, spiritual walk (Ephesians 5:18). In Jeremiah 35, God blessed the Recabites for their obedience in abstaining from intoxicants but cursed Israel for her transgressions with strong drink. Pastor Christian Wilson, Director of Victory Outreach Recovery Homes (Philippines), said, "Taking alcohol is a sin. It destroys the body, which is supposed to be the temple of the Holy Spirit."

In the nineteenth century, alcoholism, violence, and political corruption prompted activists in the United States to rally against alcohol. The Prohibition, which lasted from 1920 to 1935, was a constitutional ban on the production, sale, importation, and transportation of intoxicating beverages. However, this decree did not deter alcohol consumption but instead, emboldened criminal gangs and bootlegging.

Satan's Arsenal of Alcohol and Drugs

Satan's toolkit of intoxicants has proliferated with the widespread propagation of generic substances—tobacco, alcohol, cocaine, marijuana, and opiates. Medical marijuana is a buzzword, especially in debates on its therapeutic value.

According to the World Drug Report (2019) of the UNODC, cannabis remains to be the world's most widely used drug. Approximately 188 million people used the drug in 2017.[2] Despite its lesser addictive properties compared to cocaine or heroin, cannabis produces adverse effects. According to the National Institute on Drug Abuse (NIDA), heavy marijuana users have "lower life satisfaction, poorer mental health, poorer physical health, and more relationship problems."[3]

The growing recreational use of marijuana led to its legalization or decriminalization in some parts of the world. Cannabis is freely served or purchased in particular bars, restaurants, coffee shops, and grocery stores. Many European countries and some states in the U.S. have joined the liberal stance on pot. Surprisingly, one can purchase marijuana in groceries in North Korea. It will not be startling if cannabis someday joins the ranks of tobacco and alcohol as everyday staples.

Cannabis is a proven gateway drug to other more addictive and deadlier substances. Dr. Robert Dupont, President of the Institute for Behavior and Health and the first director of the NIDA, reported in the New York Times: "People who use marijuana also consume more, not less, legal and illegal drugs than do people who do not use marijuana."[4]

Another drug, cocaine, is a powerful stimulant drug from coca leaves native to South America. Like opium and marijuana, cocaine was first used for medicinal (also religious) purposes. Although used as local anesthesia for some surgeries, cocaine is an illegal narcotic. Globally, around 18.1 million people were past-year users of cocaine in 2017.[5] Its popularity stems from its stimulating euphoria, portability, and ease of administration. Until 1914, one could buy cocaine over the counter and in department stores for many purposes—as a tonic, toothache remedy, patent medicines, and in chocolate cocaine tablets.[6] Coca-Cola was launched in the late 1800s containing cocaine until it was removed from the drink in the early 1900s.[7]

Opiates are alkaloids (organic compounds of plants) from the opium poppy, which includes morphine, codeine, and heroin. The Sumerians used opium in 3400 BC and called it "the joy plant."[8] Initially used for medicinal purposes, these substances have strong analgesic (pain-relieving) properties but are highly addictive. Morphine is commonly used in hospitals and on the battlefield. In 2018, some 30.4 million people used opiates in the past year.[9]

The rapid development of modern-day synthetic substances, including methamphetamine, opioids, Ecstasy, LSD, and others, also widened the drug menu for users. Methamphetamine is a synthetic stimulant, frequently in tablet or powder form, that is chemically similar to amphetamine—used to treat Attention-Deficit Hyperactivity Disorder (ADHD) and narcolepsy. These illicit substances are manufactured in secret labs in many parts of the world. Its low price and portability make it the most popular illegal drug in the Philippines. In 2018, methamphetamine was also considered the primary drug of concern in all thirteen countries in East and South-East Asia, except Vietnam.[10] Moreover, in 2017, methamphetamine users who are under treatment accounted for the most significant share of people treated for drug use in the majority of countries and territories in the region.[11]

Nagayoshi Nagai first synthesized meth in Japan in 1893. It was widely used in World War II when the governments of Germany, England, America, and Japan gave their armies the drug to enhance endurance, alertness, and beat fatigue.[12] The Kamikaze pilots of Japan used this substance in their suicidal missions.[13]

Painkillers, originally prescribed to relieve pain after surgery and for trauma incidents, are now widely abused to alleviate stress and achieve euphoria. Hypnotics and sedatives, intended for anesthesia and pre-surgery procedures, are likewise misused as tranquilizers and sleeping pills.

The appalling collaboration between tolerant medical professionals and addicted patients is widely practiced. Opioids appeal to celebrities and elite members of society because of the privacy and ease of acquiring them. By opting to take opioids, they avoid the greater social and legal complications and dangers of engaging with street drugs. Approximately 57.8 million people used opioids (including opiates) in 2018.[14]

The rapid advances in the pharmaceutical industry result in the discovery of new varieties of opioids, benzodiazepines, amphetamines, and other substances. They serve as medication for certain physiological conditions, surgery, and other medical procedures. However, many are also highly addictive and abused.

Drug companies also participate in the foray of deception about addictive substances. Driven by commercialism, pharmaceutical professionals hide or downplay the dangers of opioids. They are also called the most notorious "drug dealers in suits." In 2007, Purdue Pharma, the manufacturer of Oxycontin, pleaded guilty to misleading the public on its product's addictive risk and agreed to pay $600 million in fines and other payments.[15]

> *"I have the right to do anything," you say—but not everything is beneficial. "I have the right to do anything"—but I will not be mastered by anything.*
> **—1 Corinthians 6:12**

The Bible verse above imparts a guideline on wise living regarding drugs. Certain generic substances are made by God for specific purposes, mainly for medication. Today, modern pharmaceuticals treat many diseases and enhance our health. The Apostle Paul exhorted about the use of wine for stomach troubles, "Stop drinking only water, and use a little wine because of your stomach and your frequent illnesses" (1 Timothy 5:23). Marijuana allegedly cures ADHD. Morphine is effective for urgent pain relief in hospitals and on the battlefield. Cocaine is used as local anesthesia. Central Nervous System stimulants are used for asthma and other respiratory problems.

Most natural, generic, and pharmaceutical substances are beneficial to humanity. However, taking drugs or alcohol for psychotropic or mind-altering purposes runs contrary to the biblical, beneficial aims of God and His creation.

Most natural, generic, and pharmaceutical substances are beneficial to humanity. However, taking drugs or alcohol for psychotropic or mind-altering purposes runs contrary to the biblical, beneficial aims of God and His creation.

The Father of Tricks and Lies

We know that we are children of God, and that the
whole world is under the control of the evil one.
—1 John 5:19

Long before God molded man and the earth, He created spiritual beings to serve Him and act as messengers to His people. An angel, named Lucifer, "wast perfect in thy ways from the day that thou wast created, till iniquity was found in thee" (Ezekiel 28:15, *KJV*). Lucifer means "light-bearer" and he was also called the "morning star." He became impressed with his beauty, authority, intelligence, and power (v.17). Lucifer coveted God's supremacy and position of honor.

Because of his pride and iniquities, Lucifer was cast down from heaven to earth (Isaiah 14:12), and a multitude of angels followed him. He is now commonly called Satan, meaning "adversary."

Earth is under the Enemy's jurisdiction (2 Corinthians 4:4). He sows disbelief and challenges the preeminence of God by utilizing tricks and lies to lure us into his kingdom of darkness. Addictive substances are one of his main attractions.

Satan commenced his deception to humankind at the Garden of Eden. He misled Eve, telling her she would not die if she touched and ate the fruit of the tree in the middle of the garden (Genesis 3:4). Today, the Devil relentlessly deceives users, telling them that drugs, alcohol, and tobacco will not hurt them. In his book *The Bondage Breaker*, Neil Anderson wrote:

> *God's people wrestling against dark spiritual forces is not a first-century phenomenon, nor is it an option for the Christian today; it's unavoidable. The kingdom of darkness is still present, and Satan is intent on making your life miserable and keeping you from enjoying and exercising your inheritance in Christ.*[16]

Crafty and gruesome, Satan has marked history with a trail of orchestrated drug-related fraud and mass ruin. In 1200 BC, Chavin priests in Peru administered hallucinogens and psychoactive drugs to gain control and power over their subjects. Opium was widely cultivated and used during Roman times, as Emperor Marcus Aurelius was known to be addicted to the drug. With the hallucinogenic mushrooms, the Viking warriors displayed barbaric ferocity in their battles.

The despicable rise of Nazism in Europe in the 1940s led to the Holocaust that claimed the lives of six million Jews. Adolf Hitler took cocaine, amphetamines, and morphine during WWII.[17] A deceptive and wicked spirit drove Hitler and his cohorts to unleash a historical genocide.

> *Adolf Hitler took cocaine, amphetamines, and morphine during WWII.*

During the Vietnam War in the 1960s, the U.S. military supplied the army with amphetamines, steroids, and painkillers to give them the strength to withstand the rugged combat in the jungles.

During the civil war in Syria, *Captagon* (a popular amphetamine) is reportedly widely used by fighters and people in the refugee camps. On the local TV news, we often hear of drunken fathers assault their young daughters and drug-crazed addicts commit large-scale robberies. In some bizarre cases, addicted young kids rape and kill their girlfriends, chop their bodies, and throw the body parts in a remote river. The deception of Satan subjugates millions of drug users, alcoholics, and cigarette smokers all over the world.

In 2017, approximately 271 million people, or about five percent of the total adult population in the world, used drugs at least once. Around 35.3 million also suffer from drug use disorders.[18]

The triumphant Father of Lies smiles because the drug users believe they have control over these mind-altering substances. They also deem drugs and alcohol as widely accepted remedies and comforts during desperate and difficult circumstances. This gloomy falsity robs them of what could have been godly, productive, and joyful years of their lives.

*Every form of addiction is bad, no matter whether the
narcotic is alcohol, morphine, or idealism.*
—Carl Jung, psychologist

Addicts and alcoholics with nonexistent, little, or wavering faith are unconcerned about the future. They prefer to wallow in an artificial, utopian state of mind instead of courageously facing the hard realities in life. As unbelievers and exponents of self-gratification, they openly affirm their inherent right to enjoy life to the fullest.

They hold to the common faulty rationale that smoking tobacco, taking drugs, or drinking intoxicating beverages is not an addiction, but a mere tolerable habit. Addicted people deny their hunger for these substances. Although the cravings and physiological impressions for each substance vary in degree and manifestation, the fundamental enslavement is the same. Persons hooked on meth, cocaine, heroin, nicotine, opioids, or alcohol all experience a similar syndrome of habituation, dependence, tolerance, and withdrawal attributed to drug dependency.

Addiction or alcoholism is not determined and measured by the quantity or frequency of use of addictive substances, but of *bondage*. If a person can't finish or enjoy a meal without wine or beer, there is a huge chance he is dependent on alcohol. If another person needs to smoke a cigarette after each meal, he is most probably dependent on nicotine.

Symptoms of withdrawal include irritability, nervousness, restlessness, anxiety, depression, insomnia, and hot flashes. Drug dependency exists when a person needs to take alcohol, drugs, or cigarettes to make these symptoms go away.

The Antichrist tricks people into bondage by letting them believe that dope, alcohol, tobacco, and other harmful substances are safe, moral, and acceptable in everyday living. When an addict takes drugs, the high gives him an *illusion* of power and control over his life.

Jeremiah 17:9 says: "The heart is deceitful above all things and beyond cure. Who can understand it?" Most addicts know the dire consequences of drug use, but their hearts are telling them something else.

The only good thing about hitting rock bottom is that it can't get any worse.
—Anonymous

Most addicts and alcoholics stay in denial until they hit "rock bottom"—a perception that their lives are so bad, they have nothing else to lose. They can't ignore reality any longer. But, like riding in an elevator going down, the addict can decide where he wants to step off. He knows that reaching the lowest level can be agonizing; it's enough to induce him to give up these substances early.

Oddly, many deliberately sustain their addiction until they reach their own lowest point of helplessness. Until then, they continue to sacrifice their families, jobs, possessions, and education to maintain their dependency on drugs. Satan wants them to idolize drugs and alcohol to the fullest extent for the longest possible time.

A delusion of grandeur is an anomaly experienced by addicts when high on narcotics. Despite the apparent depravity, they feel happy, ecstatic, and full of life. They are quickly lured and transported by Satan to an unholy abyss of artificial well-being through drugs. Matthew 4:8-9 says: "Again, the Devil took him to a very high mountain and showed him all the kingdoms of the world and their splendor. 'All this I will give you,' he said, 'if you will bow down and worship me.'"

Society upholds the frequent error of haphazardly judging a drug user as a "victim." On the contrary, most addicts and alcoholics are the perpetrators of their affliction, not casualties of some external conditions. Addicts exonerate themselves from responsibility by declaring they are unwilling and hopeless victims of a social problem or injustice. *"I lost my job," "my family left me,"* and *"nobody cares for me"* are some of their common justifications for drug use. Sometimes, they also blame the government and its unfair labor policies as the root of their misery and drug dependency.

This faulty paradigm deceptively absolves addicts from acknowledging the truth, confessing their responsibilities and sins, and undergoing much-needed repentance. God's wrath and their innate guilt are not removed. Worse, drug dependents may dangerously conclude they can continuously take drugs because they feel they are innocent.

The world largely views substance abuse only as a social problem—a stigma that categorizes the addict or alcoholic with prostitutes, hardened criminals, lepers, and outcasts. They are also regarded by many as immoral people, unworthy of help and redemption. God's command to love one's neighbor is replaced by society's narrow-mindedness and self-righteousness.

Diverse concepts and issues about using addictive substances remain divided and debated. For example, tolerance for drugs, alcohol, and nicotine in tobacco exists because many people regard these chemicals acceptable, even necessary, in our daily living.

Discrimination and bias in the use of these substances also prevail. For example, the public speedily denounces and labels a meth or heroin user as an addict, but tolerates a cigarette addict or alcoholic who takes the deadliest combination—tobacco and alcohol. Although the properties and effects of each material vary in character and degree, drugs, alcohol, and tobacco are all intrinsically addictive and deadly. They are also like magnets; each serving as a gateway drug to another substance.

Hypocrisy about drugs thrives in society. This pretentious thinking is recorded in the Bible during Jesus' lifetime: "The Pharisee stood by himself and prayed: 'God, I thank you that I am not like other people—robbers, evildoers, adulterers—or even like this tax collector" (Luke 18:11). The distorted prejudice on addiction and discrimination of drug users worsen the crisis and diminish the addicts' prospects for healing and recovery. Addicts feel isolated from society. These sentiments also hinder proactive and relevant drug treatment and wellness strategies.

However, most addicts are casualties of their self-inflicted drug dependency. They could not bear internal dysfunctions: boredom, curiosity, rebellion, depression, and anxiety. Satan is at work. They also find it even more challenging to persevere and move on in life due to external conditions: poverty, loss, family breakdown, and rejection. These precursors compromise their coping mechanisms and serve as practical triggers to drug use and habituation.

The Deception of Quitting and Recovery

They claim to know God, but by their actions they deny him. They are detestable, disobedient and unfit for doing anything good.
—Titus 1:16

Quitting drugs is often either a deception or a punishing struggle. Many cigarette smokers wrestle and postpone their decision to seriously cease smoking. Many addicts who declare in public their intention to stop using drugs are lying or putting on a show. On the contrary, they want to continue taking drugs or are having their options open.

At the start of their journey toward recovery, addicts often become lost in a maze or blocked by a vast and seemingly impenetrable brick wall. The feeling is akin to looking for a restroom while driving on the highway with no exit to be found. Most users prefer to take the easiest path by continuing to take drugs.

> *A frequent error or deception among drug users is the belief they have achieved recovery after they have remained clean and sober for several months.*

A frequent error or deception among drug users is the belief they have achieved recovery after they have remained clean and sober for several months. Most residents of the MRC claim that they are well after ninety days of rehabilitation. With radiant, beaming faces, they stroll proudly with their healthier bodies, which have gained back weight. They also assert they are confident and strong enough to refuse drugs after rehab.

In their minds, however, they still romanticize taking meth—with all the vivid scenes of a drug session. Many residents secretly intend to continue taking drugs after their release. They view rehab as a mere pit stop or a temporary setback in their drug-laced lives.

After overcoming withdrawal, which takes about a month, former rehab residents regret and struggle with guilt for the harm they have done to themselves and their loved ones. In a sober state, they can't comprehend how and why they physically abused their spouses and terrorized their children when they were high on meth. They also regret having been kicked out of school or losing their jobs because of drugs.

Many residents sincerely desire to figure out how to make things right when they get out of rehab. Likewise, they exhibit the right attitude toward reconciliation with their families. They demonstrate genuine intention to plan and work out the correct, necessary steps toward recovery.

However, the majority fail to concretize and act on their plans. Temptation engulfs them once they exit the gates and breathe the exhilarating air of freedom. They swiftly reach for a cigarette and puff its tantalizing smoke—like finding water in a parched desert. Later, they will drink beer and wallow in the familiar stupor of alcohol.

But these legal, seemingly harmless substances are typical fire starters and gateways to more dangerous drugs and eventual relapse. Satan immediately gets right back to work and re-enlists his former minions as returning prey.

We cannot, in a moment, get rid of habits of a lifetime.
— Mahatma Gandhi, lawyer and peacemaker

"The battle is in the mind," my physician once told me. The rehabilitation process succeeds once the addict ceases to be excited about drugs. Recovery is achieved once the former addict finds peace with God and gathers joy from things other than drugs and alcohol.

> *Recovery is achieved once the former addict finds peace with God and gathers joy from things other than drugs and alcohol.*

Many of the released residents from rehab remain in bondage because their drug cravings linger and persist. Most addicts are pleasure-seekers; many "rehabilitated" persons also stay in a paradigm of hedonism, not in graceful living. This faulty archetype is a significant vulnerability for relapse and a hindrance to a drug-free life.

The flawed affirmation from family and community because the former residents had completed "treatment" shrouds the truth that they are still in trouble. Pride, shame, and denial prevent former residents from admitting that they need further help and support after completing rehab. One sure sign of victory is when the recovering addict can unwind and enjoy a social gathering without taking drugs or alcohol where these substances are served.

The deceptive enigma of drug abuse demands godly intervention and secular wellness strategies and practices. Long-term recovery requires the inner transformation of the individual. Edward Welch stressed that other approaches could cause sobriety, but only God is "powerful enough to liberate the soul."[19]

Completely wiping out the temptation and thrill for drugs is complex and elusive—a dilemma for both addicts and addiction practitioners.

The Eight Most Common Lies of Drug Addicts and Alcoholics

1. *I am not an addict or an alcoholic; I am just a mere drinker or user.*
   The most common and popular phrase quoted by addicts and alcoholics.

2. *I can quit anytime I want.*
   This belief is easier said than done. These words are usually uttered by cigarette smokers.

3. *I only drink or use drugs to relieve stress.*
   A famous phrase of drug dependents to hide drug abuse or alcoholism. Stress also manifests if the doper or drunkard craves these substances.

4. *My drinking or drug use is my business; nobody gets hurt.*
   This belief is a fallacy—addiction and alcoholism affect family, friends, and other people.

5. *I only drink at night or take drugs at certain times.*
   Not drinking or taking addictive substances at certain times doesn't prove a person is not an alcoholic or an addict.

6. *I only drink or use drugs on weekends.*
   If someone needs or craves to drink or use drugs every weekend, that person is probably in bondage. Binge drinking and heavy drug use are frequent on weekends.

7. *My physician prescribed these medications. I am under treatment and not an addict.*
   Most opioids, tranquilizers, antidepressants, sleeping pills, and mood enhancers are addictive—a doper can't last a day without them.

8. *I only drink or take drugs in small amounts, unlike "those other people" who drink or take drugs a lot.*
   If a person compares his drinking or drug-taking habits to others, he has a problem. Addiction is a bondage, not measured by the amount of drug or alcohol consumed.

God and the Addicted Sinner

Repent: for the kingdom of heaven is at hand
—Matthew 4:17[b]

A man in his early thirties strode across the cosmopolitan roads of a busy fishing village. The salty scent of the sea filled the air above the sun-drenched streets. Capernaum, nestled on the northern shore of the Sea of Galilee, served Rome as a strategic trade route for travelers and caravans. The majority of the Jews and Hellenists in this crowded community were fishermen and farmers who wrestled with depravity and spiritual poverty.

Because a multitude of Abraham's descendants and Gentiles were living or passing through this township, Jesus chose to start His public ministry at these crossroads. Many were heathens or grappling with the Law. Unlike the rabbis who used to teach in the temples, Jesus visited homes, traversed the streets, and personally blessed the people to preach the Good News.

With all the authority given by the Father, Jesus proclaimed the imminence of the promised kingdom. He healed lepers, fed thousands of people, and drove out demons. He had to perform healing and wonders to restore the lost faith and declare that He is the Messiah. On its shining shores, Jesus handpicked His first disciples—lowly fishermen—ready and willing to drop their nets, to follow Him, and to spread the Gospel.

The very first public message of Jesus Christ in Matthew 4:17 resounded across the community, calling for the need for repentance to gain eternal life. Filled with awe, the people flocked around Jesus. They are curious to know about Him and if He was indeed the promised Messiah. The sick and troubled relentlessly followed Him, eager to obtain healing. Luke 24:47 says: "And repentance for the forgiveness of sins will be preached in his name to all nations, beginning at Jerusalem."

Today, more than twenty centuries later, that voice lingers on. Acts 17:30 declares: "In the past God overlooked such ignorance, but now he commands all people everywhere to repent." God's truth permeates through his written Word.

With hearts hardened by doubt and unbelief, humanity continues to grapple with sin. The progress of civilization and our dread for discomfort have inadvertently diminished the truth and comforts of God's grace. We have ignored knowing God through repentance and faith so we can identify His will and obtain mercy and deliverance.

Sin has mutated into a myriad of ugly forms as Satan continues to push his chief aim of luring people into his kingdom of darkness. Idolatry thrives in the drug world. Substance addiction, sustained by ancient organic substances and exacerbated by modern pharmaceutical technology, has spiraled into new ominous realms of enslavement.

From the beginning of time, God had made known His utter hatred when people turned to carved images as their deity. Worship involves sacrifice. During Old Testament times, offerings were a central practice in honoring God. Exodus 24:5 says: "Then he sent young Israelite men, and they offered burnt offerings and sacrificed young bulls as fellowship offerings to the Lord."

But, many of our ancestors sinned and turned away from God. They worshiped Baal, which involved even the sacrifice of their children (Jeremiah 19:5). Today, people turn to drugs and sacrifice their health and life in exchange for instant pleasure and gratification. God is mocked.

Drug dependents take mind-altering drugs to distort reality and escape from the wounds of their messed-up lives. The unabated use of addictive substances continues to captivate both the young and the old and has produced critical levels of concern on overall well-being and security.

Walk on the streets of Metro Manila, and the discerning eye can easily find a bunch of addicted, malnourished teenagers hanging out on alleys. They show bulging eyelids and distorted facial curvatures because of the lack of sleep. They left the graces of God and have been cast out into the wastelands.

Substance dependency is a plague that has spawned other sins. Drug users also turn into liars, adulterers, and frauds. At the MRC, many of the male residents became thieves and manipulators to satisfy their drug cravings. As a result, they left or neglected their families, were involved in promiscuous relationships, and resorted to crime. They became callous about God's laws.

> *Substance dependency is a plague that has spawned other sins. Drug users also turn into liars, adulterers, and frauds.*

Sin is a forgotten word. Repentance is an obscure notion that raises eyebrows. Addiction is a sin and dependency on dope, crack, meth, or alcohol is idolatry in its basic form. Drugs are the modern-day Baals that addicts worship. Without real sorrow and confession, repentance is insincere and fallacious. God's wrath is not removed, and the addict suffers endless denunciation and misery. Unless the grace of God intervenes, divine atonement doesn't come to light.

It All Begins with Repentance

In the same way, I tell you, there is rejoicing in the presence of the angels of God over one sinner who repents.
—Luke 15:10

TONY DELA PAZ: A DRUG DEPENDENT TURNED PASTOR

Alone in the room and without sleep for three days, Tony slowly fixed the noose of a rope around his neck. He prepared himself to jump off from a chair. He wanted to end it all—the unceasing pain, the guilt, the shame, and all the troubles he had brought to his family. His demise would finally finish his struggle with drugs, which started at the age of twelve.

A knock on the door broke the eerie air that filled his room. "Your brother is here to see you," his nephew said. Tony turned furious, knowing that his brother conspired to force him to rehab. He also had two other brothers who used drugs.

He cut the rope loose, took a knife, opened the door, and immediately lunged at his brother. He stabbed him with the blade, but his brother was able to deflect the deadly attack. They got into a scuffle, hitting each other, and rolling all over the floor. His brother overpowered him.

His uncle, a police officer, finally ordered his incarceration at Camp Crame, the headquarters of the Philippine National Police. He stayed there for three months. He could have been dead from suicide if his brother had not arrived.

Tony read and believed in the Bible before this horrible event. However, the powerful lure and pleasure from drugs caught him into a series of sobriety and relapse. As a natural leader and thrill-seeker in his younger years, he had sought fame and recognition by joining fraternities, engaging in fistfights, and using drugs. Family and financial problems exacerbated his woes in life. Because of a wayward lifestyle, he was unable to finish college.

One late night in 1987, he opened the TV, and the *700 Club* flashed on the screen. He heard a testimony of a drug addict and discerned that the story mirrored the experience he was going through. Tony cried like a baby and realized that he was a sinner and that God loves him.

Pastor Tony is now a redeemed person of God. His round spectacles and piercing gaze exude the aura of a college professor. However, he radiates the joy and warmth of being a Christian. Despite being drug-free since 1991, he honestly claims he still wrestles with other sins and temptations.

Today, Pastor Tony works as the Facility Director of Penuel Home, the drug rehab and ministry outreach of the Christ's Commission Fellowship Church (CCF). He oversees Penuel's operations and gives spiritual guidance to the residents of the facility. Pastor Tony also preaches at the CCF Katipunan.

When asked about his views about repentance, Pastor Tony replied, "Repentance happens when a person withdraws from unbelief and the acknowledgment that God is our Master." He added, "Repentance, however, is a lifelong process as we continue to face trials, temptations, and sins of many kinds. But God always convicts me whenever I go out of line, and this brings me back to repentance."

> *For the Lord your God is gracious and compassionate.*
> *He will not turn his face from you if you return to him.*
> **—2 Chronicles 30:9[b]**

Divine healing starts with an encounter and knowledge of God. An addict can't ask forgiveness from someone he doesn't know. At the very least, he needs to acknowledge that a Supreme Being, who can take over his selfish life, exists. And the more he learns about the divinity and personality of Jesus Christ, the more he becomes intimate with Him.

A vital element of repentance is sorrow. Second Corinthians 7:10 says: "Godly sorrow brings repentance that leads to salvation and leaves no regret, but worldly sorrow brings death." Grief is for sin; regret is for emotions. We don't become sorrowful when we lose our jobs, or somebody dies. But we become sorry when wrong (not sinful) things happen.

True atonement produces grief. The pain of remorse—convicting our hearts that we had hurt God and our loved ones—opens the gate to restoration. Repentance is not an emotional experience determined by the number and intensity of our groans and cries. Real contrition means a fundamental change in our hearts and minds.

Nobody is exempt from repentance. All of us have sinned (Romans 3:23). Jesus demonstrated this truth when He challenged the people, if they were without sin, to cast the first stone to a woman caught in adultery (John 8:7). Nobody stoned her, and they all left (v.9).

Repentance is also a gift of grace. Acts 11:18[b] says: "So then, even to Gentiles, God has granted repentance that leads to life." Paul exhorted Timothy: "Opponents must be gently instructed, in the hope that God will grant them repentance leading them to a knowledge of the truth" (2 Timothy 2:25).

The primary goal of recovery is the renewing of the self—to become a new creation! Through genuine remorse, the addict can overcome the wounds of the past and gather the courage to face the critical challenges of the present.

In the book, *Against the Night: Living in the New Dark Ages*, Charles Colson and Ellen S. Vaughn said:

> *Repentance is the process by which we see ourselves, day by day, as we really are: sinful, needy, dependent people. It is the process by which we see God as he is: excellent, majestic and holy…And [it] so radically alters our perspective that we begin to see the world through God's eyes, not our own. Repentance is the ultimate surrender of the self.*[1]

True repentance isn't easy. Addicts struggle through the years, hesitant and double-minded, in accepting that substance abuse is a sin. They can't easily dismiss the artificial pleasure and comfort they experience from drugs. Thomas Watson wrote, "The sinner thinks there is danger in sin, but there is also a delight, and the danger does not terrify him as much as the delight bewitches him."

A change of heart means they would lose the way of life they got used to—a nirvana with friends (usually addicts) who accept them. They also fear the unknown— a life where they find the parameters of reality and sober daily living as difficult to accept. Some will risk life and limb before they finally decide to let go of the pleasures from drugs and put their feet back on the ground. They also cast themselves as victims, not perpetrators, of addiction. They find it difficult to accept responsibility for their sins, which delays much-needed repentance.

Moreover, the wounds from their past lives are tremendous traumas that are not easily removed. They had hurt God, themselves, and their families. In the book *Victory over the Darkness*, Neil Anderson wrote, "You must learn how to resolve previous conflicts or the emotional baggage will accumulate as you continue to withdraw from life. The past will control your life as your options for handling it continues to decrease."[2]

*It was good for me to be afflicted so that I might learn
your decrees.*
—Psalm 119:71

Pain and suffering lead to repentance. The Israelites often repented after God sent them drought, plagues of many kinds, sickness, and death because of their idolatry and other sins.

*Pain and suffering
lead to repentance.*

Ultimately, the hardship experienced by a drug dependent can be a springboard for change, especially when she has arrived at rock bottom. If she reaches her lowest level of helplessness and decides that she could no longer bear the hurts and sufferings, she may finally stop using drugs. If she realizes that she could no longer also afford to sacrifice valued relationships and the essential things in life—jobs, social acceptance, health, and sanity—she may repent. She ultimately finds out that there is no other way out but to cling to God's hand.

Reaching rock bottom and making a firm decision to stop taking drugs may take years or decades to happen. However, God is patient. He has redeemed me from the tyranny of addiction after 36 years of unbelief and wavering faith. Paul spent half of his life persecuting Christians before he became the foremost missionary of Jesus. In the Old Testament, God forgave David for his grievous sins of murder and adultery (2 Samuel 12:13). Despite the length and gravity of being a sinner, God always awaits the repentant addict. The Lord declares that the forgiveness of sins precedes healing.

However, when a drug user experiences a personal encounter with God, repentance should not be delayed. We can't predict when God will again knock on our hearts. Many addicts always postpone their willingness to stop taking drugs. Despite the realization that they need God for their recovery, they continue to procrastinate and delay remorse. Instead, they extend living in a fantasy world at the longest possible time. "God can wait," they say.

Many drug users and alcoholics have hardened their hearts. They refuse to admit that addiction is a besetting sin. Zechariah 7:12 reads: "They made their hearts as hard as flint and would not listen to the law or to the words that the Lord Almighty had sent by his Spirit through the earlier prophets. So the Lord Almighty was very angry."

They often consider substance use (and abuse) as their right as free men. If they agree to some form of penalty for their substance abuse, they would only expect a mere slap on the wrist, some counseling, or at the most, a short stint in rehab. "Addiction is a sin," said Pastor Tony. "Many graduates from rehab are fully recovered [physically], but sin is not removed," he added.

> *The Lord is not slow in keeping his promise, as some understand slowness. Instead he is patient with you, not wanting anyone to perish, but everyone to come to repentance.*
> **—2 Peter 3:9**

Godly fear leads to repentance. When a user finally believes that addiction is a sin, he discovers there is a God who bears the sole power to either send his soul to Paradise or eternal doom. Matthew 10:28 states: "Do not be afraid of those who kill the body but cannot kill the soul. Rather, be afraid of the One who can destroy both soul and body in hell." The realization that he might forever rot in hell if he continues to take drugs serves as an avenue for repentance.

Addicts are selective in confessing their sins. They believe that disclosing their drug use to God is enough to earn absolution. Often, they become willing to stop taking drugs but are reluctant to let go of their other sins—gambling, manipulation, deceit, greed, and extramarital relationships. At the MRC, many residents declare they will stop using drugs after their release, but intend to smoke tobacco and drink alcohol. Drug dependents are good at compromises.

But the Bible says: "For whoever keeps the whole law and yet stumbles at just one point is guilty of breaking all of it" (James 2:10). Our God is pure, and He expects us to be holy in all aspects of our lives (1 Peter 1:16). Divine healing doesn't work selectively. It requires the total surrender of the self to God with all the sins it carries.

Besides, they are often exposed to purely secular thoughts about drug dependency. Most rehab centers expound on the Disease Model, which defines addiction as a brain disorder. This stance is supported by much of the medical profession, including prominent global institutions. With the public belief that they are sick and in need of outside help from professionals, addicts instinctively rely solely on secular treatment from scientifically expert intervention. As a result, the virtue of the addict's accountability and responsibility become diminished. Moreover, a centerpiece of this treatment modality requires the prescription of other drugs, which are often also addictive. The Psychological Model, on the other hand, states that substance abuse is a behavioral problem caused by specific genetic, hereditary predispositions, or from wrong responses to outside stimuli.

However, these secular approaches on drug dependency are helpful and useful in their specific areas and up to a certain extent.

They may proclaim spirituality as an adjunct advantage in recovery but often exclude the concept of sin as a core element in healing. Genuine repentance is not achieved. Successful recovery often involves a collaboration of faith and medicine.

> *If we confess our sins, He is faithful and just to forgive us our sins and to cleanse us from all unrighteousness.*
> **—1 John 1:9, ESV**

The deepening decadence of sin signals the imminent return of Christ. But, repentance and confession lead to sanctification. An addict needs to renounce his corrupt self and spell out in prayer his specific sins. He needs to confess to God that he stole her daughter's school lunch money, sold her wife's necklace, or pawned his motorbike to buy drugs. An injured person shows the doctor the exact wound that needs treatment.

In *Glittering Vices*, Rebecca De Young writes:

> *Rather than praying in general for forgiveness of sin, or reducing all our sin to pride or generic selfishness, we can lay specific sins before God, ask for the grace to root them out, and engage in daily disciplines— both individually and communally—that help us target them. Naming our sins is the confessional counterpart to counting our blessings. Naming them can enrich and refresh our practices of prayer and confession and our engagement in the spiritual disciplines.[3]*

Disclosure is an assertion of a core biblical and doctrinal truth. We are to declare that Calvary emancipated us from everything outside of God's will. Accepting responsibility for our wrongdoings is an integral part of repentance and confession. Proponents of twelve-step recovery programs stress the importance of the declaration of guilt and accountability as primary components in their methodology.

An addict must overcome Satan's deception that he is an unwilling "victim" of an unfair world. Passing the blame to poverty, job loss, and other harmful external factors and relationships only delays or halts the recuperation process. John writes, "If we say that we have no sin, we deceive ourselves, and the truth is not in us. If we *confess our sins,* He is faithful and just to forgive us our sins and to cleanse us from all unrighteousness. If we say that we have not sinned, we make Him a liar, and His word is not in us" (1 John 1:8–10, *ESV,* italics mine).

Repentance and confession remove guilt and shame. Isaiah 1:18[b] reads: "Though your sins are like scarlet, they shall be as white as snow; though they are red as crimson, they shall be like wool." Penitence is a prerequisite of water baptism—becoming a new creation. Acts 2:38[b] states: "Repent and be baptized, every one of you, in the name of Jesus Christ for the forgiveness of your sins. And you will receive the gift of the Holy Spirit."

Much of the problems of continuing fellowship with a holy God is that many Christians repent for what they did, not for what they are.
—Alfred Tozer, Christian author and minister

False repentance happens when a person pretends to be sorrowful or confesses his sins (only in public) just to put up a show and appease the people around him. He asks for a reprieve from God, skipping heartfelt repentance. Judas Iscariot experienced sincere regret but didn't truly repent (Matthew 27). He excruciatingly witnessed the horrifying denunciation of Jesus by the people. Judas "was seized with remorse and returned the thirty pieces of silver to the chief priests and elders (v.3)." He confessed to the chief priests and elders: "I have sinned for I have betrayed innocent blood (v.4)." There is no biblical account of Judas seeking forgiveness from God. Despite his close physical proximity to Jesus, he did not approach Jesus at that time to confess his sins. Instead, he preferred to commit suicide (v.5).

With unrepentant hearts, addicts don't make a firm and genuine commitment to follow Christ. They pretend and go through the motions of private and public remorse about their addiction, hoping to save their faces, their jobs, and the integrity of their families.

At the MRC, prayers, praise, and worship are profound. Many residents have memorized assigned verses and could quickly explain its applications for practical living. They can see the path that Christ has laid for them for their recovery and redemption. God prompts them for repentance. Yet, they find it challenging to embrace the full precepts of Christian living. The costs of taking up the cross of Christ appear to be a stigma or a heavy burden. Praying and reading the Bible is unimaginable; going to church seems tiring. Loving God and other people rather than the things of this world is unthinkable (1 John 2:15). They dread to become holy.

Repentance also means action. Paul says, "First to those in Damascus, then to those in Jerusalem and in all Judea, and then to the Gentiles, I preached that they should repent and turn to God and *demonstrate their repentance by their deeds*" (Acts 26:20, italics mine). A sinful woman showed her repentance by attending to Jesus (Luke 7). While weeping, she washed the feet of Jesus, dried them with her hair, "kissed them, and poured perfume over them" (v.38). Later, Jesus said to her, "Your sins are forgiven" (v.48).

Repentant addicts and alcoholics need to exert effort and show that they are genuinely avoiding drugs and the circumstances that trigger them to temptation and relapse. They have to change their lifestyle and mindset, make new friends, and continue to build up their faith in God. Repentance produces fruits and benefits. Matthew 3:8 says: "Produce fruit in keeping with repentance."

Unrepentant sinners have no place in the Body of Christ. In 1 Corinthians 5, Paul told the believers in Corinth to discontinue fellowship with an immoral member of the church. "But now I am writing to you that you must not associate with anyone who claims to be a brother or sister but is sexually immoral or greedy, an idolater or slanderer, a drunkard or swindler. Do not even eat with such people" (v.11). But the church is also the sanctuary for true remorseful people. Public confession and prayer bring divine healing to sinful addicts and alcoholics.

> *Public confession and prayer bring divine healing to sinful addicts and alcoholics.*

The wonderful news is that our Lord is a God of mercy, and He responds to repentance.
—Billy Graham, evangelist

Repentance poses a considerable challenge, especially during the early stages of recuperation from addiction. Besieged by many years of mental and physical affliction, the recovering addict requires joint coordination of the mind, body, and spirit to gather and maintain a repentant attitude.

First, they continue to grapple with the notion that addiction is a sin. Second, their understanding of Christ, faith, and salvation are muddled. Before they can truly understand the nature of repentance, they need the touch of God and exposure to God's Word.

Repentance can be a long-drawn process, and relapse can still happen to a penitent addict. The Devil doesn't easily give up. Despite the fallbacks, the recovering addict must not cease to continue confessing and repenting. Peter denied Jesus three times. "Before the rooster crows today, you will disown me three times," said Jesus (Luke 22:61[b]). After the third time, Peter "went outside and wept bitterly" (v.62). Not only did Peter cry, but he also had a change of heart. He exhibited true repentance after he had finally followed Jesus. Peter ferociously led the apostles, despite the constant fear of death, in proclaiming the Gospel of Christ.

Like Peter, addicts often stumble many times in search of sobriety and liberation. Overcoming addiction is lengthy, even a lifelong struggle. As a disease, the recovery of the damaged brain may take years for the cells to recuperate or grow back. According to *The Recovery Book* by Al J. Mooney, M.D., A. Eisenberg, and H. Eisenberg: "[The brain is] probably the slowest part of the body to recover from substance abuse. Many brain cells can't be grown by the body. But, fortunately, the brain can revive itself…to connect the billions of cells that remain unscathed."[4]

Sincere repentance through fasting and the changing to sack clothes are two ultimate exemplifications of true atonement. In the wicked city of Nineveh, the inhabitants repented after accepting God. Jonah 3:5 states: "The Ninevites believed God. A fast was proclaimed and all of them, from the greatest to the least, put on sackcloth."

Addicts need to plead God to smite their hardened hearts. Despite the numerous falls on the tracks, they must get up, run the race, and win the prize of freedom (Hebrews 12:1). Repentance is a continuing process. In his book, *Money Isn't God*, John White says, "The test of true repentance is permanent behavioral change. There is no such thing as instantaneous sanctification, but in repentance, major obstacles to ongoing sanctification are removed."[5] Graced with glimmering sparks of hope and faith, the addict must relentlessly pursue recovery, until God finally looks down upon him and drives him to lie prostrate and beg for the removal of his sins.

THE HEALING POWER OF REPENTANCE AND CONFESSION

There is therefore now no condemnation for those who are in Christ Jesus. For the law of the Spirit of life has set you free in Christ Jesus from the law of sin and death.
—Romans 8:1-2

Like Adam and Eve, we can't run away from God and cover our sins. The more we deny our addictions and our sins, the more we will be crippled by the grip of guilt and shame. Negative emotions can turn into vile strongholds. Only the healing power of Jesus Christ can banish the Enemy from the core of our souls.

Admitting to God that we have sinned is the first step in removing guilt and shame. We must confess to God that we have crossed his laws and trampled our bodies—the "temple of the Holy Spirit"—with dangerous substances. First John 1:9 reads: "If we confess our sins, he is faithful and just and will forgive us of our sins and purify us from all unrighteousness."

In like manner, we must also confess to other people whom we have hurt. We ask for forgiveness from our families because we left them, or we stole our daughter's lunch money to score a drug fix. In addition, we have to seek forgiveness from our neighbor for stealing his bicycle to buy drugs. It takes courage to declare our sins before people.

There is higher power when we clarify and specify the exact nature of our wrongdoings. Consequently, we must also learn to forgive others who have given us harm. Colossians 3:13 reads: "Bear with each other and forgive one another if any of you has a grievance against someone. Forgive as the Lord forgave you."

If we belong to a church, confessing before the pastor or the congregation facilitates spiritual cleansing. James 5:16 reads: "Therefore confess your sins to each other and pray for each other so that you may be healed. The prayer of a righteous person is powerful and effective." The pursuit of faith through prayer, Bible reading, and church meeting brings relief to our guilt-ridden lives.

In recovery, enrollment in after-care support or recovery groups enhances healing. In this environment, members experience similar adversities and sufferings as they help one another and share each other's secrets.

Despite being sober for many months or years, recovering addicts would have to bear the lingering stigma of addiction. Their families and the public often remain skeptical as to whether their recovery is authentic. Resolution and restoration do not come overnight, but it will happen if we keep a sincere and repentant heart. Psalm 34:5 (ESV) reads: "Those who look to him are radiant, and their faces shall never be ashamed."

Lastly, we must learn to forgive ourselves. We must stop blaming ourselves and other people for our addiction and its resulting wounds and troubles. We have to let go of the past, live for today, and look forward to the future.

The Power of Public Confession

But the tax collector stood at a distance, unwilling even to lift up his eyes to heaven. Instead, he beat his breast and said, 'God, have mercy on me, a sinner!'
—Luke 18:13

NORMAN: "ADDICTION IS A SIN, NOT A DISEASE."

Norman paced intermittently inside the living quarters of the I am Alive Christian Homes. He prayed and meditated on God's Word and some Christian literature. As an act of repentance, he committed himself to a complete fast without food and water.

The halfway house, a residential ministry outreach of our local church for substance abusers, housed volunteer individuals after their release from rehab. Five residents and a caretaker resided in the home. During his stint at the MRC, Norman was active in Bible studies and expressed his strong desire to join the ministry after his release from rehab.

Medium built and with arms laced with extended tattoos, Norman is polite and friendly. When the air gets dull, he often cracks jokes. Coming from a broken family, he hoped that the ministry shelter could help him earn back the trust and confidence of his family. David, his beloved 5-year old son, has always been a driving force for his recovery.

Out on a pass one day, he was tempted and used drugs. Dazed and confused, Norman wondered how and why he slipped back to meth after five months of complete sobriety. Despite his serious commitment to Bible studies, prayer, and ministries, he pondered how Satan knocked him out of his track. He felt confident that his recovery would go on a stretch.

After repenting and over twenty-four hours of total fasting, he claimed that his cravings disappeared. Norman immediately recovered from his relapse. Tormented with grief, he expressed remorse and confessed openly in church about his drug slip. He stood up and testified, "Addiction is a sin."

Norman remains drug-free, works in the transport industry, and continues to improve his relationship with his family. He consistently emphasizes that his past addiction was "a sin, not a disease."

> *Therefore, confess your sins to each other and pray*
> *for each other so that you may be healed. The prayer*
> *of a righteous person is powerful and effective.*
> **—James 5:16**

As an integral element of repentance, public confession heals. Proverbs 18:1 *(ESV)* says: "Whoever isolates himself seeks his own desire; he breaks out against all sound judgment." The open admission of our sins to others is a sincere effort that seeks forgiveness. It washes the decaying conscience of addicts, which was polluted by long years of bondage.

One of the main components in healing communities (TC, AA, and NA) is personal responsibility and accountability. It involves an honest and public sharing and confession of a recovering addict before a group as a healing process.

Confession may lead to open rebuke. The ensuing confrontation is not to humiliate the addict but to help him out of love and concern. Healing develops when the addict maintains humility in accepting the criticism of others. Second Timothy 4:2 says: "Preach the word; be prepared in season and out of season; correct, rebuke and encourage—with great patience and careful instruction."

In 2008, I confessed to my pastor I had used drugs again and surrendered voluntarily to him my last hidden batch of benzodiazepines. In the church, my words mumbled as I publicly confessed my relapse. Like Norman, I couldn't bear the guilt of taking drugs while being involved in church ministry. After some time,

God's ever-forgiving grace and congregational affirmation quickly eased me back to sobriety.

I also wrestled for many years in confessing my wrongdoings to my children and in asking for their forgiveness. *Why would I confess and humble myself before my children? I am their father and head of the family!* However, guilt further consumed me. I finally gathered enough courage to tell them, one by one, that I was sorry for my sins. The sense of relief was indescribable.

Every wrongdoing makes us culpable, as guilt usually breeds shame. When we declare in public even the smallest of our sins, an impactful feeling of release follows. King David committed adultery and murder. In 2 Samuel 13, he confessed openly after the prophet Nathan had rebuked him for the death of Uriah the Hittite and taking Uriah's wife Bathsheba to be his own (v.9). He said to Nathan, "I have sinned against the Lord" (v.13[a]). Nathan replied that the Lord has forgiven him and he will not die (v.13[b].)

> *He who conceals his sins will not prosper, but whoever confesses and renounces them will find mercy.*
> **—Proverbs 28:13**

In the Philippines, having an addict in the family is a huge social shame. Pride, a root component of the seven deadly sins, often restricts the open admission of guilt. Most addicts are in a state of denial, refusing to admit their addiction and confessing to their families. Internally, they may feel convicted that they are delinquents and a disgrace to society. So, they keep the problem to themselves to avoid personal and family embarrassment and, as a way to cope, they continue to take drugs.

This dilemma prevents them from getting the immediate and proper remedies they need, including the possibility of going into rehab. Addicts and their parents squelch the scandalous truth that addiction exists in the family. Arrogance drags the whole family along in the sinful state of cover-ups and deception. Satan thrives in the family home.

Social status also prevents addicts from the open admission of their bondage. Many drug users and alcoholics around the world are wearing suits and are respected by people around them. In my earlier days, I exuded a professional air of confidence and trustworthiness. However, my briefcase often contained a stash of meth and pills.

Unknown to many people, a multitude of white-collared professionals are "functioning addicts" who grapple with opioids, cocaine, or booze. In the United States, more than 11 million people abused prescription opioids in 2016.[6] These dependents dread the shame and the loss of their jobs and public standing if they openly admit that they are hooked on drugs.

> *I have not come to call respectable people to repent,*
> *but outcasts.*
> **—Luke 5:32, *GNT***

Addicts in rehab suffer a strong feeling of condemnation. They feel convicted that they have wronged their families, friends, and society. Many also sense the lowest level of worthlessness and think that they are so inadequate and unworthy of redemption. In addition, paranoia aggravates the helplessness of the addict. They harbor a lingering fear and suspicion that society continues to lurk in punishing or incarcerating them. They detest the sarcasm and blame that would be laid on them when they are out in public.

However, they remain hesitant to repent and confess their sins. Upon release, they quickly become prone to relapse. Without repentance, the easiest way out from guilt and shame is to take drugs again. Jesus came to earth to save, not the righteous people, but the outcasts—like the lepers, drug addicts, and alcoholics.

In the Parable of the Lost Son (Luke 15), genuinely penitent addicts and alcoholics are comparable to the younger sibling. He left his family and wasted away all of his inheritance in "wild living" (v.13). Later, he returned to his family and confessed to his father. "Father, I have sinned against heaven and against you. I am no longer worthy to be called your son" (v.21).

Repentance is never late. Martin Luther King Jr. once said, "I may not be the man I want to be; I may not be the man I ought to be; I may not be the man I could be; I may not be the man I truly can be; but praise God, I'm not the man I once was." We need to weep and cast ourselves down before the Lord.

Signs of True Repentance of a Drug Dependent

1. *He expresses a sincere confession of guilt before God.*
    He declares before God he is an addict and asserts that substance dependency is a sin. He admits that he places drugs and alcohol over and above God, family, work, and everything else in his life.

2. *He publicly confesses his addiction before family, friends, and other people.*
    He declares to concerned people around him that he took drugs to feed his sinful self and accepts full responsibility for his actions. He also acknowledges the damage and hurt that he had caused to others.

3. *He seeks mercy from God and forgiveness from others.*
    The drug dependent truly repents when he asks for absolution from God and other people. He also extends the same mercy to other people who he feels have wronged him.

4. *He follows God's commands and strives to increase his faith.*
    He prays with thanksgiving. Saying grace before meals is a good sign of remorse. The recovering addict always reads the Bible and regularly attends church services.

5. *He changes his mindset and behavior as fruits of repentance.*

He is earnest in avoiding temptations and triggers that lead to relapse—staying away from dangerous parties and meeting with addicted friends. He makes new friends and creates a new environment that enhances his recovery toward a born-again spirituality.

The Role of Faith in Healing and Recovery

The Pursuit of Faith

Your faith has healed you.
—Mark 10:52[b]

Two passengers sat beside each other on a transatlantic flight. After the usual courtesies and banter about the balmy weather, the subject turned to God and faith. The tall businessman, dressed in a snappy pinstripe suit, leaned sideways and quipped, "I'm a self-made man, and I don't think much about God." The mild-mannered, bespectacled Christian asked, "Where do you think your soul will go after you die?" "I don't know. Maybe we don't have souls, and I think I really don't care," the businessman replied.

After their long verbal exchange about creation, evolution, and the existence of heaven and hell, a sudden thud resounded across the aisles. The passengers gasped as successive spits of fire spewed from the plane's left engines. The captain's voice pierced through the speakers: "Ladies and gentlemen, we are going to make an emergency landing." As shrieks and cries reverberated throughout the cabin, the aircraft plummeted toward the ocean.

The believer closed his eyes, lowered his head, and prayed, "Lord, forgive me of all of my sins, and if I am to perish, please receive my soul." Amid the horror and mayhem, a shrilling voice cried out in terror, "Please pray for me!" It was the businessman.

This odd little tale depicts the irony of how many people exercise faith. When everything is fine, we coast through life without God. When trouble erupts, we remember and call to our Almighty God.

Chapels are standard features in hospitals all over the world. Inside these hallowed rooms, family members plead to God for the healing of their loved ones. They drop to their knees and pray to the Heavenly Father after the doctor had said: "Sorry, I have done my best. The patient is now in God's hands."

In a survey conducted in the United Kingdom, *The Guardian* reports that 25% of unbelievers pray when a personal crisis or tragedy occurs.[1] When life-threatening cancer, job loss, desperation, or death in the family strikes, people go back to God. However, when everything is well, they set God aside and forget to thank Him every day for their blessings. First Thessalonians 5:18 reads: "Give thanks in all circumstances; for this is God's will for you in Christ Jesus." Despite an abundant life, some people remain dissatisfied. They continue to crave and pray for more material wealth to feed their chronic discontent.

A friend once told me a revealing story of when he worked in Saudi Arabia as a construction engineer in the early 1990s. He joined a Christian congregation with around twenty Filipino members. When the Gulf War erupted from late 1990 to 1991, church attendance swelled as fear and uncertainty loomed on the horizons. With raised eyebrows, he said: "The turnout almost doubled."

Many people pray to God, worship, and praise Him only during Sunday church services. They feel that God has sanctified them in these moments. On the contrary, God rejects Sunday Christians who do not embody Christ and pursue faith every day. They are like chameleons that do good works but carouse with the Devil at the same time.

The existentialists live in a purposeless and strictly practical world—the archetype of their everyday lives. They believe that humans primarily subsist and engage in an ever-changing meaning of life through the sole exercise of free will.

Pragmatists live by the validity of ideas and beliefs based on the success of practical applications. Atheism, Darwinism, and twisted, unbiblical theology abound in many parts of the world. As a replacement for faith, these beliefs unveil man's need to bring security to their lives.

"There is no God," a fool and unbeliever would say (Psalm 14:1). How could a holy God exist if He allows the abortion of around 50 million unborn babies each year? How could God let a suicide bomber kill himself with hundreds of other innocent bystanders, both young and old, on a busy street corner? Why can't God stop all the famines, pandemics, and deadly diseases that wipe out a multitude of people on earth? These inquiries lead many people to question the validity of their faith and the existence of God.

Drug dependents and alcoholics, scarred by years of unbelief or distorted faith, are unwilling to pursue the true God.

The predominance of these anti-creation philosophies results in the breakdown of faith and pushes away the eternal truths of God's Word. Individuals who cling to these values become accessible and natural prey to addictions.

Drug dependents and alcoholics, scarred by years of unbelief or distorted faith, are unwilling to pursue the true God. As hardened hedonists, they proclaim, "Let us eat and drink, for tomorrow we die" (1 Corinthians 15:32[b]). To them, the future doesn't matter. Salvation and the resurrection of the body are abstract concepts heard only in church. For addicts, the only essential things are the pleasures of the moment.

Heroin addicts, with arms full of darkened needle marks, know death is just around the corner. A junkie utters, "I just hope I live through this day," as he wrestles and scours for his daily dose of the deadly drug. Alcoholics guzzle a bottle of whiskey and spend the day in a drunken stupor. They prefer to wallow in artificial bliss than pursue the godly joy that faith provides.

Drug addiction is idolatry. Dopers have placed their beliefs or faith on the wrong objects. They put more value on marijuana, liquor, and their drug dealers than God and their loving families. John Calvin said, "Our heart is an idol factory. In a fallen world, people constantly seek things they can worship, even though the Creator is before us in plain view."[2] The bondage to drugs also results in a myriad of negative character traits and outcomes—pride, gluttony, lust, envy, anger, and crime.

Idolatry also spawns demonic manifestations. Testimonies of residents of the MRC reveal that they experienced occurrences dealing with the occult—third-eye powers, megalomaniac prophecy, and other evil signs. These abnormalities indicate they are under satanic attacks.

Secular therapists often explain these abnormalities as psychological or psychiatric. After some time, these weird symptoms usually go away after abstaining from drugs. But the deep-seated and selfish strongholds remain in their psyche. No amount of medicinal or professional intervention can remove the evil and *deep intrusions* of the Unseen Enemy from the addict's being.

DEO SALGUERO: AN ALCOHOLIC STREET FIGHTER TURNED PASTOR

So then faith cometh by hearing, and hearing by the word of God.
—Romans 10:17, *KJV*

Deo struggled with tears as he stirred his daughter's infant food. They ran out of milk and had to settle with "am," a native term referring to the water skimmed from boiling rice. Jobless, Deo experienced, for the first time, a stinging, painful reality of life. He had no money to buy food for his family.

His mind raced back to the past. Reared from a wealthy family in Tondo, Manila, he was popular among his friends. As a young man, he became the natural leader of his friends as he often treated them in bars with liquor and other pleasures. They used to get drunk and got involved in vicious gang fights with rival groups. He landed in jail several times because of theft and violence.

Despite his carefree and wild lifestyle, Deo graduated from college with a degree in mechanical engineering. He enjoyed the "good life." He often picked up the bar tab whenever he went out with his friends to drink beer.

In the 1970s, he worked as a supervisor at Hooven Comelco (Philippines), the country's unit of the global firm dealing with aluminum products. A Christian sales manager from the company urged the unbelieving Deo, "You must be born again." Deo replied, "Should I go back to my mother's womb?" The encounter exactly reflected the verbal exchange between Jesus Christ and Nicodemus (John 3).

Because of his innate curiosity about faith, he attended a weekly Bible study at the workplace. At age 30, somebody handed him a Bible. Surprised, Deo did not realize that such a book exists. Since childhood, he had never heard about the Bible and even saw one at home or in school.

Despite having a loving family, a secured life, and a certain level of faith, Deo still felt lost and unfulfilled. He sought refuge by continuously drinking liquor, and soon turned into an alcoholic. "My mouth would salivate whenever I see a TV ad depicting people merry-making with alcohol," he remarked.

In 1980, the company he worked for closed and he was left jobless. He wrestled with the thought of providing food for his family and of sending his three children to school. He tried applying for other jobs but failed. Deo questioned why God could put him in such a predicament despite the hard work he put into to provide for his family. Amid all of these, alcohol was still running in his veins.

On this memorable day with his daughter, tears fell down his eyes. He questioned why God took away his job which made him incapable of giving his baby daughter milk. Helpless and distressed, God suddenly intervened in his life. Deo recalled the words in Matthew 6:33: "But seek first his kingdom and his righteousness, and all these things will be given to you as well." He felt a piercing message in his heart that money was his god, and the Lord was teaching him a lesson.

At that moment, Deo decided to follow Jesus. He held on to the unswerving belief that God provides to everyone who loves Him. His life changed as God answered his needs. He prayed, attended church services, and pursued faith diligently. During these times, Deo applied for an overseas job and got accepted. His employment, however, did not push through because, for the first time in his life, he discovered that he is color-blind. In another instance, he also received a telegram from the Middle East to report for work. But he declined the offer.

Deo realized that God had bigger plans for him. He trained for ministry work, discipleship, and immersed himself in the study of Scriptures. Enthusiastic, he also started a weekly Bible study right in the garage of his home in Marikina City. Over time, the number of people attending the meetings grew.

Upon the insistence of his church officers, he started Calvary Chapel in Marikina City to accommodate the growing number of believers in the locality. Calvary Chapel Costa Mesa (California, USA) is an evangelical church with around 1,000 congregations worldwide.

Today, Pastor Deo remains active in leading the local church and ministry. Since 2009, he regularly preaches to the residents of the MRC. As an epitome of a changed life, he continually stresses the importance of faith and sanctification for a drug-and-alcohol-free life. He said, "Sanctification is a lifelong aim. Faith increases by continuing sanctification."

By faith Abraham, when called to go to a place he
would later receive as his inheritance, obeyed and
went, even though he did not know where he was
going.
—Hebrews 11:8

Abraham, the father of many nations, showed utmost faith in following God. The Lord had a mission for him—to establish the Jewish state from where our Messiah would arrive. Billions of Jews, Christians, and Muslims would also later revere Him. Abraham departed his homeland and left with his family and possessions into uncharted territory. Without any doubt or questioning, he trusted God completely.

As a further show of faith, Abraham almost killed his beloved son Isaac when God tested his loyalty. In Genesis 22, the Lord instructed Abraham to offer Isaac as a burnt sacrifice in the mountains. When he was about to smite the bounded Isaac with a knife, an angel of the Lord appeared. The divine messenger said, "Do not lay a hand on the boy. Do not do anything to him. Now I know that you fear God, because you have not withheld from me your son, your only son" (v.12).

Recovering addicts and alcoholics must be relentless in their pursuit of faith. Despite the bondage and the difficulty of following Christ, obedience to God through unwavering faith opens the path to recovery and redemption.

The Healing Power of Faith

My ears had heard of you but now my eyes have
seen you.
—Job 42:5

Job had everything in life: a beautiful family, good health, and riches. As a godly man who prayed and despised evil (Job 1:1), "He owned seven thousand sheep, three thousand camels, five hundred yokes of oxen and five hundred donkeys, and had a large number of servants" (v.3[a]). He was the greatest man in the East (v.3[b]). God called him "my servant" and nobody on earth compared to him (v.8).

But Job was unaware of the battle raging in the heavenly realm. In a dialogue with God, Satan attributed Job's blessings in life to the "works of His hands" (v.10). Satan argued that Job would turn away from God if all of Job's good tidings were removed: "But now stretch out your hand and strike everything he has, and he will surely curse you to your face" (v.11). The Lord permitted Satan to test Job's faith and devotion to Him, but that Job's life would be spared (v.12).

Numerous tragedies befell Job. His ten children died (v.19), and his entire wealth was wiped out (vv.15-17). Because of the agony and loss, he tore his garments and shaved his head (v.20). Job also contracted boils in his whole body (c2:7), and his wife told him to curse God (v.9).

Despite the severe brokenness and grief, Job did not curse God. He even exalted Him. He said, "Naked I came from my mother's womb, and naked I will depart. The Lord gave and the Lord has taken away; may the name of the Lord be praised" (Job 1:21). The Lord later "restored his fortunes and gave him twice as much as he had before" (Job 42:10), including the sons and daughters he lost. Job also lived for one hundred and forty years and saw his children and their children to the fourth generation (Job 42:16).

Job epitomized true, reverent faith. Despite the intensity of his crisis and ordeals, he didn't lose faith in God. Instead, he exalted the Lord. Even when he felt forsaken, he believed that God was still with him.

> *Don't tell God how big your storm is; tell the storm how big your God is.*
> **—Anonymous**

Afflictions and troubles in life are huge roadblocks in nurturing our faith. At the MRC, about 70% of residents claim that life problems (poverty, family brokenness, and other difficulties) are the reasons they use drugs. In a sinister way, they use these adverse conditions as justifications for taking illegal substances. Yet, on the contrary, most take drugs for its sheer pleasure and thrill.

Suffering, however, often leads a drug dependent to God. When he has reached rock bottom and has no one or nothing else to cling to, faith appears. They soon grasp the words of Jesus, "Apart from me, you can do nothing" (John 15:5[b]).

Divine healing depends on the addict's measure of faith. Matthew 9 best illustrates the relationship between God and man during difficult times. Jesus asked the two blind men if they believe they can be cured. They replied, "Yes, Lord" (v.48). Jesus said, "According to your faith, let it be done to you" (v.29).

Neil Anderson writes, "If you want your faith in God to increase, you must increase your understanding of Him as the object of your faith."[3] The vigorous and persistent pursuit of faith hastens divine healing.

Faith is taking the first step even when you don't see the whole staircase!
—Martin Luther King, Jr., American minister

Drug dependents need the truth. John 8:32 says: "Then you will know the truth, and the truth will set you free." The indwelling of the Holy Spirit ushers freedom and a renewed identity in Christ—a liberation from the yoke of addiction and past sins.

Divine healing depends on the addict's measure of faith.

Divine healing starts when drug users commit themselves to knowing Christ. The pursuit of the Gospel breaks down the barriers of doubt and unbelief. Faith leads to the regeneration of the body and the indwelling of the Holy Spirit. After true repentance, faith sustains godly recovery.

Aside from lingering doubts or unbelief, addicts expect God to heal them quickly or in a certain way. In 2 Kings 5, the prophet

Elisha told Naaman to "Go, wash yourself seven times in the Jordan, and your flesh will be restored and you will be cleansed" (v.10[b]). However, Naaman got angry and said, "I thought that he would surely come out to me and stand and call on the name of the Lord his God, wave his hand over the spot and cure me of my leprosy. Are not Abana and Pharpar, the rivers of Damascus, better than all the waters of Israel? Couldn't I wash in them and be cleansed?" (vv.11-12). After some convincing from his servants, Naaman eventually went to the Jordan River, dipped in seven times, and was healed (vv.13-14).

The drug user needs to seek God and obey His will, which is specific for every believer, to achieve recovery. For example, God may deem that a recovering addict is better off without a job at the start of recovery because having money may be a trigger that would cause him to relapse. He would be better off expanding his faith by studying the Bible and serve the community. Moreover, he can't expect or demand God to heal him in six months. God has a unique way and time in dealing with the recovery of each individual.

Recovery is not a quick fix. It can be a lifelong process. It's a fallacy that an addict must be completely sober for some time before he can start effectively pursuing faith. Many addicts at the MRC declare, "I'll begin my journey of faith, pray to God, go to church, and read the Bible if I'm ready and relatively free from drugs." They also feel ashamed facing God while they are under sin or still entertain thoughts of using drugs. However, Jesus often appears during the dark moments of addiction.

> *But the seed falling on good soil refers to someone who hears the word and understands it. This is the one who produces a crop, yielding a hundred, sixty or thirty times what was sown.*
> **—Matthew 13:23**

Jesus Christ illustrated in the Gospels that God generously gives the seed of faith to anyone who believes in Him. But not all seeds grow and become fruitful. Some are scattered in the wrong places and are eaten by the birds (v.4). Some grew on stony ground but could not survive because they did not have deep roots (vv.5-6). Others grew on thorny grounds but were soon overpowered by competing, thorny plants (v.7).

In the parable, Jesus Christ is the sower who came for the atonement of our sins. However, not everybody nurtures faith. Doubt and unbelief grapple many people. Some believe in God but are reluctant in building up their faith. Because of weak faith, they become easy prey to the Evil One.

Faith is a vital component of divine healing. It rests on the continuing belief of God's existence and His love for anyone who calls His name. Idolatrous drug dependents have to leave their love of the flesh and of the things of this world (1 John 2:15[a].) They also have to let go of their occult practices, promiscuous orgies, drug dealers, and other idols. These wicked ways and vestiges perpetuate addiction and relapse.

God is holy and pure. He wants obedience and desires to weed out all our iniquities. Faith demands the addicts' submission and dependency on God. They must rely on God, not on drugs or their drug dealers. James 4:7 states: "Therefore submit to God. Resist the devil and he will flee from you." God is the Great Healer who can change their lives. An unshakable commitment to faith-building leads to full restoration and the renewal of the self.

> *For we walk by faith, not by sight.*
> **—2 Corinthians 5:7, KJV**

Genuine faith is for everyone who believes in the true God and accepts Jesus Christ as Lord and Savior. Drug addicts and alcoholics, with hearts hardened by sin, must cultivate a hunger for truth as they direly need God's Word.

Faith must be experienced through the actual practice of God's teachings. A person hooked on drugs should not rely on doctrinal knowledge from Scriptures alone. Faith is proactive.

Jesus said, "If you abide in my word, you are truly my disciples" (John 8:31 [b], *ESV*). Abiding means following the instructions of God, which often runs contrary to the world's principles. For instance, the recovering addict must love his enemies, be content with what he has, persevere amid suffering, and yield to the other commands of God.

Faith means action. In Matthew 12:13, Jesus commanded a man with the withered hand to "stretch out" his hand and was healed. Addicts ought to face their substance dependency and follow God's leadings. With sheer faith, David slew the giant Goliath with just a slingshot. Running away from any problem only exacerbates the addiction. In the book, *The Faith Factor*, Dr. Dale Matthews wrote, "Religiously involved youngsters are markedly less likely to use tobacco, alcohol, and illegal drugs."[4]

For many individuals, faith rests entirely on positive outcomes or feelings. However, belief in God should not only reside in success in life or the realm of the five senses. When people get a job promotion or the 6 o'clock news says that the GNP rose by five percent, their faith is affirmed as they remember God who blessedly provides. However, when cancer strikes or they get fired from their jobs of fifteen years, they feel abandoned and question the Almighty's love for them. Doubts or unbelief creep into them, choking their faith.

"The righteous will live by faith" (Romans 1:17[b]), not feelings. Faith can produce sensations, but such impressions alone will never result in belief. Drug addicts have relied on their senses and emotions for many years in their lives. They evade reality and sought sensory changes from chemicals. If they feel broken, they reach for pot, cocaine, or meth to ignite fireworks in their brains. If they need to control their restlessness, anxiety, or sleeplessness, they gulp alcohol or take tranquilizers to numb themselves or knock them off to sleep.

The pursuit of faith by shattering one's reliance on the senses is a huge challenge. Addicts have to gather added portions of courage and perseverance to gain confidence in God amid pain and despair. The steadfast pursuit of faith demolishes the strongholds of Satan. Drug dependents have to identify and confront the things they worship or erroneously put so much value in their lives. Faith is based on the unswerving belief of our identity in Christ and on His promises, not on our feelings or external conditions.

> *Faith is based on the unswerving belief of our identity in Christ and on His promises, not on our feelings or external conditions.*

The Barriers of Doubt and Unbelief

For those with faith, no explanation is necessary. For those without, no explanation is possible.
—Thomas Aquinas, philosopher and priest

After the death of Jesus Christ, the disciples avoided going out in public and locked themselves inside houses for fear of the Jewish leaders. One Sunday evening, the disciples gathered for an evening meal. Suddenly, Jesus appeared before them (Luke 24:36). Startled and scared, they thought they saw a ghost (v.37). Jesus said, "Look at my hands and my feet. It is I myself! Touch me and see; a ghost does not have flesh and bones, as you see I have" (v.39).

The Apostle Thomas was not with them and doubted the news that Jesus rose from the dead (John 20: 24- 25). He said, "Unless I see the nail marks in his hands and put my finger where the nails were, and put my hand into his side, I will not believe" (v.25[b]).

A week later, Jesus showed up again before them, and this time, Thomas was with them (v.26). Jesus told Thomas, "Put your finger here; see my hands. Reach out your hand and put it into my side. Stop doubting and believe" (v.27[b]). Thomas replied, "My Lord and my God!" (v.28[b]).

During the early ministry of Jesus, Thomas displayed courage and loyalty as a disciple. However, the death of Jesus brought doubts to Thomas, including his faith in Jesus' resurrection and appearance to the disciples.

Today, the world is filled with Doubting Thomases who are unsure about the existence of God. Doubt is a universal occurrence that works in different ways. When a Christian doubts, he questions the presence of God. When an atheist doubts, he fears God is real.

Skepticism is a tool of Satan to make us lose our trust and reliance on God's Word. We sometimes feel His promise of eternal life unlikely. Like Augustine, we ponder, "If there is no God, why is there so much good? If there is a God, why is there so much evil?"

In Genesis 3, Satan introduced doubt at the Garden of Eden when he tempted Eve to eat the fruit from the tree in the middle of the garden. God warned her that she would die if she touched the forbidden fruit. The serpent said, "You will not certainly die...For God knows that when you eat from it your eyes will be opened, and you will be like God, knowing good and evil" (vv.4-5). She believed the wiles of the Devil, doubted God, ate the fruit, and gave some to Adam (v.6).

In the wilderness, chaos and dangers marked the trek of the Israelites to the Promised Land. However, God had shown His love for them by guiding them and providing them with food, water, and other necessities. Clearly, the problem of the Israelites resided in their hearts—doubt, ungratefulness, impatience, and upheaval.

Because of their lack of faith, God made them intentionally wander through the desert for forty years when the journey would have taken them only eleven days (Deuteronomy 1:1-2). As a form of punishment, many also didn't reach Canaan.

Then Jesus told him, "Because you have seen me, you have believed; blessed are those who have not seen and yet have believed."
—John 20:29

In the fantasy world of drugs, God is not real. Boozers and dopers also often believe rehab and physicians would be sufficient for them to gain recovery. Many can't figure out how God can help them get out of bondage. But, Pastor Tony Dela Paz adds, "Addiction is a sin. Many graduates from rehab are fully recovered [physically], but sin is not removed."

Their addicted empirical brains often compel them that what cannot be seen or rationally proven does not exist. "I can't see God" or "Nobody came back from heaven" are some of their common remarks when the subjects about God, heaven, and hell come up. They ask, "How could a lowly Nazarene carpenter be the Messiah to save me from all of my troubles?" It is easier for drug dependents to doubt than to pursue faith and learn the truths about God. On top of doubt and unbelief, idolatry rules the mindsets of dejected addicts, which intensifies the wrath of God.

Deep in addiction, enslaved skeptics easily flock to the camps of Darwinism and the school of thought that life came from chemical reactions on warm pond billions of years ago. They cling to evolution regarding the origins of life. These notions easily cancel the existence of God and His love for addicted sinners.

However, these anti-creation beliefs are being debunked, even in the halls of modern science because the demands for updated proof and logic are not met. It becomes more profound that reason points to the direction that an intelligent, vastly incomprehensible design serves as the blueprint for the beginnings of life. God must exist.

Faith is sheer belief. A driver approaching an intersection with a green light does not stop because he believes that the other driver facing the red light would stop. Hebrews 11:1 reads: "Now faith is confidence in what we hope for and assurance about what we do not see."

Ronnie, a former meth addict and a resident of the MRC, placed his life on God's hand for his recovery. Today, he has a loving family and holds a job as a security officer. He once remarked, "'To believe is to see' and not 'to see is to believe.'"

A study funded by the Swiss National Science Foundation reported that "Young Swiss men who say that they believe in God are less likely to smoke cigarettes or pot or take Ecstasy pills than Swiss men of the same age group who describe themselves as atheists. Belief is a protective factor against addictive behaviour."[5]

> *Doubt isn't the opposite of faith; it is an element of faith.*
> **—Paul Tillich, philosopher and theologian**

Faith is a product of free will—a gift from God. Our Heavenly Father does not force Himself to be known, understood, loved, and worshiped by man. Instead, God wants us to believe that He is "The way and the truth and the life" (John 14:6).

Most addicts and alcoholics who come to God are searching for a fresh start, hoping that God can repair their brokenness and desperation in life. However, the biggest obstacles that loom on the horizons are relentless doubt and unbelief. Hebrews 11:6 states: "And without faith it is impossible to please God, because anyone who comes to Him must believe that He exists."

However, doubt and faith can co-exist. Skepticism does not necessarily mean the absence of faith. You can only doubt what you already believe. Uncertainty about God and His teachings are some of the most common struggles in the life of a Christian. Charles Spurgeon said, "I do not believe there ever existed a Christian yet, who did not now and then doubt his interest in Jesus. I think, when a man says, 'I never doubt,' it is quite time for us to doubt him."

Questioning what we believe can result in stronger faith if we look for answers to our inquiries and take the right steps in resolving them. God's Word is the source of truth. Some people feel their dilemma is doubt, but their actual problem is unbelief. They do not have faith to doubt from the start.

Billy Graham, who was called "the greatest evangelist," harbored doubts. In 1949, before a large crusade in Los Angeles, he grappled with uncertainty whether he could fully trust the Bible. Finally, he said, "Father, I am going to accept this as Thy Word—by faith! I'm going to allow faith to go beyond my intellectual questions and doubts, and I will believe this to be Your inspired Word."[6]

The Bible is full of prominent characters whose faith wavered. Abraham laughed and doubted when God told him that his wife, Sarah, would bear a son. "Will a son be born to a man a hundred years old? Will Sarah bear a child at the age of ninety?" (Genesis 17:17). David had strong faith, yet he often questioned and doubted God numerous times. In prison, John the Baptist questioned if Jesus was the real Messiah. He sent two of his disciples to ask the Lord, "Are you the one who is to come, or should we expect someone else?" (Luke 7:19[b]).

In his book, *The Case for Faith*, Lee Strobel writes:

> *Many spiritual seekers have legitimate questions concerning Christianity and need to pursue answers that will satisfy their heart and soul. Yet, I think some seekers get to the point where they are subconsciously raising smokescreens to mask their deep-seated motivations for rejecting the faith.*[7]

Relentless doubt inhibits the growth of faith and delays divine healing. Unbelief denies the existence of God and rescinds any remedy from our loving Father. One can't approach God in doubt or unbelief. Divine healing is founded

Relentless doubt inhibits the growth of faith and delays divine healing.

on the atonement by our Savior and Lord Jesus Christ so we can receive eternal life and deliverance.

A sick person can't effectively seek medical treatment if she doesn't have confidence in her doctor and refuses to follow prescriptive orders. She must pray, ask, and seek for faith, and believe that Jesus Christ is our Healer and Savior. When Jesus Christ began his earthly ministry, He often and importantly emphasized belief as a primordial pursuit of man. Healing is a result of faith.

Persistence is key. Hebrews 10:23 (*GW*) says: "We must continue to hold firmly to our declaration of faith. The one who made the promise is faithful." When addicts plea for God's help, they should not doubt God. James 1:6-8 says, "But when you ask, you must believe and not doubt, because the one who doubts is like a wave of the sea, blown and tossed by the wind. That person should not expect to receive anything from the Lord. Such a person is double-minded and unstable in all they do."

On the other hand, unbelief can serve as a springboard for vigorous faith. C.S. Lewis, the author of *Mere Christianity*, once a professed atheist, became an ardent believer in God.

The life of Paul had shown the defining transformation of a Roman officer, who killed and persecuted Jews, from a blatant unbeliever to one of the most prominent disciples of Jesus Christ. He declared, "Even though I was once a blasphemer and a persecutor and a violent man, I was shown mercy because I acted in ignorance and unbelief" (1 Timothy 1:13). The relentless pursuit of faith leads to sanctification that breaks down all walls of doubt and unbelief in our Creator.

Deceptions About Faith and Divine Healing

1. *I am a total sinner. God wouldn't heal me.*
   God heals anyone who repents and accepts Jesus Christ as Lord and Savior.

2. *It is not God's will to heal me.*
   God loves all of us and is always willing to help anyone who believes Him.

3. *I always pray, but my addiction remains.*
   Prayer alone does not always result in divine healing.

4. *I always read the Bible and go to church; I believe I am healed.*
Reading the Bible and going to church do not prove deliverance has been attained.

5. *I am healed because I no longer take drugs; I just drink alcohol and smoke pot.*
Divine healing happens when the tyranny of all addictive substances is removed.

6. *My faith is so small; I can't be healed.*
God can heal any person with the smallest faith.

7. *Miracles are no longer real.*
Miracles occur every day.

8. *Doctors and medicines are not part of divine healing.*
The Scriptures support physicians and medicines as components of God's provision for healing.

9. *I only need a doctor or somebody else to cure me of my addiction.*
Recovering addicts who think they don't need God rarely achieve real, long-term recovery. Many also end in relapse.

10. *I did not take drugs or alcohol for five years; I no longer need divine healing.*
Divine healing is a lifetime covenant with God.

11. *I did not use drugs or drink alcohol for many years, but I still crave these substances. Maybe, I am healed.*
People who crave for drugs and alcohol are still in bondage; divine healing is not yet achieved.

12. *I have followed God, but I can't feel any healing.*
Divine healing is usually progressive because the building up of faith takes time. God's healing is also not sensory, but the holistic cleansing of body, soul, and spirit.

The Building Blocks of Faith

If you have little knowledge about God and His Word, you will have little faith. If you have great knowledge of God and His Word, you will have great faith.
—Neil Anderson, author and minister

As Jesus entered the village of Capernaum, He was approached by Jewish elders sent by a centurion whose slave was sick and at the point of death. They pleaded Him to heal the servant because the deserving centurion "loves our nation and has built our synagogue" (Luke 7:5). Jesus agreed to come to the house of the centurion (v.6).

The centurion, being a Roman and enemy of the Jews, knew his predicament. However, he had faith in Jesus and believed in the miracles that the Messiah performed. With utmost humility, he sent friends to say to Jesus, "Lord, don't trouble yourself; for I do not deserve to have you come under my roof" (v.6[b]). The centurion also remarked that he was not worthy to come to Jesus (v.7[a]). "But say the word, and my servant will be healed" (v.7[b]). When the messengers returned to the house, they found the servant healed (v.10).

In this incident, divine healing surpassed the boundaries of distance, social status, race, nationality, and spiritual state. The centurion belonged to the higher class of citizens, and the slave was a foreigner with "small value" and probably an unbeliever who had not heard about Jesus Christ. But Jesus healed the slave. He affirmed the centurion's faith and said, "I tell you, I have not found such great faith even in Israel" (v.9[b]).

The Bible emphasizes the "measure of faith" as a vital gauge in our relentless pursuit of God. Paul said, "We ought always to thank God for you, brothers and sisters, and rightly so, because your faith is growing more and more, and the love all of you have for one another is increasing" (2 Thessalonians 1:3). But, nobody can claim he has attained the maximum level of faith. No one has reached the perfection of Jesus.

Faith is like a spiritual bank account. God has given us an initial deposit of faith as a gift. The Apostle Paul proclaimed that God had allotted faith to each one of us (Romans 12:3). By harnessing and sharing our faith with others, we increase our trust in God and enjoy a spirit-filled life.

An utmost belief in the divine authority of Jesus is exemplified by the attitude and action of the woman who had been bleeding for twelve years. She touched the cloak of Jesus (Matthew 9:20[a]). She said, "If I only touch his cloak, I will be healed" (v.21). Jesus told her, "Your faith has healed you" (v.22[a]).

The seed of faith planted in man begets the responsibility and willingness to nurture our complete reliance on God. God's Word brings Christ into our hearts and the equipping power of divine healing. Brother Job, a friend in our local church, once told me, "Nurturing faith is like riding a bicycle. You must keep on pedaling. Otherwise, you will fall."

The Measure of One's Faith

The kingdom of heaven is like a mustard seed, which a man took and planted in his field. Though it is the smallest of all seeds, yet when it grows, it is the largest of garden plants and becomes a tree, so that the birds come and perch in its branches.
—Matthew 13: 31-32

The mustard seed, a popular spice and one of the smallest seeds, measures around one to two millimeters in diameter. Technically not a tree, the mustard plant can grow up to six to twenty feet high, with rare plants reaching thirty feet, spreading its branches quickly.

The parable of the mustard seed illustrates faith that starts small and grows in measure. As we grow in faith, we become closer to the likeness of God. We also turn more resilient from the wiles of the Enemy. Above all, we become faithful disciples of Jesus Christ.

At the start of recovery, addicts may possess some measure of faith. Despite the anguish and darkness in their lives, they may see a flicker of light or a beam of hope from God. But, fostering faith to achieve recovery takes time. Pastor Deo Salgado remarked, "Sanctification is often a slow cleansing of the addicted, sinful person." Despite the faith, the power of Satan may still dominate their lives. Their trust and obedience to God are sometimes eclipsed by many kinds of temptations and drug cravings.

Mustering faith requires focus and a change of attitude and lifestyle. For example, praying before meals is an excellent start to exercise faith. Carrying a Bible in public places or transport may be unlikely or uncomfortable for recovering addicts. However, as serious students of God's Word, holding a Bible anywhere must bear no shame or discomfort.

According to a study conducted by the University of Michigan Addiction Research Center, "Those who had reported an increase in daily spiritual experiences were less likely to participate in heavy drinking, as were those who had experienced an increase in feelings that their lives had purpose."[1]

Divine healing is a total surrender of all our iniquities and worldly attachments to God. If an addict or alcoholic manages to stay sober but could not let go of his other besetting sins, deliverance is not achieved.

In another aspect, the cessation of cursing is a considerable lifestyle change. The majority of the residents of the MRC swears and utters repeated sinful profanities. I often challenge them to test their willingness to pursue faith by watching their language. I challenge them, "If you can stop cursing, you can also stop taking drugs." Surprisingly, they would find it may be more difficult to stop cursing than to give up drugs.

Addicts feel the need for restoration but are reluctant to pursue faith because they are still using or wrestling with withdrawal symptoms. In these times, they need all the love, hand-holding, and support in their early struggles of faith and recovery.

Comparing our level of faith with other people shows weakness. God detests spiritual pride. Romans 12:3 says: "For by the grace given me I say to every one of you: Do not think of yourself more highly than you ought, but rather think of yourself with sober judgment, in accordance with the faith God has distributed to each of you." We should not get jealous when other people claim they are experiencing joy and spiritual awakening. We ought to cultivate faith and work out our salvation (Philippians 2:12).

Jesus often admonished his disciples for their lack of faith. In Matthew 8, Jesus calmed the storm and rebuked the apostles for fear of the strong wind when they were on a boat. Jesus said, "You of little faith, why are you so afraid?" (v.26[a]). Jesus also healed a boy after the apostles failed to drive out evil spirits (Luke 9:40-42). Nevertheless, the disciples eventually fulfilled the mandate of Jesus, proclaimed His kingdom, and performed healings, signs, and wonders.

> *Then he touched their eyes and said, "According to*
> *your faith let it be done to you."*
> **—Matthew 9:29**

After Jesus raised the daughter of a synagogue leader in Capernaum, two blind men followed Him saying, "Have mercy on us, Son of David!" (v.27). Jesus asked them if they believed that He could heal them (v.28[a]). They replied, "Yes, Lord" (v.28[b]). "Then he touched their eyes and said, 'According to your faith let it be done to you' and their sight was restored" (v.29).

Divine healing rests on the level of one's faith. The Bible emphasizes that dynamic belief in God and His precepts is key to accessing God's supernatural power. Unlike the two blind men, addicts remain skeptical that God can heal their deep-seated drug addictions. Sadly, it often takes many years before addicts put their full belief and trust in the Lord.

Escaping from the clutches of Satan and moving toward our Creator require consistent prayer in conjunction with reading God's Word and worship through songs. Only then, can the Lord respond through His mercy and grace to bring about recovery.

As our faith increases, we begin to throw off our bondage to the "cares of this life." In the book *Addiction and Grace*, Gerald May M.D. wrote, "Faith is the human component of that mysterious interweaving of divine grace and human intention that can vanquish the power of attachment."[2] With God's help, the time will eventually come when we finally lose our romance with drugs, alcohol, and other addictive substances. Only then will we begin to enjoy life as a responsible person and a faithful child of God.

Prayer: The Source of Authority

Ask and it will be given to you; seek and you will find; knock and the door will be opened to you. For everyone who asks receives; the one who seeks finds; and to the one who knocks, the door will be opened.
—Matthew 7:7-8

The sky was still dark as Jesus started his walk to find a quiet place to pray (Mark 1:35). Leaving the disciples to their slumber, He made His way up the mountain where He would find the isolation and quietness He needed. As the Messiah, Jesus needed to commune with His Heavenly Father. He had to unburden Himself from the pressures of teaching an unbelieving public and plead with God for strength and guidance. Above all, He needed to exalt the Father as His Creator. In the stillness at the crack of dawn, Jesus Christ prayed.

> Most addicts and alcoholics seldom pray. Often, to them, God doesn't exist or even matter.

Unlike Jesus, many drug addicts and alcoholics have different priorities upon waking in the morning. Meth addicts scramble to retrieve their hidden stash of meth and lock themselves in the bathroom for their initial early morning kick. Alcoholics scuttle to the cupboard to take a quick swig of whiskey. Only then can they face the mundane tasks of the day, like having breakfast and preparing to go to work. Isaiah 5:11 reads, "Woe to those who rise early in the morning to run after their drinks, who stay up late at night till they are inflamed with wine."

Drug dependents and alcoholics are mired in sin, contaminating their sacred bodies with deadly substances. Having lost sight of the difference between right and wrong, they're more likely to steal, manipulate, engage in promiscuity, and commit adultery. Addicts are also often idolatrous—making drugs the primary object in their lives. Once stoned, high, or drunk, they become creatures with no need for faith. Pride, denial, and self-justification more easily consume them and harden their hearts against the idea that addiction is a sin.

Most addicts and alcoholics seldom pray. Often, to them, God doesn't exist or even matter. As atheists, hedonists, and idolaters, they believe only in themselves, drugs, money, and their drug dealers.

Their addiction becomes a life-dominating problem, and they spend many years or even decades wandering in the desolation and isolation of drug dependency. Eventually, they will reach rock bottom, and when they do, they'll realize that they must surrender themselves to God.

Prayer is the key to unlocking the addict's plight. It breeds humility, which reveals to the addict that he or she is the lesser being before an Almighty God.

Is anyone among you in trouble? Let them pray.
—James 5:13[a]

On the Day of Atonement, only the High Priest could enter the Holy of Holies to seek forgiveness for the sins of the Israelites. Once a year, a feast day was celebrated with animal sacrifice as required by God (Leviticus 16). Thus, through the atoning death of Jesus Christ and His holy name and authority, we have direct access to God in prayer and worship.

The daunting times of addiction and recovery are filled with many assaults by Satan attempting to win back his former minion. An empty wineglass on the dinner table could send a stinging signal to the gut of an alcoholic. A stream of cigarette smoke from a passerby could suggest an enticing line of meth or crack to a doper. Television, with its vast array of suggestive shows and commercials, might elicit addictive thoughts that bring relapse.

Recovering addicts have to contend with addiction triggers every day. Temptations and flashes of cravings are like lightning that strikes suddenly out of nowhere. These intrusions can lead the recovering addict to the dangerous cliff of relapse.

Prayer is the first aid to halt the enticements of the Unseen Enemy immediately. When an individual admits his powerlessness, renounces the drugs, and cries out for strength and help from God to thwart the Evil One, he gains strength.

True prayer is measured by weight, not by length. A single groan before God may have more fullness of prayer in it than a fine oration of great length.
—Charles H. Spurgeon, preacher

Prayer, also the most common form of worship, is essential for an addict to express his faith in the Almighty. Luke 16:10[b] says: "If you are faithful in little things, you will be faithful in large ones." Intermittent prayers are the baby steps toward repentance and the nurturing of faith. A healthy prayer life demonstrates a person's commitment to God that unveils the most significant promise of salvation.

When an addict prays, he seeks God's truth and mercy. Despite his wretchedness, he also declares that addiction is a sin and accepts that there exists the highest power that rules over him. He pleads God for the renewing of his mind.

To overcome the temptations that he contends with every day, the addict learns to rebuke evil spirits. Second Corinthians 10:4 says: "The weapons we fight with are not the weapons of the world. On the contrary, they have divine power to demolish strongholds." Spiritual warfare involves intense praying.

Divine healing is the consistent aim of an addict's prayer. He has learned that rehab and other secular approaches were not sufficient in the deliverance of his trampled body and soul.

Lord, teach us to pray.
—Luke 11:1[b]

One dilemma of a recovering addict is the manner on how to pray. He wrestles in praying to the true God in the right way. He possesses a seed of faith and wants to communicate with God, but often wonders what his prayers should contain.

The Lord's Prayer in Matthew 6:9-13 encompasses all the essential components of prayer: worship, confession, thanksgiving, and petition. Jesus prayed:

Our Father in heaven, hallowed be your name, your kingdom come, your will be done, on earth as it is in heaven. Give us today our daily bread. And forgive us our debts, as we also have forgiven our debtors. And lead us not into temptation, but deliver us from the evil one.

At the beginning of one's prayer life, God helps those who show sincere faith and intention. Romans 8:26 says: "In the same way, the Spirit helps us in our weakness. We do not know what we ought to pray for, but the Spirit himself intercedes for us through wordless groans."

PRAYING IN HUMILITY

> *And when you pray, do not be like the hypocrites, for they love to pray standing in the synagogues and on the street corners to be seen by others. Truly I tell you, they have received their reward in full. But when you pray, go into your room, close the door and pray to your Father, who is unseen. Then your Father, who sees what is done in secret, will reward you.*
> **—Matthew 6:5-6**

A recovering addict needs to approach God with humility and repentance. To always confess one's sins will lead to godly sorrow and divine healing. In the book *Enter His Gates*, Charles Stanley wrote, "Prayer becomes the spiritual scalpel that lifts off the stifling layers of self-preoccupation."[3]

An addict cannot gain God's grace and favor if he has unconfessed sins. Isaiah 59:2 says: "But your iniquities have separated you from your God; your sins have hidden his face from you, so that he will not hear." Unforgiveness, pride, and idolatry are some of the sins that serve as obstacles in our communication with God. Seeking forgiveness from God for all of our sins is integral in our prayers to be connected with God again.

A spirit of humility and mercy is a crucial element so God will hear us as we pray. Isaiah 66:2[b] reads: "These are the ones I look on with favor: those who are humble and contrite in spirit, and who tremble at my word."

We also have to follow God's commands if we seek answers from our prayers. First John 3:22 says: "And receive from him anything we ask, because we keep his commands and do what pleases him."

While we look for forgiveness from God, we must also truly forgive others. Our Father in Heaven doesn't listen when we come to him in a spirit of revenge, resentment, or hatred. Matthew 6:14-15 reads: "For if you forgive other people when they sin against you, your heavenly Father will also forgive you. But if you do not forgive others their sins, your Father will not forgive your sins."

SEEKING GOD'S WILL

> This is the confidence we have in approaching God:
> that if we ask anything according to his will, he hears
> us.
> **—1 John 5:14**

We often wrestle with the thought of praying in line with God's will. How can I possibly know God's will? Do my groans seeking healing for my sick sons elicit God's approval? Is asking for a job all right with Him? However, we soon arrive at the discernment that sometimes our petitions are granted and other times, they are left unanswered.

John 9:31 reads: "We know that God does not listen to sinners. He listens to the godly person who does his will." Sin blocks our prayers to God. But, listening to our prayers doesn't always mean that God would positively act on them. He may deny our prayer because it would cost us and other people harm. On the other hand, God may grant our prayers at a later time. God may deny a recovering addict who prays for a job because having money at the time would only serve as a trigger for a drug relapse.

We can't comprehend God's mind. God's plan is often not the same as our aims in life. Isaiah 55: 8-9 reads: "For my thoughts are not your thoughts, neither are your ways my ways...As the heavens are higher than the earth, so are my ways higher than your ways and my thoughts than your thoughts."

Many recovering addicts pray for restoration—mending of broken family ties, getting their jobs back, and being accepted to society. Their prayers do not focus on repentance and divine healing. They are more concerned about the wellness of their existence than the deliverance of their souls.

Aligning our petitions with God's will is key to answered prayers. A person who only prays whenever there is a financial or a health crisis is not abiding in God. We also pray for the wrong motives—to win the lottery, to have our wrinkles removed, or to get a lifetime supply of drugs. James 4:3 says: "When you ask, you do not receive, because you ask with wrong motives, that you may spend what you get on your pleasures."

Instead, we ought to often exalt and thank God, ask for forgiveness, and seek His guidance in our daily lives. Colossians 3:2 reads: "Set your minds on things above, not on earthly things." A Spirit-filled prayer life is the cornerstone of a happy relationship with God. Prayer should often go beyond the self—an act of worship by which we express our adoration and confidence in God.

> *A Spirit-filled prayer life is the cornerstone of a happy relationship with God.*

ESTABLISHING A ROBUST PRAYER LIFE

Pray without ceasing.
—1 Thessalonians 5:17

Jesus Christ was a man of prayer. He prayed in public and moments of solitude. Jesus also prayed during significant events in His ministry—before choosing the twelve disciples until His crucifixion and death at Calvary.

The daily life of a recovering addict and alcoholic must be charged with sincere, not shallow, prayers. The Greek word for "without ceasing" is *adialeiptos*, meaning constantly recurring, not nonstop.

A 2014 study of the Pew Research Center reveals:

More than half (55%) of Americans say they pray every day, while 21% say they pray weekly or monthly and 23% say they seldom or never pray. Even among those who are religiously unaffiliated, 20% say they pray daily. Women (64%) are more likely than men (46%) to pray every day. And Americans ages 65 and older are far more likely than adults under 30 to say they pray daily (65% vs. 41%).[4]

The Bible shows time patterns on when to pray: upon waking up, before meals, before going to sleep, before any important activity, and in spiritual warfare. In Daniel 6:10, Daniel prayed three times a day. King David also prayed three times a day. Psalm 55:16-17 reads: "As for me, I call to God, and the Lord saves me. Evening, morning, and noon I cry out in distress, and he hears my voice." In Matthew 14:19, Jesus looked up to heaven and gave thanks before he broke the bread to be eaten by His disciples and followers. Through prayer, the recovering addict's dependence and daily walk with God is magnified.

Despite their willingness to regularly pray, many recovering addicts from the MRC find difficulty praying at home. For example, they often find it awkward to say grace before meals in the presence of their unbelieving family members. But in due time and with persistence in prayer, God uses these moments in allowing other members of the family to become followers of Jesus Christ. Many Christian homes have developed through the initiative of a recovering, praying addict.

Praying and reading the Bible or some Christian literature before going to sleep is also beneficial. This spiritual nightcap also requests God for safety during sleep and in shedding off all the material, secular junk absorbed during the day. Proverbs 3:24 says: "When you lie down, you will not be afraid; when you lie down, your sleep will be sweet."

We must be relentless in our prayers. Winston Churchill, former Prime Minister of the UK, exuded inspiration and courage during World War II. Faced with the threat of the military might of Germany, he said, "Never, never, never give up." In an earlier time, Jesus told his disciples to "Always pray and not give up" (Luke 18:1[b]).

The parable of the persistent widow illustrates the message of Jesus that those who persevere boldly in their prayers will be heard (vv.5-13). The woman kept on badgering the judge until she got a favorable outcome. "And will not God bring about justice for his chosen ones, who cry out to him day and night? Will he keep putting them off?" (v.7).

A consistent prayer life also does wonders for our well-being. In his book, *God, Faith, and Health*, Jeff Levin Ph.D. wrote, "Frequent prayer, whether public or private, is associated with better health and emotional well-being and lower levels of psychological distress."[5]

Diligence and persistence in prayer are not the same as vain repetitions. When a son asks for a bicycle from his father, he does so several times before his request is granted. Repeated prayers found in Scriptures are worthy. The Psalms are filled with repeated prayers. During Sunday worship, we often sing the chorus multiple times. Matthew 6:7 (*KJV*) says: "But when ye pray, use not vain repetitions, as the heathen do: for they think that they shall be heard for their much speaking." The phrase "vain repetitions" is a translation of the Greek word *battalogeo*, which means to stutter. Other versions of the Bible translate the word as "babbling" (*NIV*) and "empty phrases" (*ESV*). Jesus described these vain repetitions as prayers of pagans. The Lord seeks simplicity in our prayers that comes out of our hearts.

An addict must also learn to pray for other people. Intercessory prayer expands his own active prayer life and diminishes an addict's obsession with the self. He should pray for his aching and broken family, fellow drug users, and pushers.

As we keenly study the Bible and surrender to Christ, His will progressively replaces our own. Luke 22:42 (*KJV*) reads: "Father, if it is Your will, take this cup away from Me; nevertheless not My will, but Yours, be done."

The Serenity Prayer

*God grant me the serenity to accept the things I
cannot change; courage to change the things I can;
and wisdom to know the difference. Living one day
at a time; enjoying one moment at a time; accepting
hardships as the pathway to peace; taking, as He did,
this sinful world as it is, not as I would have it; trusting
that He will make all things right if I surrender to His
Will; that I may be reasonably happy in this life and
supremely happy with Him forever in the next. Amen.*
—Reinhold Niebuhr

God's Word: The Source of Truth

*For the word of God is alive and active. Sharper than
any double-edged sword, it penetrates even to dividing soul and spirit, joints and marrow; it judges the
thoughts and attitudes of the heart.*
—Hebrews 4:12

Penuel Home: A Sanctuary of Healing

Two large aqua-colored steel panels greet the eyes of visitors at the
sprawling compound of Penuel Home. Tall, perennial trees surround the area, and a wide escalating, sloped driveway leads to the
main hall. The half-court basketball strip that lies on the far left of
the parking space adds vibrancy to the hallowed place.

On the main hall entrance, a big Bible lies open on top of an
old wooden rectangular table. Comfortable sofas and side chairs
for guests and residents of the home dot the living area. A book-
shelf filled with books about healing, addiction, and recovery
stands at one end of the main room. The place resembles a blend
of a quaint, family home, and the structure of a traditional school-
house.

Penuel Home is the recovery ministry facility of Christ's Commission Fellowship Church. As an all-male residency program, it

started as a support group under the Precious Hope Foundation of CCF in 2001 and became a recovery facility in 2006.

In the heart of the bustling city of San Juan, the place exudes a mixed aura of suburban air and peaceful seclusion. The main building houses the office, dormitories, kitchen, and living room while auxiliary rooms serve as functional areas for Bible study and fellowship.

The afternoon Bible study session commenced with around twelve residents sitting in front of a widescreen monitor. Pastor Tony Dela Paz motioned everybody to lower their heads for the opening prayer. Later, he opened the study on the Book of Galatians. The meeting examined the true Gospel as revealed by Jesus Christ in contrast to the false teaching espoused by some believers. Pastor Tony kept the course engaging as he cracked random jokes. He also held the topic on track by naturally veering the biblical narratives into its relevance to addiction, recovery, and divine healing.

Residents are encouraged to memorize verses and note their significance to specific situations in their lives. As a Christian rehab, the Holy Bible is the cornerstone of Penuel Home's recovery program.

Man shall not live on bread alone, but on every word
that comes from the mouth of God.
—Matthew 4:4 [b]

The Bible is an excellent resource in recovery ever written. It contains the stories of beloved characters who overcame life pains, tragedies, loss of loved ones, defeat, sickness, and desperation.

The Bible is an excellent resource in recovery ever written.

God's children are afflicted because of sin and the lack of truth about God and His teachings. Hosea 4:6 says, "My people are destroyed from lack of knowledge." However, with God's help, they turned out triumphant, recovered, and healed. Job endured the loss of his loved ones and prized material possessions. He also suffered from boils and skin diseases. However, through faith, God restored him with health and wealth far beyond what he lost.

We read about the accounts of Joseph, David, and the apostles who became heroes and revered figures of men. In the New Testament, we learn about the lepers, the demon-possessed, the blind, the lame, and the sick that got well because of the healing power and miracles of Jesus Christ.

Today, over 100 million Bibles are sold or given annually all over the world. However, the book remains a mystery to most people. Yet, its authenticity has been verified and corroborated by numerous archeological findings and biblical prophecies. As the essential book in the world, the Bible provides holistic principles on how to lead happy, triumphant lives by loving God and our neighbors. It clarifies the uncertainty and dangers of the world. Its prophecies reveal the future. Most importantly, it unveils God's promise of eternal life in the coming Kingdom of Heaven. Luke 21:33 declares: "Heaven and earth will pass away, but my words will never pass away."

As the ultimate source of truth and knowledge, the Bible is an indispensable tool for recovering addicts in the journey toward healing. John 14:6 reads: "I am the way and the truth and the life. No one comes to the Father except through me." It contains not only passages that explain how divine healing conquers all sorts of enslavement but also measures on how to renew one's mind. Former U.S. President Ronald Reagan said, "Within the covers of the Bible are the answers for all the problems men face." A consistent daily intake of Scripture ensures a steady flow of divine wisdom, which empowers us to face the adversities of everyday life.

Prayer is talking to God while reading the Bible is letting God speak to us, allowing Him to take over our lives. Idolatrous addicts, desperately thirsty for a higher power, satiates their innate plea for help by leaning to God.

Knowledge comes from the world, but wisdom comes from God. President Theodore Roosevelt once said, "A thorough knowledge of the Bible is worth more than a college education." God sets forth the tenets of daily living, family relations, work, and other social interactions, including the practice of good manners and right conduct in the Scriptures. George Washington, the first president of the United States, also remarked, "It is impossible to rightly govern a nation without God and the Bible."

The truth from Scriptures exposes the truth of God and the lies of the Enemy. In *The Bondage Breaker*, Neil Anderson writes:

> *Freedom from spiritual conflicts and bondage is not a power encounter; it's a truth encounter. Satan is a deceiver, and he will work undercover at all costs. But the truth of God's Word exposes him and his lie. His demons are like cockroaches that scurry for the shadows when the light comes on. Satan's power is in the lie, and when his lie is exposed by the truth, his plans are foiled.[6]*

Through Bible reading, the soul of the addict is searched for iniquities. The Holy Spirit impresses and reveals all the sins he had committed during his lifetime, especially in the times of his addiction. Surprisingly, he also discovers that his previous bad habits and actions, which he had dismissed or taken lightly for granted, are likewise sinful. He finds out that his ingrained, incessant habit of cursing and swearing is abominable to God.

John 3:16 echoes the central message of the Bible: "For God so loved the world that he gave his one and only Son, that whoever believes in him shall not perish but have eternal life." The realization of the promise of salvation removes the addict's perceived worthlessness of sober daily living. The cares and worries of this world fade into insignificance (Luke 21:34). The joy of life and hope of heaven replace the wounds, loss, and heartaches that overwhelm most drug dependents.

THE WISE AND FOOLISH BUILDER

> *Therefore everyone who hears these words of mine and puts them into practice is like a wise man who*

> *built his house on the rock. The rain came down, the*
> *streams rose, and the winds blew and beat against that*
> *house; yet it did not fall, because it had its foundation*
> *on the rock. But everyone who hears these words of*
> *mine and does not put them into practice is like a fool-*
> *ish man who built his house on sand. The rain came*
> *down, the streams rose, and the winds blew and beat*
> *against that house, and it fell with a great crash.*
> **—Matthew 7:24-27**

The knowledge of God and His Word sustains divine recovery. Charles H. Spurgeon said, "A Bible that's falling apart usually belongs to someone who isn't." Like the Wise Builder, recovering addicts need to strengthen their faith by having a stable and truthful foundation of Scriptures.

In addition, they need to put biblical teachings into practice. Loving God takes precedence over loving others and oneself (Matthew 22:37-39). Despite the difficulty, loving one's enemy is a command. Knowledge must lead to action. Otherwise, like the Foolish Builder, recovering addicts would soon falter and end in relapse.

Joining a Bible group study is integral in achieving a deeper appreciation of the Word. American evangelist Billy Graham said, "The first tool God has given us to strengthen our faith is the Bible... If our faith isn't rooted in the Bible, it will wither like a plant pulled out of the soil." Through a communal discourse on the doctrines, the Holy Spirit descends on the addict and illuminates his inquiries. The Lord uses pastors, teachers, ministers, and believers in turning a hopeless, vanquished addict into a faithful disciple.

At the start of the recovery, the personal supervision of the addict is most beneficial. Jesus Himself labored for three years in close contact with the twelve apostles. He lived with them. Paul also carefully taught Timothy: "With the help of the Holy Spirit who lives in us, protect the Good News that has been entrusted to you" (2 Timothy 1:14, *GW*).

God speaks to us through Scriptures, and following God's voice leads to healing. Psalm 107:20 reads: "He sent out his word and healed them; he rescued them from the grave." The recovering addict should keep the Bible as a daily companion. Read a verse or a chapter in the morning and before going to bed. Study, not read, the Bible. Thomas Paine said, "The Bible is a book that has been read more and examined less than any book that ever existed."

Keep a concordance and commentary ready and supplement your reading with other Christian literature. The world is filled with knowledge and diverse interpretation of Scriptures. Study all the Scriptures on a topic to gain more insight and understanding of doctrines. Ask and pray for the Holy Spirit to guide you in your reading and discernment as He is the source of truth (John 16:13).

The Importance of Quiet time

Setting a "quiet time" is an excellent habit toward addiction recovery. As an intrinsic part of daily life, it is a commitment of time carved out by the recovering addict to personally commune with the Creator. It includes prayer, personal Bible study, worship, meditation, and notes or journal taking. The plea for divine healing is the main component of quiet time. He should also pray, by intercession, for his family, friends, addicted friends, and drug dealers. Pastor Tony Dela Paz remarked, "Daily quiet time is needed after rehab to achieve full recovery."

Like Jesus, recovering addicts need a secluded place or spot early in the morning, free from distractions. A thirty-minute quiet time right after waking up would be an ideal schedule. In these golden moments, the recovering addict humbles himself before God and delightfully hears guidance and gain strength and wisdom from Him for the perilous day ahead. Psalm 119:105 reads: "Your word is a lamp for my feet, a light on my path." They need God to thwart all the temptations and wiles of the Unseen Enemy.

Bible reading is a lifelong commitment and enjoyment. As we grow in Christ, we grow in wisdom and maturity. Hebrews 5:14 says: "But solid food is for the mature who, by constant use, have trained themselves to distinguish good from evil."

Most recovered addicts turn out to be highly knowledgeable of the Scriptures. Their intense sincerity in knowing God and building up their faith through prayer and Scripture reading have firmly established their identities in Christ.

Praise and Worship: Exalting God

God is a Spirit: and they that worship him must worship him in Spirit and in truth.
—John 4:24, *KJV*

King David and the Israelites eagerly awaited the arrival of a gold-covered wooden chest. The Ark of the Covenant, built by the Israelites at the foot of Mt. Sinai, contained God's commandments written on two tablets of stones handed down by God to Moses. It was considered the holiest vessel among the Israelites. In one of their battles, the Ark was captured by their nemesis, the Philistines. However, after some time, the Philistines thought that the Ark had brought them misfortune and thus, returned the Ark to Israel. David, as king of a united Israel, sought the Ark so that all could worship God in one place. He planned to build a sanctuary for the Ark, but it was his son, Solomon, who completed the construction of the temple.

Upon seeing the Ark, David leaped and danced with joy as he praised God. "Wearing a linen ephod, David was dancing before the Lord with all his might, while he and all Israel were bringing up the Ark of the Lord with shouts and the sound of trumpets" (2 Samuel 6: 14-15). As a king, David could have looked ridiculous and undignified for his actions, but he set those established conducts aside. Instead, David jumped and danced as an expression of joy for the Lord as the whole kingdom praised and worshiped God.

Today, a multitude of Christians all over the world continue to exalt God through singing, dancing, shouting, crying, praying, fasting, or by walking in the Spirit every day. Whether alone, in groups, or in a church congregation, these acts of veneration honor and please God.

> *But mark this: There will be terrible times in the last days. People will be lovers of themselves, lovers of money, boastful, proud, abusive, and disobedient to their parents, ungrateful, unholy, without love, unforgiving, slanderous, without self-control, brutal, not lovers of the good, treacherous, rash, conceited, lovers of pleasure rather than lovers of God.*
> **—2 Timothy 3:1-4**

In 1969, a different kind of praise and worship took place in the state of New York. Woodstock, a three-day outdoor music festival held on a 600-acre dairy farm in the Catskill Mountains, ushered a new way of escapism and hedonism. At its height, the concert attracted around 400,000 people. People smoked opium and marijuana, snorted cocaine, tripped on LSD, took psychedelic mushroom, and walked around naked. Because of their sheer number, the authorities couldn't arrest and contain them.

Woodstock was a milestone in Rock and Roll history. It revolutionized the conduct of musical concerts, which also served as a backdrop for communal drug-taking and bacchanalian freedom. As a counter-culture movement of the hippies against society and the Vietnam War, it started the trend wherein drugs, alcohol, and hedonism are central components of the concert experience. Gyrating drug-laced fans idolized the performers, fainting, and throwing themselves to the audience in a frenzied stupor.

Drugs and the sexual revolution in the 1960s reflected a change of social structure from tradition to irresponsible innovation in many parts of the world. The *Roe v. Wade* case became a revolutionary event in the United States, which legalized abortion in many states. It reinforced the folly that people can worship their bodies and pursue their lusts and other desires of the flesh by removing the unwanted consequences of their wrong actions. Today, the legalization or tolerance of the killing of unborn babies, sex outside of marriage, same-sex marriage, and the use of harmful substances for recreation have become widely accepted.

> *Common scenarios in present-day drug-laced revelries mirror ancient pagan practices.*

Common scenarios in present-day drug-laced revelries mirror ancient pagan practices. Our ancestors revered the sun, trees, animals, unknown spirits, and many types of false gods. The Bacchanalia during the Greco-Roman period was an act of worship for Bacchus, the Roman God of wine, through hedonism, ecstasy, and drunkenness. In these rites, participants indulged in excessive wine drinking, intemperance, and orgies.

Today, man's folly remains the same. Many people worship false deities, pleasure, celebrities, rock stars, drugs, money, pet animals, and themselves. Our ancestors sacrificed goats, oxen, and human babies in giving honor to their God. Nowadays, addicts sacrifice their souls, bodies, and sanity to the Evil One in exchange for pleasure from drugs.

Drug dens mirror and even surpass the decadent carousing of the past. Addicts freely exchange needles and girlfriends, mindless of the world around them. Opioids, cocaine, Ecstasy, pot, and other party drugs are readily available (even legal) in many bars and other places. These cultic, self-indulgent scenarios reveal that Satan is their lord.

> *Will we worship our own desires or will we worship the true God?*
> **—Edward Welch, author**

The Old and the New Testaments emphasize the fundamental value of praise and worship in our everyday lives. In the original Greek and Hebrew texts, worship means to prostrate oneself, to fall or bow down, and to pay reverence. As a form of fellowship, it is the highest form of honor and respect that we can give God.

In Luke 7:36-38, we see the solemn acts of a sinful woman when she served Jesus—"As she stood behind him at his feet weeping, she began to wet his feet with her tears. Then she wiped them with her hair, kissed them, and poured perfume on them" (v.38).

On the other hand, in the original Greek and Hebrew texts, praise means to celebrate, to boast, to sing, to confess, and to give thanks. Praise is a public declaration of thanksgiving for God's goodness. Psalm 9:1-2 says: "I will give thanks to you, Lord, with all my heart; I will tell of all your wonderful deeds. I will be glad and rejoice in you; I will sing the praises of your name, O Most High."

In the Old Testament, praise and worship included the use of musical instruments. To honor God, the Israelites also offered gift offerings through animal sacrifices, considered a vital component in their worship practices.

In the New Testament, Jesus Christ gave his life to bring redemption to humanity. As the Lamb of God, He died on the cross as the ultimate sacrifice for all sins. First Corinthians 5:7[b] says: "For Christ, our Passover lamb, has been sacrificed." The former sacrifices were aimed to please God, but the death of Jesus redeemed humankind and opened the gates of salvation.

Our acts of worship also produce beneficial results in terms of overall health. In a study at the Duke University Medical Center, researchers revealed, "People who regularly attend religious services appear to have a healthier immune system than those who don't."[7] Jeff Levin further wrote:

A principal means of experiencing positive emotions, especially feelings of love and forgiveness, is by religious worship and prayer. Through the experience of public and private rituals, religion may ease dread and anxiety, reduce tension and aggression, allay fear, and moderate loneliness, alienation, and feelings of inferiority. Many of these negative affects, or feelings, have been found to be risk factors for illness.[8]

AN ANTIDOTE FOR ADDICTION

I can safely say, on the authority of all that is revealed in the Word of God, that any man or woman on this earth who is bored and turned off by worship is not ready for heaven.
—A.W. Tozer, Christian author and minister

The journey to sanctification entails persistence and perseverance. A drug dependent always wrestles with the thoughts and questions about God. How can I praise God if my family left me? How can I possibly worship God if all I think about is drugs? How can I praise God if I am jobless? These nagging difficulties block the addict's quest in exalting God.

It may be incomprehensible how an addict who indulges in sinful practices can worship the true God at the same time. It may also appear paradoxical for the addict to praise and worship God when his life is turned upside down. But sufferings can be the springboard to bring drug dependents back to the Creator who provides relief and deliverance. Despite experiencing the agonies in life, we are called to worship God.

In Acts 16, the magistrates threw Paul and Silas into prison after they were accused of unlawful practices. The two disciples were "stripped and beaten with rods" (v.22[b]). At midnight, they prayed and sang hymns to the Lord (v 25[a]). Despite the anguish, they worshiped God. "Suddenly there was such a violent earthquake that the foundations of the prison were shaken. At once all the prison doors flew open, and everyone's chains came loose" (v.26). In like manner, true worship unshackles the tyranny of addiction.

Drug addicts and alcoholics are idolaters. The first thing that comes to the mind of a meth head when he wakes up in the morning is meth. Where can I get or borrow the money to buy the drug? What can I sell, pawn, or steal to raise cash? Where is the meth available? Is meth at the dealer fake or genuine? These are the burdensome and tedious concerns that assault the addict every day.

Determined to get high, he cranks his body and prepares for the grueling day ahead in the hunt for drugs. He spends around two hours looking or hustling for money so he can buy drugs. He then wastes another two hours scouring the town for a good source of meth. Finally, he gets the drug and takes it home or settles in a drug den and goes tripping in a spooky realm of fantasy. By late afternoon, when the drug wears off, he goes for another boost of the drug to maintain the high. At night, he finds trouble getting sleep.

The rigorous and punishing routine with drugs consumes most of an addict's daily life. To him, family, job, health, and God do not matter—only drugs. Behind these enslavements and deceptions lurks the Evil One.

> *Do not get drunk on wine, which leads to debauchery. Instead, be filled with the Spirit, speaking to one another with psalms, hymns, and songs from the Spirit. Sing and make music from your heart to the Lord.*
> **—Ephesians 5:18-19[a]**

Music is a powerful vehicle that can lead unbelieving addicts to God. It is a potent expression of the creativity given by God to man to praise and worship Him. Music transcends ethnicity and language barriers and forms a unified, blended hymn of voices and sounds from instruments.

Addicts and alcoholics are intrinsically fond of music. It enhances the drug experience and gives added exhilaration to the overall drug trip. Praise and worship often serve as the gateway to recovery for drug dependents. Many rehab and treatment centers commend music therapy because of its benefits. It improves

Christian music is an excellent and proven avenue to lead addicts to Christ.

the addict's abilities to distinguish and accept diverse emotions and promotes self-awareness and relaxation.

Christian music is an excellent and proven avenue to lead addicts to Christ. It moves their hearts in ways that their addicted brains can't comprehend. Songs of praise and worship shift their fondness of crass, worldly music to a joyful fellowship with God. Many addicts who have successfully recovered maintained their sobriety because they often included songs of God in their playlists or have actively participated in music ministries. Levin further adds, "Participation in worship and prayer benefits health through the physiological effects of positive emotions."[9] Music, as a form of praise and worship, is one of the most effective paths towards faith-building and the ultimate expression of our love for God.

> *Therefore, I urge you, brothers and sisters, in view of God's mercy, to offer your bodies as a living sacrifice, holy and pleasing to God—this is your true and proper worship.*
> **—Romans 12:1**

No longer are we required to offer burnt offerings of bulls, goats, and grains to God to please Him. As disciples of Jesus Christ, we also no longer need to go into a church building, to perform rituals, or to rely on a priest or someone else to worship God.

However, addicts and alcoholics go against the present teaching of God. They sacrifice their minds and bodies in exchange for immediate gratification from drugs. They pollute their bodies with all sorts of deadly chemicals, making themselves unworthy as the dwelling place of the Holy Spirit. Their praise and worship are erroneously directed to Satan.

But we are called to be "holy and pleasing to God" every day and everywhere. We are God's temple. First Corinthians 6:19-20 says: "Do you not know that your bodies are temples of the Holy Spirit, who is in you, whom you have received from God? You are not your own; you were bought at a price. Therefore, honor God with your bodies."

We can't rightfully praise and worship God if we don't audibly and visibly express our honor to Him. We exalt God with our hearts and lips. Our exaltations to God should become a constant lifestyle that goes beyond what we do in Sunday church services and spiritual gatherings.

The COVID-19 pandemic does not impede our praise and worship. We glorify God in our hearts, minds, and lips, and in the company of believers on online congregational meetings and events.

The road to recovery is a huge challenge to traverse. Switching the object of worship from addictive substances to the true God requires repentance and belief. The depth of our faith and the truthfulness of our worship depend on our knowledge of God. Neil T. Anderson writes, "It's what you believe and who you believe in that will determine whether or not your faith will be rewarded."[10]

Praise and worship change the landscape of the addict's search, bringing him to a sense of awe towards a higher entity. When addicts exalt God, they push Satan away from their lives through the power of the Holy Spirit. Worship obliterates the altar of addiction. Our exaltations to God can produce miracles that break the oppression of addiction. When faced with trials and adversities, the Evil One may batter our addicted minds and bodies. But he cannot imprison our praise and worship to God.

We have to worship Him now as we are destined to exalt Him in heaven. Praise and worship is the bedrock on which we live our lives. Without both, we can't adequately serve the Master.

Praise and worship is the bedrock on which we live our lives.

6

CHAPTER

Essential Elements of Healing and Recovery

The Willingness to Change

Do you want to get well?
—John 5:6[b]

At the pool of Bethesda (known for its healing properties), Jesus Christ approached a man paralyzed for 38 years. The blind, the lame, and other persons with disabilities gathered around the pool, waiting for the water to stir so they could dip themselves into it and get well. The unnamed man showed frustration because no one helped him go to the pool and felt victimized when overtaken by somebody else when the waters were stirred (John 5:7).

Jesus challenged the person with paralysis: "Do you want to get well?" With negativity and uncertainty, he told Jesus about his predicament in going to the pool. In his mind, he wanted to recuperate. But he was resigned to the idea that healing may not be forthcoming. Out of compassion, Jesus commanded him to "Get up! Pick up your mat and walk" (v.8). He was immediately cured (v.9). In this passage, Jesus demonstrated that healing comes from steadfast faith and a firm, decisive action to get well. It requires collaboration between God and a sick, troubled man.

Today, the call of Jesus for change resounds amid illness and despair. Resignation, hesitation, and double-mindedness grapple addicts when thoughts of recovery arise. They suffer from mental paralysis, unable to chart the right steps in their lives. Deciding to stop taking drugs and gathering enough willpower to change their lifestyles are their most elusive concerns. They are tremendously challenged in choosing between continuing to serve the Devil by gratifying themselves with mind-controlling drugs or pursuing a faith that brings true peace and meaning.

Like the paralyzed man, addicts easily yield to complacency and uncertainty. They find difficulty in bearing a proactive stance and claim their birthright for God's healing in their lives.

Beneath their addiction, they consciously know that their flings with unreality are momentary. They also hold on to a veiled hope that things will get better on their own someday. However, the lure of drugs and alcohol are so enticing that the decision to change is often put on hold.

Begin with the end in mind.
—Stephen Covey, author and psychologist

Drug addicts, alcoholics, and cigarette smokers grapple with addictive substances. They know the costs and consequences of addiction and the possible further damage that might occur if they refuse to quit. Many also believe that addiction violates God and society. But life is full of difficulties, suffering, and boredom. To drug dependents, only drugs make sense, and its use becomes the default alternative in life.

The brutal tyranny to addictive substances makes the willingness to stop taking drugs a large obstacle to overcome. Addicts and alcoholics will risk life, limb, and their families in exchange for drugs and alcohol. Dr. Marvin Seppala of the Hazelden Ford Foundation said, "The drug use becomes recognized [by the brain] as more important than survival itself."[1]

Abstinence is not enough, and it is not the same as real recovery or healing. Abstinence deals with behavior, while recovery means a change of lifestyle. Going past the withdrawal and detoxification process and staying sober do not define victory.

Healing is transformative, requiring a vast amount of dedication and effort for change to take place. It also means changing what we believe. Having a clear vision, by striving for true freedom, is paramount in the attainment of long-term recovery. Psalm 29:18[a] says: "Where there is no vision, the people perish."

> *But if serving the LORD seems undesirable to you,*
> *then choose for yourselves this day whom you will*
> *serve, whether the gods your ancestors served*
> *beyond the Euphrates, or the gods of the Amorites, in*
> *whose land you are living.*
> **—Joshua 24:15[a]**

Many residents of the MRC don't take recovery seriously. In contrast, getting out of rehab as soon as possible is their primary aim. They gleefully count the number of days left in their term like a "rocket launch countdown" instead of celebrating the glorious days of sobriety they have attained. Barely serious in achieving recovery, many are "just passing the time" as a short prison term.

However, they actively participate in the structured program of the center, like Bible studies and life skills seminars. When asked by the staff, pastors, and visiting parents regarding their recovery, they quickly gather a somber composure. A firm snap follows, "Yes, I'll not take drugs again." However, in the deep recesses of their minds, they are undecided about whether to stop or worse, they are resolute to continue taking drugs after rehab. They put up a charade through their words, assertions, and actions to the delight and satisfaction of the outside world.

Some addicts enter recovery because of coercion. Despite their unwillingness to stop taking drugs, they forcibly proclaim their addiction and accept help to satisfy the pressures and concerns of their families. In reality, they are just "buying time" and plan to go back to drugs as soon as possible. Many residents, especially those from jail for drug possession or small-time pushing, are treating rehab like a vacation. They also have some loot of meth stashed somewhere in their houses, which they would later use or deal to others.

You cannot easily spot the minority who are seriously determined to stop using drugs. They know their frailty as they burn with questions and indecisiveness. However, deep in their souls, reason tells them they have to change. Indecisiveness is dangerous. Drug dependents suffer from ambivalence that impedes their firm resolve to quit. They also reject thoughts against leaving the escape and pleasure from drugs. Indecisiveness means continuing to take drugs.

However, the time will ultimately come when they have to decide whether to serve the cravings of their addicted flesh or to serve the Almighty God, who bears the sole power to bring remedy to their brokenness. Reaching a firm decision to stop taking drugs is the gateway to liberation.

Recovery is not for people who need it; it's for people who want it.
—Anonymous

Decision-making comes from free will—a gift from God. Recovery starts when drug addicts and alcoholics have firmly stopped using drugs or drinking alcohol completely. They finally become willing to accept and embrace the needed changes in their messed-up lives. Like the paralyzed man, they need to depart from their victim mentality and ferociously work out their recovery.

Addicts must concede that they have lost control over their lives and are powerless over their addiction. The idea of surrender is often scary as this means the recognition and the public admission that they are drug dependents. Addicts must rid themselves of apathy, setting their minds on the finish line. Despite the falls and stumbling blocks, they should get up and continue to run the race toward sobriety.

Recovery means deciding on the right choices and actions in life. Addiction is the result of wrong decisions. Psychologist Jeff

Schaler, author of *Addiction Is a Choice*, wrote, "Addiction is a behavior and all behaviors are choices."[2] It means staying away from your addicted friends and drug dealers and making new friends that foster sobriety. Many recovered addicts acted on their willingness to change by voluntarily submitting themselves to rehab. They knew that rehab was the best choice for them.

The willingness to change must reside in the heart, mind, and soul. Addicts need to have a firm resolve to stop taking drugs because they know that they are worshiping the god of this world whenever they do so. Joshua

> *The willingness to change must reside in the heart, mind, and soul.*

exhorted the Israelites to leave their idols and worship the true God (Joshua 24). Drug dependents need to turn to God, revere Him, and plead for help. As they learn more about God and how to keep drugs and alcohol from controlling them, they also discover how to manage their behaviors, actions, and emotions.

A Change of Lifestyle

If you can quit for a day, you can quit for a lifetime.
—Benjamin Alire Sáenz, poet and novelist

Next to the greater focus of stopping the use of drugs, recovering addicts also need to change their mindsets and ways of living. Recovery involves the decision to fight the internal mental and bodily drug urges and cravings, and the giving up of other adverse habits and emotions related to drug use. In addition, a change in the external environment is needed.

Recovery requires a massive chunk of determination by deciding to allow the outside world to make alterations in our lives. Despite the daunting thought of having new friends, we need to connect to the community. We have to cut ties with our addicted friends and cultivate new friendships with people who can support our goals of sobriety. We also need to spend more time with our families as they are most concerned about our recovery.

Changes in daily life become inevitable as we seriously pursue recovery. Having a vigorous prayer life, for example, is a big step away from our old idolatrous selves. We have to avoid places where we used to go: drug dens, bars, nightclubs, back alleyways, gambling rooms, drug-infested neighborhoods, and drug-rich workplaces. Continued participation in family therapy sessions, NA or AA, and other after-care programs is a clear sign of commitment. We can consider getting back to work, if advantageous, in a conducive atmosphere for healing. We may also have to change jobs or careers to escape from temptations and triggers.

A balanced lifestyle is a goal for people in recovery. Recreation should be healthy, wholesome, and pro-sobriety. Leisure activities that hint at substance abuse should be avoided. We also need to have proper sleep, nutrition, and exercise, which were all grossly neglected in the past. Pursuing self-enrichment activities such as reading books, going back to school, and taking vocational courses on the improvement of life skills enhance recovery.

We must also fix the damages in our relationships with others. Making confessions, amends, and resolutions will clear or lessen the guilt, shame, and other negative thoughts and emotions that hinder recovery.

Applying changes in our past daily routine is challenging. In many cases, addiction recovery requires a complete life change. It means having to re-examine ourselves and conclude that we have to leave our familiar comfort zones.

The route toward recovery is different for everyone. We must have an open mind regarding our options. Rehab, whether short or long term, works for many addicts. However, recovery in the comforts of our homes or under the supervision of the family or church can work just as well. Others may seek help from AA, NA, outpatient or hospital services, and other support groups. Recovery is also not a one-time thing. Many successful long-term recoveries only happened after multiple rehabs, treatments, or support programs.

In sum, we must alter our depraved lifestyles. Each addict has a different story and circumstance. However, all who have successfully achieved recovery happened because they were willing to change. The firm decision to stop taking drugs is the critical first step towards recovery.

Free Will: The Power of Choice

You, my brothers and sisters, were called to be free.
But do not use your freedom to indulge the flesh;
rather, serve one another humbly in love.
—Galatians 5:13

In 1942, the Nazis arrested Viktor Frankl, a Jewish psychiatrist, together with his parents, wife, and brother, and sent to the Thereisienstadt concentration camp. Within six months, Frankl's father died. In three years, they moved Frankl between four concentration camps and finally to the dreaded Auschwitz facility where his brother and mother died. His wife died in Bergen-Belsen, a facility that housed women and minors, including the famous survivor and diarist Anne Frank.

In these camps, he witnessed or experienced the horrors of nakedness, hunger, abject loneliness, and certain death in the gas chambers. Frankl and the other prisoners overcame utter fear and severe depression through positive memories, scenes, and thoughts.

He survived the genocide and Holocaust at Auschwitz. In this infamous prison in Poland, around 1.1 million died out of the 1.3 million prisoners. Most died in the gas chambers while the rest died because of disease, starvation, fatigue from forced labor, and medical experimentation.

In his book *Man's Search for Meaning*, Frankl wrote:

> *We who lived in concentration camps can remember the men who walked through the huts comforting others, giving away their last piece of bread. They may have been few in number, but they offer sufficient proof that everything can be taken from a man but one thing: the last of the human freedoms—to choose one's attitude in any given set of circumstances, to choose one's own way.[3]*

In those dark moments, Viktor Frankl observed that, even in the worst possible conditions, an individual still possesses the freedom to choose his or her attitude toward suffering. He learned that the Nazis could not take away from him his freedom of choice. With a positive mindset, he chose to be courageous and persevering in his most trying moments at the concentration camps.

> *And the Lord God commanded the man, "You are free to eat from any tree in the garden; but you must not eat from the tree of the knowledge of good and evil, for when you eat from it you will certainly die."*
> **—Genesis 2:16-17**

God gave us the preeminent gift of free will. At the Garden of Eden, God told Adam that they could eat anything from any tree except the "tree of the knowledge of good and evil." The crafty serpent approached Eve and challenged her if God really told her the command and its fatal consequence if they disobeyed Him (Genesis 3:1-3).

Poised to attack Eve's innocence, the serpent immediately hurled a punch of doubt by telling her she would certainly not die if she ate the fruit (v.4). Instead, her "eyes will be opened, and you will be like God, knowing good and evil" (v.5). Eve succumbed to the trickery of the serpent, ate the fruit, and gave some to Adam (v.6).

When questioned by God, she claimed that the serpent tricked her (v.13). God blamed the serpent but declared that Adam and Eve were guilty and accountable for their wrongdoing. God punished Eve, Adam, and the serpent (vv.14-19).

The wrong choice of our first parents marked the origin of sin on earth. Despite their disobedience that led to the fall of humankind, God did not remove our freedom to choose. Made in His image, God designed us with liberty in all our thoughts and actions. However, God inherently commands us to make the right choices.

We possess the freedom to select what food to eat, what clothes to wear, and how to spend our time. We can also decide between going to church and getting drunk with our friends in a bar on Sunday mornings. We can choose to be sacred or sinful. God seeks our worship, but He never forces faith and obedience.

Addicts and alcoholics embrace the distorted notion that they possess the inalienable right to do anything they want. Engulfed with pride, they proclaim, "This is my own life and body. I can do everything as long as I don't hurt anybody else." These statements reek of pride and deception.

Irresponsible exercise of free will yields unwanted consequences and even tragic outcomes. Drug dependents hurt themselves, their families, and others. The freedom of choice entails the responsibility of choosing right from wrong.

> *"I have the right to do anything," you say—but not everything is beneficial. "I have the right to do anything"—but I will not be mastered by anything.*
> **—1 Corinthians 6:12**

How we exercise our free will determines the small and significant outcomes in our lives. The power of choice manifests in the selection of the toys we play in our childhood days, the studies we pursue, the careers we take, the spouses we marry, the lifestyle we espouse, and the faith we seek.

Different diseases surround us. We can prevent most of these ailments if we choose to live wisely—avoiding cigarettes and drugs. Heart disease, the number one killer disease, can be averted by having a healthy way of life—the right food, proper rest, and exercise.

Addiction is a matter of choice. An individual possesses the inherent power to refuse or stop taking drugs or alcohol from the onset to the severe stage of abuse. Despite the strong drug cravings, a person can rally his internal, willful drive to conquer addiction. Christopher Ringwald, the author of *The Soul of Recovery*, wrote, "Throughout the treatment field and recovery movement, people call addiction a disease over which a person has no control, but then prescribe solutions that involve a great deal of personal initiative."[4]

The case of the addicted cigarette smokers who stopped smoking on their own proves that addiction is a choice. Millions of heavy smokers have also quit smoking with no professional help. A multitude of veterans, hooked on heroin during the Vietnam War, also gained sobriety by sheer will power. About 75 percent of them kicked off the habit once they returned home to the United States.[5]

In the same way, a multitude of former drug addicts and alcoholics achieved recovery by merely choosing to stay sober. They *resolved* to stop smoking, ceased taking drugs, and quit drinking alcohol, and succeeded. While many have sought help because the severity of addiction had stunted their power to choose, the overriding decision, responsibility, and effort came from within themselves. Despite its reduced and tainted measure, the power of choice still resides in them.

In a study conducted by neuroscientist and author Carl Hart, addicts were given a choice between taking 50mg of methamphetamine or five dollars in cash. The addicts chose and took the drug about half of the time. However, when the money was raised to twenty dollars, they took the money, not the drugs. Dr. Hart said, "Addicts can and do make rational decisions."[6]

Sin is a matter of choice. In spite of the hardship, torment, and brokenness, drug addicts and alcoholics can rise above any extreme predicament and choose not to fall from grace. Like Victor Frankl, they can change their helpless mindsets, make the right decisions, and survive the imprisonment of addiction. God gave us free will—not so that we can do everything we want—but to have the power to do what God wants.

> God gave us free will—not so that we can do everything we want—but to have the power to do what God wants.

Recovery Means Action

"Go," he told him, "wash in the Pool of Siloam" (this word means "Sent"). So the man went and washed, and came home seeing.
—John 9:7

While walking with his disciples, Jesus saw a man who has been blind since birth. The apostles asked, "Rabbi, who sinned, this man or his parents that he was born blind?" (John 9:2). The Lord replied that neither of them sinned and that the encounter would show to the world the healing power of God (vv.3-5). Jesus spat on the ground, mixed some mud with His saliva, and placed it on the man's eyes (v.6). "Go," he told him, "*wash* in the Pool of Siloam" (this word means "Sent"). So the man went and *washed*, and came home seeing" (v.7, italics mine).

The story of the man born blind in the Gospel of John illustrates the element of action as a principal part of healing. God does not always cure our troubles and diseases in an instant. Divine healing requires faith, trust, and dynamic action, as exemplified by the blind man following the instructions of Jesus in going to the pool and washing his body. Cooperation and participation were involved in the curing.

Drug addiction is a sin, and divine healing happens when there is a holy collaboration between God and man. Healing becomes elusive when the recovering addict ignores God's guidance and commands. The Bible tells us to "pray without ceasing" (1 Thessalonians 5:17) or to avoid seeing addicted friends. However, we often set aside God's ways and persist in our bad habits.

Another obstacle to recovery is complacency. With drugs, addicts are mistakenly pleased and content with themselves and their ways of living. But God and their loved ones are not delighted with their rebellion.

Complacency leads to inaction. In many cases, erroneous drug-induced contentment breeds sloth. Because of addiction, many drug dependents avoid the normal routines in life, like doing household chores and having a job. They prefer to remain idle, eagerly waiting for the next drug trip. Rebecca De Young, Ph.D. adds, "Sloth is opposed to the great Christian virtue of diligence—that powerful sense of responsibility, dedication to hard work, and conscientious completion of one's duties."[7]

Victimization leads to complacency and sloth. The popular notion among addicts is that they are not at fault for their addictions. This would mean placing the burden of guilt on others. When we do not own the responsibility for our actions, we are denying ourselves of repentance and the necessary changes that will lead to restoration.

Procrastination is the nemesis of recovery. Postponing the decision to stop using drugs and follow the right precepts for recovery delays healing. If asked when they will stop using drugs, many addicts would reply, *"I'll stop when things get better," "I'll turn sober when I get my family back,"* or *"I'll stop when I get a job."* These eyebrow-raising and abstract replies reflect indecisiveness and inaction until they reach rock bottom.

As masters of "delaying tactics," drug addicts sit around and wait for life to unfold before them. They believe they can still afford to bear the costs and outcomes of addiction in their lives. Gerald

May, M.D. writes, "The mind is infinitely ingenious at complicating the process of quitting. When what is needed is direct, clear-cut refusal to perform the addictive behavior, the mind invents such convoluted and entangled complications that the addicted person finds himself thrashing about helplessly in an ocean of details."[8] Drug dependents feel they haven't had enough. This deadly mistake often leads to greater misery and tragedy.

> *Everyone then who hears these words of mine and does them will be like a wise man who built his house on the rock.*
> **—Matthew 7:24, ESV**

According to the 72-Hour Rule, if you don't act on your decision in the next 72 hours, you would probably not start at all. If you don't fix the broken cabinet within that period, you would probably fix it a year or a decade later. By that time, it is so broken, you have to replace it. Postponing the act to stop taking drugs is a dangerous syndrome that affects all who are reluctant to gain recovery.

Addiction, with its repercussions, is bound to get worse before the addicts get better. Healing doesn't happen overnight. Recovery may take years and may include a series of relapses. In the book *Celebrate the Temporary*, Clyde Reid wrote, "Don't wait. You'll end up waiting forever. Celebrate the now with all its pains and difficulties."[9]

Staying active is vital. Laziness is the work of the Devil. Engaging in productive work, exercise, and hobbies like painting and music enhance recovery. When confronted with intense drug cravings, cleaning the house all day long is therapeutic. Volunteering in community programs and participating in spiritual retreats and seminars lift the spirit. Above all, engaging in spiritual and ministry work brings us closer to God. Busyness reduces or erases drug cravings and diminishes powerful triggers that lead to relapse.

Exclaiming positive remarks like "I will live a life of sobriety" in contrast to passive, negative words like "I don't want to take drugs anymore" reinforce recovery. Positivity opens to the recovering addict proactive good choices and opportunities, while negativity creates distressing thoughts that hinder capabilities to move on in life. The paralyzed man would not have experienced healing if Jesus didn't intervene and debunked the man's negativity.

Stagnation is a primary hallmark of relapse. In the absence of any favorable decision and the active pursuit of recovery, liberation does not happen. Recovery from addiction is a matter of steady growth and the aggressive pursuit of a drug-free, wholesome, and happy life.

The Importance of Responsibility and Accountability

Do your best to present yourself to God as one approved, a worker who does not need to be ashamed and who correctly handles the word of truth.
—2 Timothy 2:15

As cupbearer to King Artaxerxes of Persia, Nehemiah had borne the weight of great responsibility, accountability, and power in the empire. Aside from being a private servant, the king relied on him as a trusted confidant and consultant. But Nehemiah longed for the welfare of his fellow Israelites. In Nehemiah 2:4-8, he approached the king and requested to allow him to rebuild the walls of Jerusalem. The king granted his request, and Nehemiah successfully led the rebuilding of the walls, with the Israelites celebrating and dedicating themselves to God through public prayer, praise, and worship (Nehemiah 12:27).

Nehemiah displayed responsibility and accountability from the start to the end of the rebuilding project. He told the king his objectives and whereabouts—the details, the logistics, and the workforce. He declared the schedule of his absence and when he was likely to return. Nehemiah showed utmost dependability as a leader and submitted himself to the king openly and transparently.

In the quest for recovery, the sense of transparency and accountability for our actions and decisions are crucial for success. Responsibility means the removal of our sense of victimization—that it is not our fault why we got addicted to drugs. Accountability means opening and submitting ourselves to others regarding the state of our recovery. It also implies our commitment to pursuing sobriety and overcoming our thoughts of helplessness.

He that is good for making excuses is seldom good for anything else.
—Benjamin Franklin, one of the founding fathers of the United States

Recovery is difficult. But, not owning our failures block us from effectively moving in the right direction. Despite the bondage, the recovering addict always possesses the inherent control and power over himself. Being responsible for our actions will increase our self-confidence and earn the trust of the outside world.

The major burden for recovery rests on the addict or alcoholic. First, she must realize and admit that addiction is idolatry—that she puts herself and drugs above God and other people. Second, she must "put to the death" the exact transgressions that enslave her (Col. 3:5). Lastly, she needs to rely on God's Word as the primary source of defense and offense in the battle against addiction.

God illustrated in the Scriptures the essential virtue of responsibility. At the time of the creation, God told Adam to tend, protect, and keep the Garden of Eden (Genesis 2:15-17). Jesus knew the frustration and hesitation of the paralyzed man of 38 years. He had to stir up the mind of the disabled man and prod him into taking responsibility for his care. Despite the hardships of recovery, Jesus exhorts drug addicts to muster strength and take charge of themselves. Responsibility is the bedrock on which a successful recovery stands.

> *So then, each of us will give an account of ourselves to God.*
> **—Romans 14:12**

We live in a world where we need to belong and be part of a group or community. Submission is a crucial element of accountability. Aside from primarily giving in to God, the addict must allow the outside world to check up on him and monitor his progress toward recovery.

Recovery requires honesty, openness, and the willingness to yield to others. Addicts detest being accountable to somebody or a group. But recovery requires honesty, openness, and the willingness to yield to others. Engulfed with pride, guilt, and shame, addicts loathe having to open themselves to someone and give a regular account of their progress and activities. They feel this is an intrusion to their privacy and an invasion of their adopted fundamental right of doing what they want.

But, recovering addicts need other people because wholeness and change cannot be sustained in solitude. A working system of accountability enables them to share their struggles and progress in deep trust and confidentiality. Hebrews 10:24 reads: "And let us consider how we may spur one another on toward love and good deeds."

Wrestling with sin, they need to confide and connect with someone or a group of people to help them in their crucial steps toward freedom. In addition, they should welcome suggestions and accept rebukes and reprimands from others, especially when things seem to go off track. They must also appreciate the applause and praise for every positive step they achieved toward recovery.

Seeking an "accountability partner" is an essential component of recovery. The addict agrees to be answerable to someone and "give account" of his actions. It involves the opening up of one another with the sharing of one's innermost thoughts. The partner can be a pastor, health specialist, life coach, parent, friend, or support group that also agrees to help and monitor the recovery process. Romans 14:1 reads: "Accept the one whose faith is weak, without quarreling over disputable matters." Having a former drug addict as an accountability partner is highly advantageous. Such a person would be able to empathize and relate well with the recovering addict who may have feelings of isolation and rejection.

On top of monitoring the addict's daily state, the accountability partner prays in a petition to God for matters in recovery. Together, they can also beseech God for continued healing with gratitude for each progress and milestone. First Thessalonians 5:11 says: "Therefore encourage one another and build each other up, just as in fact you are doing." The recovering addict can also maintain a written journal tracking the slips and falls he encountered on his journey toward sobriety.

Peter displayed a sense of accountability when he stayed with the disciples after he publicly denied Jesus three times (John 18). Better still, Jesus showed an exemplary role as an accountability partner for his fallen disciple. In John 21, Jesus helped Peter go through his guilt and shame by pointing out his mistakes and summoning him back to lead the ministry of evangelization.

Support is the backbone of recovery. After rehab, support groups provide the right environment and inputs for the recovering drug dependent. These groups also serve as a viable alternative for rehab. Support groups offer a system of accountability. These communities are popular, not only because of their effectiveness in providing a social setting for discussion but also because of the anonymity it provides.

Recovery Takes Time

*It does not matter how slowly you go as long as you
do not stop.*
—Confucius, Chinese philosopher

One day, a leper approached Jesus and begged him on his knees, "If you are willing, you can make me clean" (Mark 1:40[b]). Out of love and compassion, Jesus touched the man. "Immediately the leprosy left him and he was cleansed" (vv.41-42). But Jesus was not finished with him. The Lord gave the leper specific instructions "with a strong warning" about his healing: not to *tell* anyone about the miracle, *present* himself to a priest as testimony and proof of healing, and *offer* a gift of sacrifice as required by Mosaic Law (vv.43-44). Instead, the former leper defied the instructions by not acting on them, and immediately spread the news of the healing power of Jesus Christ (v.45).

Divine healing is not always a one-time act. In drug recovery, healing is often a gradual process that requires many changes in the life of the recovering addict. In addition, it means the continuing submission to God according to His specific will and instructions. After the physical curing from addiction, God leads us to transformation and alterations in our lifestyles. Sanctification involves the passage of time as our omniscient God knows what is best for each of us.

CURING VS. DIVINE HEALING

*Wounds don't heal the way you want them to, they
heal the way they need to. It takes time for wounds to
fade into scars. It takes time for the process of healing
to take place. Give yourself that time. Give yourself
that grace. Be gentle with your wounds. Be gentle with
your heart. You deserve to heal.*
—Dele Olanubi, writer

Curing is not the same as healing. Even wounds take time to repair. Curing is confined to the recuperation and treatment of physical ailments. As a chronic condition, the treatment and remission of cancer require repeated surgeries and other management methods. The treatment protocol of one patient may differ from another. The same concept applies to addiction recovery.

In his book *God's Touch*, Bruce Epperly wrote, "There is a profound difference between curing and healing. Healing reconnects us with God, others, and ourselves. To be healed is to experience God's shalom and wholeness, regardless of one's physical or social condition."[10]

As a disease, the recovery of the hijacked brain may take years for the cells to recuperate or grow back. Many addicts in treatment also suffer from mental disorders. Studies show that one in four American adults with a mental illness also has substance abuse disorder.[11] Treatment of this type requires a more considerable amount of time. Recovering addicts also grapple with the pains of withdrawal and social adjustment before they can pull through from the clutches of addiction.

Divine healing transcends and encompasses both the rejuvenation and renewal of mind, body, and soul. In another study, neuroscientist Andrew Newberg, M.D. and Mark Robert Waldman wrote in their book *How God Changes Your Brain*:

> Our research team at the University of Pennsylvania has consistently demonstrated that God is part of our consciousness and that the more you think about God, the more you will alter the neural circuitry in specific parts of your brain. That is why I say, with the utmost confidence, that God can change your brain.[12]

True recovery is not only about graduating from a six-month stint at rehab or staying away from alcohol for two years. It involves the miraculous transformation of a former wretched addict into a new being, cleansed from all sins and impurities. An anonymous quote reads, "Recovery didn't open the gates of heaven and let me in. Recovery opened the gates of hell and let me out!"

Aside from the cessation of drug-taking, recovery involves a continuing inventory of our moral compass through relentless confession and reparation of sins. It also includes asking for forgiveness from God and from other people we had hurt. In a reciprocal manner, it also entails the forgiving of others who had hurt us. Dr. Karl Menninger, a famous scientist, once said that "If he could convince the patients in psychiatric hospitals that their sins were forgiven, 75 percent of them could walk out the next day."

In his book, *The Biology of Desire: Why Addiction is not a Disease*, Dr. Marc Lewis revealed that recovered addicts preferred they were *freed, not cured*, from addiction. He wrote, "Having overcome their addictions by dint of hard work, intense self-examination, and the courage and capacity to regrow their perspectives (and their synapses), they'd rather see themselves as having *developed* through addiction and become stronger as a result (italics mine)."[13]

> *But small is the gate and narrow the road that leads to life and only a few find it.*
> **—Matthew 7:14**

Recovery is hard. It is comparable to coming out of a cave where the addict had lived in a dark abyss of isolated depravation for many years. Going back again to society, seeing the sunlight, and mingling back with "normal" people is a treacherous and painful struggle toward normalcy and liberation.

God does not zap us to recovery.

Healing is progressive and entails many actions. God does not zap us to recovery. Pastor Deo Salgado said, "The sanctification process happens without you knowing it." It requires a change of heart, mind, and lifestyle. Rebecca DeYoung Ph.D. wrote, "When we want to re-form our character from vice to virtue, we often need to practice and persevere in regular spiritual disciplines and formational practices for a *lengthy period of time* (italics mine)."[14]

Initially, the recovering addict immediately faces the specter of withdrawal from substance abuse. He experiences hallucinations, and his body undergoes body aches, nervous fits, and breakdowns. The torment alone is enough to make the recovering addict terminate his intent to recover. To relieve the aches and mental anguish, he takes drugs again and isolates himself back into his cave. Sometimes, protracted withdrawal from drug abuse takes years.

A journey of a thousand miles begins with a single step.
—Laozi, philosopher

The long voyage to sobriety is lined with dangerous traps and potholes. Setbacks are bound to happen: you may unintentionally hurt someone, run out of money, or experience a debilitating disease. Recovery from addiction is a dangerous journey where temptations lurk on every corner. The Unseen Enemy does not easily give up. These obstacles are the reasons why successful recovery takes time. Recovering addicts also suffer from past hurts and strongholds which obstruct God's healing.

Many addicts have false or unrealistically high expectations of recovery. They believe that they are healed after three months of rehab. Passing the detoxification and withdrawal stage does not mean recovery. They are deceived when they say that they are already well enough because the cravings have lessened in frequency and intensity. Beaming with radiant faces, they have also regained physical health and body weight.

With a great deal of enthusiasm and determination, recovering addicts feel they are ready to face the world. However, they soon realize that severe drug cravings still haunt them. In the book, *The Addicted Brain*, Michael Kuhar, wrote:

Studies using brain-imaging techniques have shown that continued use of drugs causes long-lasting changes in brain chemistry and function... Levels of energy metabolism (indicated by light areas in the image) are compared in a normal subject, a cocaine user who has not taken cocaine for 10 days, and one who has not taken cocaine for 100 days. It is clear that even after 100 days of abstinence, the brain has not returned to normal.[15]

Many face extreme difficulties in meeting or resolving their life issues after rehab. They can't figure out how to reconcile with their strained families and accept the failures they experienced. The hardships in sustaining lasting recovery soon compromise their willingness to stay sober. The lack of perseverance and resolve for recovery eventually lead to relapse.

RELAPSE: BOUND TO HAPPEN

For though the righteous fall seven times, they rise again, but the wicked stumble when calamity strikes.
—Proverbs 24:16

After rehab or successfully quitting on their own or through other means of recovery, former users and alcoholics and their families dread one thing: relapse. With their bodies back in shape and their cheeks once again glowing pink with health, recovering addicts often let their guards down. They feel they are well and ready to resume a normal life. But Jeremiah 17:9 says: "The heart is deceitful above all things and beyond cure. Who can understand it?"

Because of pride and complacency, they hesitate to take further steps to enhance their recovery by putting safeguards to avoid triggers and temptations. Overconfidence with their short-term gains engulfs them, making them unaware of the drug cravings that are slowly creeping back into them. Filled with arrogance, they think they are well enough to resist temptation and bravely face the world on their own.

Away from the safe confines of rehab, people in recovery face the harsh realities of life. They return to their hurts and problems—joblessness, separation from the family, or mere boredom.

Real triggers, trials, and temptations loom over their sober heads. Also, they meet their addicted friends and drug dealers whenever they pass the notorious street corner in town.

Despite their willingness to make changes in their lives and to place safeguards in avoiding triggers and temptations, the specter of relapse becomes real. Soon, their prized sobriety crumbles, as they backslide and fall back to addiction.

Relapse is a common setback among people in recovery. In his book *Free from Addiction*, Morteza Kaleghi Ph.D. wrote, "Half the time they slip into heavy, sustained use, and 90 percent have short-lived relapses before getting back on the road to wellness."[16] The medical sector claims that addiction is a chronic, progressive, and "relapsing disease." According to the NIDA of the United States, the relapse rate for those facing drug addiction is from 40 to 60 percent.[17]

Relapse often takes over by surprise. Parents rashly celebrate and lose their guard after their children have stayed sober for a few months after rehab. They gasp with shock to learn that their loved one had slipped. Kaleghi adds, "There is a 70 percent chance that a patient will relapse within a year of leaving treatment."[18]

Despite the strong commitment and guarded efforts, the alcoholic goes back to the bottle, and the addict re-visits the drug den for a whiff of meth. They revert to their past sinful habits, old hang-ups, and hurts. Addicts in relapse also tend to be bolder in their drug use and the sourcing of their supply. They consume more drugs and alcohol, and become more daring in deception, trickery, and breaking the law. Their spiritual state has also spawned more vile spirits to assault them.

Relapse is comparable to an aftershock after a big earthquake. It can surface many times over a long time. In 2014, Academy Award-winning actor Philip Seymour Hoffman died with a syringe in his arm in his New York apartment of acute mixed drug intoxication of heroin, cocaine, amphetamine, and benzodiazepines. TMZ reported that he'd been sober for 23 years but had relapsed.

> *Total abstinence is key to long-term recovery.*

Total abstinence is key to long-term recovery. Controlled or moderate drug use and drinking is dangerous for those prone to addiction and especially to people in recovery. While some drug users and alcoholics practice "managed drinking and drug use," most will soon go back in full-blown relapse. Substance dependency is not defined by the volume of drugs or alcohol consumed and its frequency, but by bondage.

A study conducted at the University of Gothenburg in Sweden, reveals that those who drink in moderation are less likely to achieve their goal, while those who aimed at totally quitting drinking achieve greater success. The 90% of patients who went for total abstinence were still sober two and a half years after treatment while only 50% of those who practiced controlled consumption succeeded in recovery.[19]

Deliverance from drug addiction is often a work-in-progress, as our Great Healer slowly peels away the layers of our old addicted identities. There is no "quick fix." Mothers weep and question why their son would have to go back to rehab for the third time. But, real recovery entails perseverance, patience, and time. Often, multiple rehabs or other recovery methods are needed to finally achieve deliverance.

> *Our greatest glory is in never failing, but in rising up every time we fail.*
> **—Confucius, philosopher**

Relapse is not necessarily a failure but shows the greater need for God and an openness to changes in recovery plans and strategies. Backslides can be lessons learned toward resilience and healing because we gain spiritual maturity from our relapses.

Pastor Tony Dela Paz of CCF expressed that the most successful long-term recoveries involve a series of relapses. He only became clean from drugs in 1991 after fifteen years of addiction to drugs, alcohol, and sexual promiscuity with several drug relapses.

Addiction is a sin, and humanity is under the grip of Satan. As the fallen creation of God, we all sin and "fall short of the glory of God" (Romans 3:23). Idolatry, deceit, manipulation, love of money and possessions, and various addictions engulf us every day. Humanity is under bondage by the flesh, and the pursuit of a spirit-filled life is a constant challenge.

However, God loves us. Despite our rebellion, He always awaits our faith and loyalty. Repentance is crucial and relapse is a lesson of consecration. Like the depraved Israelites, we experience affliction if we are away from Him. Through these trials, we would finally reach the land of sobriety and reap the joy that comes from divine healing.

Through our relapses, we become sanctified so we later come out in shining glory. Like gold, we are refined by the fires of our backslides. First Peter 1:7 reads: "These have come so that the proven genuineness of your faith—of greater worth than gold, which perishes even though refined by fire—may result in praise, glory, and honor when Jesus Christ is revealed."

Real recovery means the driving out of evil spirits that reside in our bodies and minds. Ephesians 5:18 reads: "Do not get drunk on wine, which leads to debauchery. Instead, be filled with the Spirit." Instead of pursuing God and building up our faith, we remain complacent, idle, and spiritually vacant. Our unholy openness attracts more evil spirits that quickly lead us back to relapse.

Removing the desire to take drugs takes time. It means the renewal of the heart and mind. Also, the length of recovery differs depending on the clinical severity of one's dependence, such as the total length of drug use or addiction, the drug of choice, and the frequency and duration of drug binges. Secular treatment groups such as AA and NA often call sober, former drug dependents as "recovering" not "recovered"—regardless of the length of time they abstained from drugs.

The constant building of faith is the cornerstone of avoiding relapses. Prayer, Bible reading, and praise and worship are keys in repelling temptations and cravings that lead to relapse. Enrollment in after-care or support groups provides the right environment in pursuing recovery with peers. Pastor Tony Dela Paz comments, "Regular and structured drug testing, ideally twice a week for some time after rehab, is a good deterrent for relapse."

We should not be scared of relapse. With a firm resolve, we can start again. With God's help, we will become victorious warriors of Christ.

Lessons in the Wilderness

Remember this and never forget how you aroused the anger of the Lord your God in the wilderness. From the day you left Egypt until you arrived here, you have been rebellious against the Lord.
—Deuteronomy 9:7

After 430 years of slavery in Egypt (Exodus 12:40), God freed about three million Israelites and promised them a "land flowing with milk and honey" in Canaan (Exodus 3:8). However, they have to cross the desert where there was no food, water, and shelter. Moses led them by faith that God would supply all of their needs.

Because God loved His people, He allowed them to bring herds of cattle, food, jewelry, and clothing to sustain them at the beginning of their journey (Exodus 12:31-35). God also turned bitter water into something fit to drink (Exodus 15:25), rained down manna from heaven, and sent quails to their camps (Exodus 16).

However, the Israelites soon got impatient and disgruntled. They complained about the food, water, and the lack of spices. Numbers 11:4-6 reads: "The rabble with them began to crave other food, and again the Israelites started wailing and said, "If only we had meat to eat! We remember the fish we ate in Egypt at no cost—also the cucumbers, melons, leeks, onions, and garlic. But now we have lost our appetite; we never see anything but this manna!" The scouts sent by Moses to spy on Canaan also lied. They spread unfounded fear to the people by saying that Canaan was occupied by giants and fortified by massive walls (Numbers 13:28).

Consumed with bitterness and doubt, they turned away from God. They also made a golden calf to worship (Exodus 32). God said, "How long will this wicked community grumble against me?" (Numbers 14:27). God had to teach them a lesson in faith and obedience.

Because of their idolatry and ingratitude, God punished the stubborn Israelites. What was supposed to be a trek of only eleven days to cross the desert took them forty long years (Deuteronomy 1:1-2). With young children and the elderly, they wandered in the wilderness and faced war and hardships of many kinds.

Because of God's wrath, only Joshua, Caleb, and those who were below twenty years saw the Promised Land (Numbers 32:11-12). Even Moses failed to reach Canaan because of his episodes of unfaithfulness (Deuteronomy 4:21).

The Bible records past ordeals and breakthroughs of great men in the desert. They received God's revelations but experienced intense spiritual struggles at the same time. The number forty is also significant in most of these experiences. Moses led the stubborn Israelites in the wilderness for forty years. He fasted and prayed for forty days and nights. Elijah traversed the wilderness with no food for forty days until he reached Horeb (1 Kings 19:8). Pursued by Saul, David hid in the desert before God made him king (1 Samuel 23:14). Jesus Christ fasted in the desert for forty days and nights before His temptation by the Devil (Matthew 4:1-3).

God leads most people into the desert once or many times in their lives to test their faith. Barren land is a place of trial, encounter, and restoration. Comparable to the trek toward the Promised Land of the Israelites, addicts and alcoholics relentlessly drift in the desert of addiction. God seems nowhere to be found.

Whether self-inflicted or induced by external circumstances, addicts end in dismal helplessness. Many become jobless, homeless, and separated from their families. Society rejects them, and some have contracted AIDS, tuberculosis, cirrhosis, or other deadly diseases. Countless addicts had died due to overdose or committed suicide.

People need God. Despite having loving families and decent, secure lives, people remain dissatisfied and so, they turn to drugs and alcohol. They seek pleasure from substances and other dangerous pursuits like gambling and extramarital relations. A lingering void engulfs them as something seems to be missing in their lives.

Unlike Job of the Bible, who remained steadfast in faith despite severe, tragic troubles, many addicts reject the existence of a loving God. They shift the blame towards Him for their sorry, impoverished state. Moreover, they embrace Satan and glorify sin. Scared to deal with the challenges and pains of life, they numb themselves with drugs.

Meth, alcohol, marijuana, and pills are the quickest routes to chase their troubles away. Many addicts have reached rock bottom. The only choice is to climb to the light of freedom or to stay in the dark abyss of addiction. Most choose the latter option. As a result, addicts and alcoholics find themselves trapped in a chasm of brokenness and helplessness.

Gerald May, M.D. wrote:

> *In the desert, they [Israelites] expressed all the characteristics of addiction and of the addicted personality to a degree that was as agonizing for God and as frustrating for Moses as it was for them. They experienced the stress and fear of withdrawal symptoms, longing for the old days of slavery. They hoarded more of their manna than they needed, and it rotted. They deceived themselves with idolatry and excuses. They made resolutions to obey God's commandments, only to apostatize when left to themselves.*[1]

The unfaithfulness, ingratitude, and idolatry of the Israelites brought God's anger. In like manner, the sufferings of addicts, including the torment of chronic addiction, are often God's retribution for their heretic and rebellious ways. Despite the defiance, God longs for the return of His lost children.

Coming out from the wilderness of substance abuse is difficult. Recovery is often long and treacherous. Addicts and alcoholics also often think that God's deliverance is elusive and probably untrue.

However, desperation in the desert can make them entirely rely on God to reach liberation. Addicts feel the urgent need to recover. They know that they have to clean up their acts to get their messed-up lives in order. Isolated and rejected, they need to regain the love and trust of their families and friends. In addition, they yearn to get back to work, earn a decent income, and lead a healthy lifestyle—all in a sober state.

But then again, their sincere aims of getting their lives back in order seem to be an almost impossible task. Their minds play tricks on them—with Satan whispering that sobriety is pain-filled and boring. Similar to Eve's temptation, the Devil insists that drugs are the best way out of their dull, troubled lives.

They hesitate to stop taking drugs as they undergo a myriad of troubling barriers toward freedom. Most addicts wrestle with homelessness, poverty, rejection, family separation, joblessness, hedonism, lingering drug cravings, temptations, or just plain boredom.

They often ponder, *"How can I face life alone? My family left me." "How can I live without any job or money?" "How can I be sober when all of my friends drink alcohol or take drugs?" "How can I recover when my body doesn't stop craving for drugs with all the surrounding temptations and triggers?" "Can I really be happy without drugs?"*

In addition, the aches of withdrawal from taking drugs and alcohol often become unbearable. The gut-wrenching and raw-nerve sensations are agonizing enough that taking drugs again is the quickest way to obtain relief. These torrents of nagging distresses are real challenges to get their lives back in order.

Functional addiction also delays healing. Unknown to many people, addicts conceal their addiction by masquerading as a "normal" person. With the capability to provide for their families, addicts acquire the "license" to continue living in their addictive ways. The malady of functional addiction captivates and deceives other people for years or decades.

But, recovering addicts can learn the lessons from the desert experience of our forefathers. Despite all the hardships, brokenness, and grief, we can all look up to God and plead for deliverance. Faith is the launching pad of recovery. The unswerving belief in God guides us to cross the desolation of addiction toward a changed life.

Suffering Is Not an Excuse

Whoever believes in the Son has eternal life, but whoever rejects the Son will not see life, for God's wrath remains on them.
—John 3:36

Like the Israelites, drug addicts have earned the ire of God because of their sins and debauchery. Drug addicts and alcoholics are prone to idolatry and hedonism. Most only love themselves, drugs, pleasure, and drug dealers. To satisfy their addiction, they also break God's commands and the laws of man. They forsake their families, engage in illicit and extramarital relationships, and manipulate other people. Because of drugs, they rob stores, assault people, or commit heinous crimes like rape and murder.

Romans 1:29-31 reads:

They have become filled with every kind of wickedness, evil, greed and depravity. They are full of envy, murder, strife, deceit and malice. They are gossipers, slanderers, God-haters, insolent, arrogant and boast-

ful; they invent ways of doing evil; they disobey their parents; they have no understanding, no fidelity, no love, and no mercy.

Many MRC residents openly declare that their first order of business after their release is to find a job. The family is delighted. The wife beams with joy that his husband has finally shown a semblance of responsibility. The children are also grateful that their loving father would again bring food to the table.

However, beneath this façade lurks a charlatan with the vile intention of continuing to take drugs. For a few weeks, he forces himself to stay sober and shows off his responsible self. The time will eventually come when he would once again snort meth or drink alcohol. God is repeatedly mocked. He has to teach the addicted sinner a lesson.

I have told you these things, so that in me you may have peace. In this world you will have trouble. But take heart! I have overcome the world.
—John 16:33

People always question the existence of pain, suffering, and death. Even among the faithful flock of God, many believers ask why bad things happen to them. *"Why do I suffer from diabetes and cancer at the same time?"* *"How can a loving God allow the murder of innocent schoolchildren in a class by a raving, crazy gunman?"* *"Why did God allow my beautiful child to get hooked on drugs?"*

The nagging questions about God and His love for humanity puzzle us. However, hurts and suffering are parts of our mundane lives. At the Garden of Eden, Adam and Eve disobeyed God by eating the prohibited fruit. As a result, humanity fell from the graces of God. He drove us out of Paradise, took away the immortality out of our lives, and subjected us to many kinds of toils and pains (Genesis 3).

Since then, we have lived in a fallen, sinful world. We continue to suffer from the consequences of the sins of our first parents.

They broke our holiness in God's image, which gives us the right to live in the Garden of Eden. We now suffer from disease, suffering, addiction, and death. But God has great plans for us. The Lord said to Moses, "Now leave me alone so that my anger may burn against them and that I may destroy them. Then I will make you into a great nation" (Exodus 32:10).

Jesus Christ came to earth to bear all the sins of humankind. He also proclaimed our salvation and the coming Kingdom of Heaven, where all sufferings and death will be removed. Until that time, despite our faith and godly obedience, we will continue to experience pain. We will also wrestle with the existence of evil, as Satan continues to mess our lives with temptations that lead us to sin.

Since times past, drug addiction is an arena where the conflict between God and Satan come about. In this battleground, pain, misery, disease, and relationships are involved and deeply affected. In his book *Lifelines for Tough Times*, Mike Fabarez wrote, "Because sin became a part of the human equation, suffering is a part of the human experience."[2] But with God, we can learn to deal with and rise above our broken conditions.

Taking drugs, which gives temporary relief and respite from our life wounds, is a quick unholy remedy to resolve our conflicts. When food, jobs, education, or shelter are lacking, people turn to drugs. Young people seek refuge from substances when love, trust, and guidance don't thrive in the family home. Street children flock to the sidewalks and sniff glue to chase away hunger and create a world of their own. They also commit petty crimes. Rich kids, tormented by sheer boredom, take pleasure from drugs.

When addicts fail to deal with life troubles, the attainment of long-term sobriety would turn into a seemingly impossible task. When the right attitudes and actions are not taken, the cycle of chronic dependence, short-term sobriety, and relapse perpetuates.

Drug-induced delusion causes addicts to believe that life should be a constant flow of blessings and good feelings.

Their darkened hearts demand a consistent run of pleasure and merry times. But life consists of joy and pain. Sometimes the skies are sunny, and other times it rains. Sometimes we cry, other times we laugh.

A famous saying goes, "No pain, no gain." A bodybuilder faithfully goes to the gym and endures the ache from lifting weights but is later rewarded with better health and muscle tone. Hardships in life are not always punishment from heaven. God has his ways to test our faith to build our resiliency and morality. Helen Keller said, "Character cannot be developed in ease and quiet. Only through experience of trial and suffering can the soul be strengthened, ambition inspired, and success achieved."

Pains and sufferings can be blessings in disguise. Gold and diamonds are refined by fire. First Peter 1:6-7 reads:

> *In all this you greatly rejoice, though now for a little while you may have had to suffer grief in all kinds of trials. These have come so that the proven genuineness of your faith—of greater worth than gold, which perishes even though refined by fire—may result in praise, glory and honor when Jesus Christ is revealed.*

Wong Ming Dao, an exceptional Chinese leader, led a Christian revival movement in China during the twentieth century. Because of his disloyalty to the government, the authorities imprisoned him for 23 years. Without a Holy Bible, his unswerving faith in God sustained him through the dark, long years. He later wrote in his book, *A Stone Made Smooth*: "When silver is refined in the fire it does not experience pain because it has no feeling. However, when people are refined it means pain indescribable. Yet unless you are refined in that way, your life will not be purified and enriched like unadulterated silver."[3]

Pain is part of the human equation. Remember the torment and the genocide suffered by the Jews in

> *Pain is part of the human equation.*

the concentration camps of Auschwitz, the horror of the atomic bombings in Nagasaki and Hiroshima, and the Death March in Bataan during World War II. In addition, keep in mind the 430 years of slavery and misery suffered by the Israelites. However, many survived the Holocaust and other catastrophes. We, too, can overcome the wounds and tragedies of addiction.

Jesus Christ came to earth to save sinners, drug dependents, and alcoholics. He said, "I have not come to call the righteous, but sinners to repentance" (Luke 5:32). Real troubles and other false justifications are not to be used as excuses to take drugs. However, sufferings can lead a sinful addict to deliverance. Martin Luther King Jr. once said, "Only in the darkness can you see the stars." God heals and God saves.

My son, do not make light of the Lord's discipline, and do not lose heart when he rebukes you, because the Lord disciplines the one he loves, and he chastens everyone he accepts as his son.
—Hebrews 12: 5-6

God knows the frailty of humanity. Our loving Father in Heaven also disciplines us. God punishes us for our sins to prepare and make us better for the future.

Discipline is paramount. A loving father disciplines his child to righteous living. He strictly implements a computer gaming ban on certain hours of the day so the child can have the proper time to study. A mother whacks the sides of his naughty son because he stole some money from the kitchen drawer, with the stern message that he should not do it again. Proverbs 13:24 reads: "Whoever spares the rod hates their children, but the one who loves their children is careful to discipline them." We must also have discipline in our daily lives, not only in the big things but also in the small ones. For example, in our diet, too much fat or sugar intake can result in disease.

Despite their faith in God, recovering addicts and alcoholics remain vulnerable to temptations, drug cravings, and relapses. To make them stronger in the recovery process, God often subjects them to painful tests and trials.

Repentance is key. Suffering and pains linger after forgiveness from God was sought. However, these are often refining fires to mold godly character. Recovering addicts must embrace God's discipline and learn from them. Hebrews 13:7 says: "Endure hardship as discipline; God is treating you as his children. For what children are not disciplined by their father?"

In our fallen world, the Scriptures reveal that life is a struggle and sufferings are inevitable. We suffer now because all creation was subjected to God's wrath because of sin (Romans 8:18-20). But, we can all rejoice in our present sufferings, and gather joy amid the hurts and trials in our lives. We confront and learn the paradox that true happiness comes in the midst of suffering.

We will soon reach our future glory because "the creation itself will be liberated from its bondage to decay and brought into the freedom and glory of the children of God" (Romans 8:21). Jesus suffered the ultimate pain of crucifixion and death for our sake. The desert experience teaches faith, humility, endurance, and the revelation of a sovereign God who controls everything. We must lift God's anger in our lives to achieve true recovery. Jesus Christ is the key to remove God's wrath.

There Is Virtue in Not Giving Up

Therefore, since we are surrounded by such a great cloud of witnesses, let us throw off everything that hinders and the sin that so easily entangles. And let us run with perseverance the race marked out for us.
—Romans 12:1

On the way to the place of prayer, a woman fortune teller exasperated the disciples by following them for three days. She shouted,

"These men are servants of the Most High God, who are telling you the way to be saved" (Acts 16:17[b]). Knowing that the woman was driven by evil spirits, Paul rebuked the demon, "In the name of Jesus Christ I command you to come out of her!" (v.18[b]).

Because the woman can no longer make money, her master seized Paul and Silas, brought them to the authorities, and accused them of advocating acts against Roman law and practices (vv.19-21). The magistrates ordered them to be stripped, beaten with rods, flogged, and thrown to prison (vv.22-23). Under heavy guard, the guards put them in isolation with their feet locked by heavy chains (v.24).

Yet, Paul and Silas prayed and sang hymns to the Lord (v.25). After a strong earthquake, the ground shook, the prison doors opened, and all the prisoners' chains turned loose (v.26).

Paul epitomized courage and perseverance. In his ministry, he was imprisoned, whipped with cords and rods, and pelted with stones numerous times. He was also shipwrecked on three occasions, experienced hunger and sleepless nights, and faced starvation and death repeatedly. But he remained steadfast in the faith and sang praises to God amid many sufferings and trials. C.S. Lewis once said, "Hardships often prepare ordinary people for an extraordinary destiny."

Do not be afraid of those who kill the body but cannot kill the soul. Rather, be afraid of the One who can destroy both soul and body in hell.
—Matthew 10:28

Many recovering addicts and alcoholics are living in apathy and fear. They dread facing real-life pains. Crippled with helplessness, they can't muster the ways in rising above their fears and sorrows. Satan relentlessly sows the seeds of discouragement: "You can't make it, you're a loser," "It's useless to go sober," "Better take drugs," and "You can stop sometime in the future."

Like lepers, addicts feel they are social outcasts. Their friends and neighbors stay away from them, and other people avoid having anything to do with them. When sober, they suffer from the wreckage of the past that perpetually haunts them. Besides, they also loathe the reality of family separation, joblessness, and the feeling of dire unworthiness.

Afflictions and uncertainties paralyze addicts with fear of the present and the anxiety of the unknown future. Meth addicts also suffer from paranoia, fearful that the world is out to get them. Proverbs 28:1 reads: "The wicked flee though no one pursues, but the righteous are as bold as a lion." Drug addicts also experience other mental disorders that impair their faculties to cope with life situations. Rejection, pain, worthlessness, and uncertainty can be so overwhelming that taking drugs becomes a quick and easy remedy to banish fear.

> *Be strong and courageous. Do not be afraid or terri-*
> *fied because of them, for the LORD your God goes*
> *with you; he will never leave you nor forsake you.*
> **—Deuteronomy 31:6**

Courage does not necessarily mean the absence of fear. It means having the right attitude and taking action despite fear. Our troubles or external difficulties can crush us, or we can choose to dig deep within ourselves and find the strength to persevere and meet these challenges. Napoleon Bonaparte once said, "Courage isn't having the strength to go on—it is going on when you don't have strength."

Angie, my beloved wife with disabilities, was probably the most courageous person I knew. She was plastered in bed most of the time for eighteen years due to a massive stroke she contracted in 2002. She also developed stage-four breast cancer in 2016. Despite these infirmities and disease, she possessed the devotion to pray and muster the daily joy of a godly life until her death in May 2020.

Anyone who gathers courage and perseveres in trials is a hero. David slew the giant Goliath with a simple slingshot. Thomas Edison failed about 8,000 times in his experiments. He tried about 1,000 times before he finally succeeded in making the first light bulb. He once said, "I didn't fail 1,000 times. The light bulb was an invention with 1,000 steps." U.S. President, Abraham Lincoln failed in business, lost his sweetheart, had a nervous breakdown, got defeated in congress, senate, and the vice presidency before he got elected. He said, "I am profitably engaged in reading the Bible. Take all of this Book upon reason that you can, and the balance by faith, and you will live and die a better man."

Jesus Christ, our Savior, summoned all the courage and determination to fulfill the will of the Father. He was humiliated because of His cause and was constantly in fear for His life. He got beaten by a whip of cords, took up the heavy cross, crucified, and gave up His life in Mt. Calvary for the sins of all humanity.

With God's help, protection, and guidance, recovering addicts can defeat their fears and live a life full of courage and determination. Second Timothy 1:7 (*KJV*) says: "For God hath not given us the spirit of fear; but of power, and of love, and of a sound mind." Whatever we face, we must have faith and confidence in Him. Furthermore, 2 Corinthians 6:10 reads: "sorrowful, yet always rejoicing; poor, yet making many rich; having nothing, and yet possessing everything." Like Paul, we find joy not by denying the troubles in our lives but by facing them.

Never give up.
—Winston Churchill, prime minister of the United Kingdom

It takes the heart of a warrior to recover from addiction. Robert Frost said, "The best way out is always through." We have to dig deeper into our inner selves and gather all the resources to build up strength. We invoke our right as a child of

> *It takes the heart of a warrior to recover from addiction.*

God and defeat the onslaught of the Enemy. To put ourselves on the path of clean and healthy living, we must also overcome guilt, denial, and shame.

Healing takes time. In Mark 8, Jesus put some spit on the blind man's eye and asked, "Do you see anything?" (v.23). The blind man replied that his vision was not clear—"I see people; they look like trees walking around" (v. 24[b]). Once again, Jesus put his hands on the eyes of the man, and he could now see clearly (v.25). In the same manner, recovery takes time and often involves a series of attempts. Recovering addicts and their families must not lose heart for the arduous path ahead of them. There may be a need for a second or third rehab, but we should not lose faith because of these chronic relapses.

The attainment of real recovery is a huge challenge. Crossing over from addiction to sobriety is difficult and takes time and perseverance. Gene Heyman Ph.D., author of *Addiction: A Disorder of Choice*, wrote, "Addiction is not a chronic disorder, but a limited and, after some years, perhaps, a self-correcting disorder."[4]

Recovery is often uncomfortable. Prayer, meditation, and Cognitive Behavior Therapy (CBT) help in developing courage. But with perseverance, the rewards of liberation are gratifying. Recovering addicts learn to rise above the ridicule and scathing indictment of being looked upon as outcasts.

Slaying the giants in our lives means change. Addicts grow when they persevere through the discomfort of changes in their behavior and lifestyle. Most addicts hate the distress of incarceration. They do not persist and make the most out of their treatment. Instead, they count the days like serving a simple jail sentence.

The fight for recovery is long, and the specter of relapse haunts us. We are besieged with thoughts that our efforts of recovery are futile and feel that taking drugs is better than sobriety. The temptation to use drugs again seems the better alternative.

However, we must persevere. Relying on our proud and self-righteous nature is a sure tripwire to backsliding back to addiction and alcoholism. Helen Keller once said, "We could never learn to be brave and patient, if there were only joy in the world." Addicts who persevere in the storms of addiction not only overcome the barriers of drug dependency, but also grow as a child of God.

The Blessedness of Gratitude and Contentment

Were not all ten cleansed? Where are the other nine?
Was no one found to return and give praise to God
except this foreigner?
—Luke 17:17-18

On His way to Jerusalem, Jesus met ten men stricken with leprosy (v.12 [a]). As social outcasts, the lepers kept some distance since the disease is contagious. They suffered from skin sores, numbness, paralysis, and other debilitating conditions. They called Jesus in a loud voice, "Jesus, Master, have pity on us!" (v.13). Jesus said, "Go, show yourselves to the priests" and they were healed (v.14).

One of them, a Samaritan, came back to Jesus and praised Him in public (v.15). He threw himself at the feet of Jesus and thanked Him (v.16). Disappointed, Jesus questioned why only one out of the ten healed lepers came back to express his gratitude.

In the desert, the Israelites' unfaithfulness and ingratitude showed. Instead of thanking God for their deliverance from centuries of slavery, they whined and complained about many things. They grumbled about the lack of food, water, onions, and garlic. Despite God's daily provisions of manna and quails, they neglected to thank Him for their sustenance. They disregarded the blessed promise of security of reaching the Promised Land of Canaan.

But godliness with contentment is great gain. For we brought nothing into the world, and we can take nothing out of it. But if we have food and clothing, we will be content with that.
—1 Timothy 6: 6-8

Today, much of humankind exhibits ingratitude. The pursuit of more material wealth and possessions directs us every day. Despite the sufficiency of God's blessings, we forget to thank God for what we have and complain in our hearts that we need more of everything.

Instead of saying grace over dinner, we take fancy pictures of our nicely plated meals for upload on social media. How often do we throw our gaze at our neighbor's garage and squirm to see he has a second brand-new car? We forget to thank God that we have shoes until we see a man with amputated feet. It is ironic to realize that as our possessions multiply, our discontent also increases.

In 1863, Abraham Lincoln once said:

We have grown in numbers, wealth and power as no other nation ever has grown; but we have forgotten God! We have forgotten the gracious Hand which preserved us in peace, and multiplied and enriched and strengthened us; and we have vainly imagined, in the deceitfulness of our hearts, that all these blessings were produced by some superior wisdom and virtue of our own.

Drug addicts are masters of ingratitude and discontent. The whispers of Satan on Eve's ears that things are not good enough reverberate in the souls of present-day drug dependents. The majority of the MRC residents are in rehab because of bondage to worldly desires of the flesh and inability to cope with life pains. Plenty of them belong to a loving family and have decent jobs.

Despite the blessings they have, they remain unfulfilled, ungrateful, and dissatisfied. When high, they feel ecstatic and gratified. Rich kids take drugs out of sheer boredom, exploring new and artificial pleasures from chemicals. Addiction perpetuates as they compare sobriety with the hard realities of life to the escape and thrill that addictive substances provide.

Many addicts find it difficult to express gratitude considering that they have lost many things in their lives—family, material possessions, jobs, and respect from others. Overwhelmed with grief, some commit suicide.

> *I am not saying this because I am in need, for I have learned to be content whatever the circumstances. I know what it is to be in need, and I know what it is to have plenty. I have learned the secret of being content in any and every situation, whether well fed or hungry, whether living in plenty or in want.*
> **—Philippians 4:11-12**

Drug addicts and alcoholics feel that God is unfair and blame Him for their perceived deprived state. First Timothy 6:6-7 says: "But godliness with contentment is great gain. For we brought nothing into the world, and we can take nothing out of it."

They forget our holy God, who bears the sole right over all things in creation. As the Potter, he shapes us according to His will and purpose. Isaiah 64:8 *(ESV)* reads: "But now, O Lord, you are our Father; we are the clay, and you are our potter; we are all the work of your hand."

Discontented people are highly prone to drug abuse. Drug dependents only find joy and contentment in drugs. However, they know each drug episode is only temporary, often wondering if true happiness can happen without drugs.

Addicts and alcoholics may not openly grumble about their sorrows. But, inside of them, they possess deep-seated feelings of unbelief, worthlessness, and discontent. They also harbor strong doubts that true contentment and joy reside in having faith in God.

As Paul experienced, real and sustained happiness can be discovered and learned. Despite the inadequacies, infirmities, and troubles in our lives, we can also find contentment. Hebrews 13:5

says: "Keep your lives free from the love of money and be content with what you have, because God has said, 'Never will I leave you; never will I forsake you.'" Contentment can be found by "sitting still" and knowing that God is our Lord and provider of all things.

> *Though the fig tree should not blossom, nor fruit be on the vines, the produce of the olive fail and the fields yield no food, the flock be cut off from the fold and there be no herd in the stalls, yet I will rejoice in the Lord; I will take joy in the God of my salvation.*
> **—Habakkuk 3:17-18, *ESV***

Gratitude emanates from a humble heart. Pride, the root of the deadly sins, obstructs us from expressing our thanksgiving to God and other people. James 4:6[b] *(KJV)* reads: "God resisteth the proud, but giveth grace unto the humble." Narcissism, rooted out of pride, engulfs drug addicts. Also considered as a personality disorder, addicts crave an entitlement that entails the need for excessive attention and admiration. They believe that the world owes them many things in life.

In West Africa, people belonging to the Masai tribe know the correlation between gratitude and humility. They lay their foreheads to the ground whenever they want to give thanks to other people. They say, "My head is in the dirt." Another African tribe expresses gratitude by sitting quietly in front of the hut of a person to whom he is thankful. They say, "I sit on the ground before you."[5]

Idolatry thrives in the hearts of many drug addicts. In their hearts, God does not exist, and giving thanks to an unseen being is a myth. Self-centeredness also prevents them from seeking help from God for deliverance. They also find it challenging to ask for help from other people.

In his book, *The Pursuit of God*, Alfred Tozer wrote:

> *Our woes began when God was forced out of His central shrine and "things" were allowed to enter. Within the human heart, "things" have taken over. Men*

have now by nature no peace within their hearts, for God is crowned there no longer, but there in the moral dusk stubborn and aggressive usurpers fight among themselves for first place on the throne.[6]

Instead of being grateful to God for their blessings in life, addicts and alcoholics focus on what they don't have, grumble, and complain. They look for contentment in the wrong places. Drugs and discontent have forced God out of their hearts.

Their sense of vanity impedes gratefulness, contentment, and the need for divine intervention and much-needed help from others. Philippians 2:3 says: "Do nothing out of selfish ambition or vain conceit. Rather, in humility value others above yourselves."

Gratefulness is an elusive subject to addicts and alcoholics. Because of covetousness and discontent, they envy the "sober and successful happy people" around them. Only in the darkest moments of despair or in the depths of reaching rock bottom do they find God and the need to become grateful. Contentment and gratefulness come from faith even when life seems unfair.

Contentment and gratefulness come from faith even when life seems unfair.

Despite all the sufferings and hardships, the Bible says, "Draw near to God, and he will draw near to you" (James 4:8[a], *ESV*). Job cried out, "Naked I came from my mother's womb, and naked I will depart. The Lord gave and the Lord has taken away; may the name of the Lord be praised" (Job 1:21).

Bruce Epperly wrote, "The same attitude of thanksgiving that broadens the spirit and connects us to God may also transform our experience of pain and bring us greater well-being. We thank God for the wonder of all being, for despite appearances to the contrary, God is working gently in all things."[7]

Scriptures illustrate the biblical correlation between faith, gratitude, and contentment. The more we express our gratitude, the more satisfied we become. In addiction recovery, simple prayers of thanksgiving reduce the discontent in our hearts. First Thessalonians 5:18 reads: "Give thanks in all circumstances; for this is God's will for you in Christ Jesus."

Cultivating Gratefulness and Contentment

1. *Be Thankful*
   Gratefulness starts when we thank God for the miraculous gift of life. Every day is a blessing. We thank Him in our prayers for the protection and for the food and water we take. We see a glass of water as half-full, not half-empty.

   Despite the tragedies and losses, we also thank God for His goodness. We are separated from our families and homes because of drugs, but we are thankful that God takes care of them.

   At the start of recovery, we often have to push ourselves into prayer and the relentless pursuit of faith. However, we will soon learn that real joy and contentment resides in God, not in our relationship with others, our social status, or the number of our possessions.

2. *Practice Gratefulness Anytime and Anywhere*
   We don't only thank God in the confines of our homes or during our scheduled prayers or Sunday services. We should be grateful to God in our places of work, the mall, or the markets. Whether done in prayer or a simple utterance of "Thank you, Lord Jesus," the spirit of contentment heals our broken souls.

   Be appreciative also of other people. We express our gratitude to our family, office mates, neighbors, the bagger who helps us with our groceries, and the doorman who welcomes us.

In addition, we should help others. By sharing our resources and time with other people in need, we will discover that we are not alone in the realm of affliction and despair. Through our efforts of outreach, we learn to be content. We find fulfillment when we volunteer in community programs like feeding outreaches, street cleaning, or drug ministries and prevention campaigns.

3. *Pray and Rejoice Always*
The Bible tells us to "Rejoice always, pray without ceasing, give thanks in all circumstances; for this is the will of God in Christ Jesus for you" (1 Thessalonians 5:16-18, *ESV*). Paul exhorts that despite the different pain, anxiety, and suffering we experience, we should "Be joyful in hope, patient in affliction, faithful in prayer" (Romans 12:12). We pray and rejoice at home, in the car, on the bus, and in our workplaces. Each day of recovery is a blessing.

4. *Stop Comparing Yourself to Others*
Envy is an enemy of joy and contentment. Proverbs 14:30 (*ESV*) says: "A tranquil heart gives life to the flesh, but envy makes the bones rot." Comparing ourselves to others—regarding our possessions, social status, our physical attractiveness—would always lead to discontent. Contrasting ourselves to people who gained sobriety obstructs our recovery. Each of us is unique in God's eyes. Our true value comes from faith and the strength of our character.

5. *Practice Abstinence*
By practicing restraint on the many aspects of our lives, we cultivate joy and contentment. Abstain from deadly substances such as tobacco, alcohol, and drugs. We should take control of our daily habits, diversions, and recreations—food, TV, and social media. Sobriety is an opportunity for the addict to experience the real joy they would not have even dreamed was possible.

Regular fasting is an excellent measure to recovery and in gaining the right perspective about contentment in life. By going on without the essential food and water, we appreciate the blessings in our lives we usually overlook or take for granted. Fasting is a cornerstone of healing and divine recovery.

6. *Read the Bible*
    The Scripture is an oasis of joy and contentment. Despite the adversities and sufferings experienced by the people in the Bible, they found joy and satisfaction in God.

    Job found peace in God despite the loss of his family and possessions. Paul found purpose and joy despite all the sufferings, hard work, and death threats he encountered. Jesus Christ experienced His most solemn and divine purpose, despite the whiplash of cords and death on the cross. The passages of the Bible douse the spirits of grief and discontent suffered by drug addicts and alcoholics.

7. *Attend Church Services Regularly*
    The congregation of saints enhances joy and contentment. Matthew 16:18 (*ESV*) says: "And I tell you, you are Peter, and on this rock I will build my church, and the gates of hell shall not prevail against it." The spirit of God thwarts the evil intents of Satan who sows unbelief and discontent in the hearts of recovering addicts.

    In the church, we are surrounded by grateful and satisfied people. Many are also struggling sinners or people who conquered addiction. The communal spirit of praise and worship breeds joy that overcomes our struggle with discontent and ingratitude. During this pandemic, online meetings, Bible studies, and other church activities are great alternatives in our pursuit of God.

Conquering Deadly Sins and Negativity

To flee vice is the beginning of virtue.
—Horace, lyric poet

In 1933, a man from Austria with humble beginnings became the chancellor of Germany. He organized the Nazi Party, which pushed widespread propaganda that denounced the existence of the Jews. As a creative and intelligent but brutal dictator and chief architect of World War II, Adolf Hitler instigated the death of over 50 million people.

The Holocaust, the systematic genocide of the Jews in Europe between 1941 and 1945, resulted in the death of around six million Jews in gas chambers and through harsh labor in concentration camps. With his eloquent intoxicating words, Hitler seduced the masses, politicians, and the industrialists into following him as their divinely appointed leader. Consumed with pride, he craved for power and superiority.

But, unknown to many people, Adolf Hitler was a drug addict. A National Geographic TV documentary, *Nazi Underworld - Hitler's Drug Use Revealed*, disclosed that Adolf Hitler took a combination of drugs during World War II. Dr. Theodor Morell, Hitler's personal physician, confessed to the Allies that he gave the dictator a combination of opiates, morphine, barbiturates, and amphetamines.[1]

Behind the rise of Nazism was rampant drug use not only in the military sector but also by the public who served as the backbone in building Germany's war machine. In the book *Blitzed: Drugs in the Third Reich*, German author Norman Ohler also disclosed how Hitler used drugs, which was then cheaper than coffee, in achieving the aims of Nazi Germany. Generals, soldiers, pilots, factory workers, and housewives used cocaine, methamphetamine, heroin, and alcohol to gather confidence and euphoria and to boost their morale and productivity. He wrote, "Soldiers were awake for days, marching without stopping, which wouldn't have happened if it weren't for crystal meth; so yes, in this case, drugs did influence history."[2]

Heinrich Boll, the first German to be awarded the Nobel Prize for Literature in 1972, wrote in his letters about the widespread use of Pervitin, an early branded version of meth during World War II. This drug gave soldiers the stamina and strength to weather harsh days in the front lines with little sleep, hunger, and trauma. It was also reported that 35 million units of Pervitin and similar substances were shipped to the army and air force troops between April and July 1940 alone.[3]

As one of the most wicked men in history, Hitler exhibited extreme pride. Driven by narcissism and obsession, he glorified himself and proclaimed the Aryans as the supreme race to inhabit the whole earth. Hitler had no true God and put himself at the center of his life. He was also paranoid and suffered from schizophrenia, anxiety, delusions of persecution, and illusions of omnipotence and messiahship.[4] Hitler's pride triggered heinous atrocities in the whole of Europe.

The mad outbursts of drug-crazed Hitler and the horrors of the Holocaust, depicting images of dead bodies of millions of Jews piled up in concentration camps, testify that no sober person can commit such terrible atrocities.

Pride: The Father of All Sins

There are six things the LORD hates, seven that are detestable to him: haughty eyes, a lying tongue, hands that shed innocent blood, a heart that devises

wicked schemes, feet that are quick to rush into evil,
a false witness who pours out lies and a person who
stirs up conflict in the community.
—Proverbs 6:16-19

Before the creation, an angel named Lucifer rebelled against God. He wanted to be God. Because of his pride and covetousness, God cast him down to earth, along with his insurgent followers (Isaiah 14:12-15).

At the Garden of Eden, pride also led Eve to eat the forbidden fruit. The Devil tempted her that she could be like God (Genesis 3). Jesus Christ denounced the Pharisees, not for their knowledge and obedience of the Law, but because of their haughtiness and pride (Luke 18: 11-14). In his work the *City of God*, St. Augustine of Hippo (354-430 AD) wrote, "Pride is the commencement of all sin because it was this which overthrew the devil, from whom arose the origin of sin; and afterwards, when his malice and envy pursued man, who was yet standing in his uprightness, it subverted him in the same way in which he himself fell."

Pride is the excessive belief in one's capabilities, without regard for others. It blocks a person's ability to recognize the authority and grace of a sovereign God. Pride also begets the other deadly sins: lust, gluttony, greed, wrath, envy, and sloth.

Drug addicts are inherently engulfed with pride. They believe they do not need God or anybody else to rule them, much less help them in times of need or trouble.

Pride is the vilest of the vices. C. S. Lewis said, "The essential vice, the utmost evil, is Pride. Unchastity, greed, drunkenness, and all that, are mere flea-bites in comparison: it was through Pride that the devil became the devil. Pride leads to every other vice: it is the complete anti-God state of mind."[5]

Meth and other drugs produce megalomania and paranoia—extremely distorted forms of pride and feelings of omnipotence. When high on drugs, they feel a sense of superiority and belief that they can do anything they want. With distorted feelings of invulnerability, some also jump from the top of buildings or commit bizarre actions and crimes. Like the depraved Nazis, drug dependents exhibit gruesome pathological and behavioral changes in their personalities.

History records the significant role of addictive and mind-bending substances in wars and conquests of people, tribes, and nations. Today, the same vile spirit pervades in our homes and on the streets. We hear on TV about the drug-crazed father who raped and killed his six-year-old daughter or the addicted rapist who cut his victim into body parts. Terrorism is also known to have been fueled by drugs. News reports indicate that suicide bombers take drugs to gather courage before they blow up themselves and other people. Our witness to the reprehensible curse of addiction in our family homes and the havoc we see in our community attest to the wickedness that addiction brings to our ranks.

Pride, as written in the Bible, differs from the good pride we sometimes feel and experience in a positive way. It can also mean a good sense of gratification for some hard work or achievement. For example, we become proud when our child garners an honors medal, when we finish some difficult task, or when our country wins in the Olympics. In contrast, the biblical connotation of pride equates to the obsession of the self and an extreme groundless sense of entitlement and importance. The Pharisees of the Bible exhibited insidious pride when they highly pontificated themselves over the people.

Pride goes before destruction, a haughty spirit before a fall.
—Proverbs 16:18

Drug addiction encompasses all of the deadly sins illustrated in the Bible. Drug dependents feel they are superior over many people. They believe that they don't need God or others in their lives, especially in recovery (*Pride*). Drug addicts covet and steal money and things from their families and other people (*Envy*). They need more of their drug of choice and money to satisfy their chronic addiction (*Greed*). They require excessive amounts of the drug, stocking up their supply to ensure a continuous high (*Gluttony*).

Laziness consumes the drug addict. They reject holding a regular job or can't cope with the normal routines of work. They also can't effectively perform chores or housework (*Sloth*). Drugs lead them to promiscuity and adulterous relationships (*Lust*). Finally, they possess blatant indifference to an unfair world and other people who do not contribute to their goals of sustaining their addiction (*Wrath*).

The horde of unholy spirits that plague drug addicts makes recovery elusive and a continuous challenge. The cleansing of the addicted sinner and the healing of his soul requires thorough supplication and pleading to God for forgiveness and recovery. The removal of pride and the other consequential sins requires utmost faith, repentance, and time.

> *For by the grace given me I say to every one of you:*
> *Do not think of yourself more highly than you ought,*
> *but rather think of yourself with sober judgment, in*
> *accordance with the faith God has distributed to each*
> *of you.*
> **—Romans 12:3**

Pride is a massive obstacle for people in addiction recovery. Despite the bondage, they continue to cling on to the belief that they are well. Satan deceives them that taking drugs is a form of entitlement. They feel they deserve to be happy by popping pills or getting drunk.

> *Pride is a massive obstacle for people in addiction recovery.*

Overconfidence in recovery leads to relapse. Some recovering addicts beam with pride, prematurely thinking and proclaiming that they are freed from addiction after some months of sobriety. However, their minds say otherwise as they still entertain thoughts of drug use. Real recovery has not yet been achieved.

Breaking down pride and other deadly sins or vices requires the cultivation of virtues. Pursuing the Great Commandment (Matthew 22:36-40), of loving God before others and the self, vanquishes the root of the seven sins. Also, exercising the cardinal virtues (1 Corinthians 13:13) and the other biblical ethical values empower us to live godly lives, away from the influence of evil. Rebecca De Young wrote, "According to the Christian tradition, everyone needs faith, hope, and love, as well as practical wisdom, justice, courage, and temperance in order to become all God intended him or her to be as a human being."[6]

Putting God in the center of our lives to replace Satan vanquishes idolatry and addiction. When addicts and alcoholics believe in the good promise of salvation and eternal damnation in hell, godly fear arises and pride obliterates. Faith begins as they experience the utmost need to bow down before a holy God. Neil T. Anderson wrote, "Until we deny ourselves that which was never meant to be ours—the role of being God in our lives—we will never be at peace with ourselves or God, and we will never be free."[7]

Wherefore let him that thinketh he standeth take heed lest he fall.
—1 Corinthians 10:12, *KJV*

Humility breaks down the walls of pride. Addicts must accept and confess they are in bondage and that they need help. Humility controls the ego and removes boastfulness. It entails faith and the admission that God is superior and we are weak in His sight.

In recovery, addicts must take the proper actions and rely on hard work toward recovery for a long time. First Peter 5:6 says: "Humble yourselves, therefore, under God's mighty hand, that he may lift you up in due time." They also have to realize that relapse is a vulnerability, and are humbly willing to start all over again if a drug slip occurs. Ephesians 4:2 reads: "Be completely humble and gentle; be patient, bearing with one another in love."

We must remove pride from our dark and sorry souls. Healing happens when we worship our holy God and seek guidance and forgiveness from others. The price of recovery is the absolute reliance on God and a firm dedication to an entirely new way of life.

The Evil Sin of Denial

The heart is deceitful above all things and beyond cure. Who can understand it?
—Jeremiah 17:9

We may not easily recognize him or her—the drug addict or alcoholic. He or she may be our admired CEO, neighbor, doctor, plumber, street sweeper, or even our working mom. But, beneath the façade of sobriety, respectability, and admiration, lurks a hidden monster that controls their lives.

In contrast, we witness the alcoholic and homeless street bum who roams in our neighborhood, the doped teenagers hanging around on street corners, or the depressed street kid who sniffs cheap glue on the sidewalls. Many of these people share one thing in common. They deny they are addicts or alcoholics.

In Luke 22, the Apostle Peter denied he knew Jesus Christ. He feared for his life as the Romans might harm or kill him if he was identified as a follower of Jesus. Despite his earlier insistence that he would not forsake Jesus in the critical moments, Peter relented. He denied Jesus three times.

Like Peter, many drug addicts and alcoholics refuse to accept that they are in bondage. Because of the myriad of reasons, they also convince themselves and others that they are not in any way under the rule of dangerous substances. Above all, they erroneously or forcibly believe that taking drugs or getting drunk is not wrong, but only a respite from the hard reality and grind of life. However, habits soon turn into enslavement. The Bible says that addiction goes against God's precepts. They will "not inherit God's kingdom" (Galatians 5:20-21, *GW*).

Denial is a common first defense reaction when addicts are confronted with the truth, especially when it comes to drug abuse and alcoholism. As a powerful coping mechanism, denial delays the admission of reality. Filled with pride, drug dependents also believe they are in full control and proclaim, "I can stop anytime I want."

Substance abusers are masters of lies and deception. Most alcoholics deny they are enslaved to liquor; most addicted cigarette smokers deny they are addicted to nicotine; most drug dependents deny they are hooked on drugs. Homer said, "Hateful to me as the gates of Hades is that man who hides one thing in his heart and speaks another." They rationalize that they have only some habits that do not harm them or others.

Drug dependents are good at making excuses. They often say, "I have to entertain clients," or "It's a weekend." They utter these alibis and scapegoats to protect their deadly habits. Worse, the legality of tobacco, alcohol, prescription drugs, and marijuana (in some areas and situations) gives them the license and legitimate justification for taking them. Despite the clear, strong warning on cigarette packs that smoking is dangerous to their health, smokers rationalize and deny tobacco's lethal effects.

Deception is a matter of the heart. The brain tells the addict or alcoholic that taking alcohol or drugs is wrong, while the heart feels otherwise. Through manipulation and deceit, they camouflage and weave themselves into a lifestyle that can free them from the prying eyes of their family and the public. In worse instances, the family members act as enablers and codependents by cheering on the addicted worker who provides earnestly for the family.

However, a close scrutiny on the life of our loved ones would reveal hints of addiction and alcoholism. They often come home late, and their clothes exude the smell of alcohol and drugs. A significant portion of their pay goes to these deadly substances. Even wealthy stockbrokers run out of money because of drugs. They also spend little time with the family and more time with their friends. Yet, when asked if they are well, they quickly reply, "I'm fine" or "Everything is okay."

> *Quitting smoking is easy; I've done it hundreds of times.*
> **—Mark Twain, writer**

Addicts are skilled in propagating half-truths. If they manage to survive a whole week without drugs and alcohol because of a particular sickness, they will use this condition as evidence that they are not in bondage. A short stint of sobriety tells them they have full control of their lives. In addition, they see themselves as victims who face more struggles and pains in life than anybody does. Hence, they justify their drinking and drug use to cope with the hard realities of life.

The public shame that comes with admitting that they are under bondage also exacerbates denial. According to Christopher Ringwald, "Most active alcoholics or addicts know they are in trouble even when they do not want to admit it publicly... The issue becomes a stumbling block, especially for people whose entire success makes them unwilling to declare failure."[8] The deceptive state of denial can last for many years or decades, which robs the drug addict or alcoholic of what could have been more godly, fruitful, and joyful years of their lives.

In drug recovery, sobriety can co-exist with a state of denial. A person who has ceased taking drugs or drinking alcohol for some time may still have strong cravings or thoughts of using drugs and drinking. Yet, she falsely claims she is totally free from addiction. This deceptive posture often leads to relapse.

> *Woe to you, teachers of the law and Pharisees, you*
> *hypocrites! You are like whitewashed tombs, which*
> *look beautiful on the outside but on the inside are full*
> *of the bones of the dead and everything unclean. In*
> *the same way, on the outside you appear to people*
> *as righteous but on the inside you are full of hypocrisy*
> *and wickedness.*
> **—Matthew 23:27-28**

Hypocrisy engulfs the denying addict or alcoholic. She wears a mask and pretends to be something she is not and behaves in a way contrary to what she believes. Like the hypocritical Pharisee, she compares herself to others who she believes are the real addicts or alcoholics. She points to the homeless man sprawled on the sidewalk, with a bottle of liquor in his hand, as the true alcoholic, not her. She thinks that the malnourished teenager standing on the street corner with distorted facial curvatures is the real drug addict, not her.

God detests hypocrisy. The self-righteous says in Luke 18:11[b]: "God, I thank you that I am not like other people—robbers, evildoers, adulterers—or even like this tax collector." The pretense and comparing of a drug dependent to others feeds and perpetuates the denial of addiction.

THE DECEPTION OF FUNCTIONAL ADDICTION

They live a double life. Like chameleons, many alcoholics and drug dependents appear sober and productive. Some turn out to have sterling jobs, are promoted to higher positions, and are given awards and accolades.

However, unknown to most people, alcohol or drugs are constantly running in their veins. Some secretly pop pills every five hours or sneak a drink or two during lunchtime. Many are efficient in the workplace during the day but turn into monstrous drinkers and drug users at night. The outside world does not mind that they drink alcohol on weekends or take marijuana at some social gatherings. The public believes that "they deserve to be happy."

Functional addiction thrives in our society. The world tolerates this anomaly with the belief that people are inherently entitled to the fruits of their hard work. A 2007 study by the U. S. National Institute of Alcohol and Alcoholism revealed that around twenty percent of alcoholics are highly functional, well-educated, and have good incomes.[9] Shamsa reports, "Combined data from 2008 to 2012 indicate that an annual average of 8.7 percent of full-time workers aged 18 to 64 used alcohol heavily in the past month, 8.6 percent used illicit drugs in the past month, and 9.5 percent were dependent on or abused alcohol or illicit drugs in the past year."[10] The opioid crisis has destroyed and enslaved the lives of millions of "respectable" working men and women. According to the CDC, 2018 data shows 128 people in the U.S. die every day from opioid overdose.[11]

Like the famous fictional characters of Dr. Jekyll and Mr. Hyde, the personality of the functional addict is split into two—the sober professional—and the other, an addicted or alcoholic wrongdoer. High-functioning addicts and alcoholics can be found in company boards, academe, medicine, law, and critical government positions where stress levels are elevated. Pills, cocaine, and liquor rule their lives. The charade goes on for years or decades. They look happy and prosperous on the outside but suffer from the inner punishing struggles of addiction and alcoholism.

In his book, *Empowering Your Sober Self: The LifeRing Approach to Addiction Recovery*, Martin Nicolaus writes:

> *The person in the grip of dependency on an addictive substance is a person in conflict, with a personality that has split into two antagonistic camps. There is the old, original person, the person that existed before addictive substances became a priority. And there is the more recent person, the addict, who lives in the person's mind and body like a parasite, sucking up more and more resources, and driving the person toward premature death.[12]*

I was a functioning alcoholic in my corporate working life for around twenty years. A bottle of whiskey was often tucked in my table drawer to enable me to sneak a drink or chase away hangovers. I also stacked cologne, energy drinks, and hangover remedies to remove intoxication and cover the smell of alcohol from my body. My drinking friends and I also drank too much alcohol almost every day after work. Business meetings and dinners became avenues for more alcohol. We couldn't last for around three days without having too much to drink. Yet, no one among us dared to admit that he was an alcoholic.

The masquerade perpetuates as secret addicts and alcoholics become proud that they can harness excellent productive work and provide for their families. A successful career becomes the primary justification for indulging in chemicals. They believe that they have no problem that needs to be addressed. In their minds, they think they are not in any way considered an "addict" or "alcoholic." However, deep in their souls, they wrestle with the truth: they are held captive by addictive substances.

There is nothing concealed that will not be disclosed,
or hidden that will not be made known.
—Luke 12:2

Managing functional addiction takes skill and effort. Frequently, the shame of hiding addiction can be thrilling as it involves a high level of expertise, like walking on a tightrope. However, the addiction soon overpowers the drug users, and troubles start to surface. They skip work because of hangovers or bungle due to drug cravings. Eventually, they reach rock bottom and experience total helplessness and brokenness.

The deception ends as the drug dependents reach a state where they could no longer bear the pains and consequences of their "habits" that are hugely affecting themselves and others. Functional addicts and alcoholics often find it difficult to seek help until they arrive at total helplessness and experience severe withdrawal symptoms, like gut-wrenching stomach cramps or blackouts.

Functional addiction is trickier to address when the drunkards or drug addicts bear greater responsibilities in their careers. Corporate CEOs, lawyers, physicians, or school principals may find more difficulty in accepting their dire state. They dread failure and the thought of losing the prestige and social status they carry. Besides, they believe that they are prominent figures who bear much responsibility. As success is paramount in their lives, they refuse to admit they are in trouble and do not take the needed time off for recovery.

A prominent manifestation of denial and deception exhibited by recovering alcoholics and addicts is called "dry drunk syndrome." Initially coined by the AA for alcoholics, the concept also applies to drug addiction. Clinical specialists suggest that this phenomenon is part of "post-acute withdrawal symptom." Because they have stayed away from drugs and alcohol for a considerable length of time, they believe they are fully recovered from substance addiction. But they still often think and romanticize drugs and alcohol. In addition, they display the behavior, language, and actions attributed to alcoholics and drug users. Real recovery is not yet achieved as they are also always bothered by thoughts of drugs and alcohol. Soon, they usually end up in relapse.

DENIAL IN THE FAMILY

*If we claim to be without sin, we deceive ourselves
and the truth is not in us.*
—1 John 1:8

Denial is one of the primary behaviors that families espouse when they discover that a loved one is hooked on drugs or alcohol. They refuse to admit that a real problem exists and that their addicted son has lost control over his habits. Thinking that there is no crisis at all, they believe that rehab or another form of treatment is unnecessary.

Because of public shame, families hide or justify the addiction in the family. In many cases, they also do not know how to handle the drug situation, which makes denial the quickest, safest reaction. Hence, addiction becomes a family problem.

Enabling and codependency support and exacerbate denial. Families condone the drinking and drug use of a loved one because they believe that the habit is only occasional and will soon go away. Some parents join their son in drinking and using drugs at home so he would not go outside into dangerous places. Others may contribute to the addiction by taking over the personal responsibilities of the affected member, like paying off his debts and expenses or doing laundry for him. Because of guilt and the feeling of being responsible for the addiction of their loved one, enabling and codependent parents deny the problem. Instead, they try to make up by doing things that only worsen the trouble and perpetuate denial.

> *If we confess our sins, he is faithful and just and*
> *will forgive us our sins and purify us from all*
> *unrighteousness.*
> **—1 John 1:9**

> *Denial is the first*
> *obstacle to healing.*

Denial is the first obstacle to healing. A lie is the biggest threat to the road to recovery. This lie is not what someone else will tell us, but rather one that we will say to ourselves. We tell ourselves that we have changed, even when we haven't. As the Father of All Lies, Satan plants many types of deceptions in our hearts.

Drug addiction is a sin. The first step in recovery is to acknowledge the truth that one is under the oppression of drugs or alcohol. First John 1:10 reads: "If we claim we have not sinned, we make him out to be a liar and his word is not in us." Repentance means that we confess to God that we are sinners who had broken many of His laws by having a separate life of our own—especially through seeking joy and refuge from addictive substances.

The addict must also admit to other people, especially to their families, that they have a drug problem and that they need help. He should take personal responsibility for his actions and cease blaming others for his plight. On the other hand, family members must stop hiding the truth that addiction exists in the family home. Codependency and enabling must be expelled in their midst. Honesty removes denial. The Bible says: "The Lord detests lying lips, but He delights in people who are trustworthy" (Proverbs 12:22).

Addicted employees must not hesitate to tell their superiors that they need to take some time off for treatment. They should also not be afraid that they would lose their jobs because of their honesty. It is difficult to hold on to a job and wrestle with addiction at the same time. Recovery must be made as soon as possible.

Aside from rehab, they can opt to enroll in recovery and support groups like *The 12-Step Circles*. This outpatient option means that drug dependents need not necessarily leave their work. In these settings, addicts and alcoholics realize that they are not alone in their struggles and in seeking recovery. Denial is addressed as they share their lives and secrets.

Above all, addicts and alcoholics should depend on God. Divine healing happens when we have a true encounter with God. John 8:32 says: "Then you will know the truth, and the truth will set you free."

Dealing with Guilt and Shame

Fixing our eyes on Jesus, the pioneer and perfecter of faith. For the joy set before him he endured the cross, scorning its shame, and sat down at the right hand of the throne of God.
—Hebrews 12:2

187

Raul (not his real name) distanced himself from the rest of the crowd at the MRC. A middle-aged man with a sturdy physique, he looked withdrawn in our weekly Bible studies. After several months, Raul finally gathered the courage to disclose that his wife committed suicide. Consumed with guilt, he believed his wife took her own life because of his gunrunning and drug-laced deeds.

We visited him after his release at his relative's house, which was near the rehab center. Raul still showed signs of brokenness and aimlessness, as he couldn't decide to go home and face his children. He also couldn't ascertain what he would do in his life. He opted to remain with his relative in dismal seclusion. Beaten with grief and guilt, Raul later moved out alone to an undisclosed distant province.

Guilt and shame are the most debilitating state of feelings after we realize that we have hurt God, ourselves, and others. These negative emotions isolate us from other people and hinder our faith and trust in God.

Guilt is a natural feeling that comes from our conscience when we have committed a sin or a big mistake. Shame, on the other hand, is a feeling of degradation and humiliation that results from our wrongdoings. Disgrace, borne out of pride, leads to a sense of unworthiness and a loss of self-respect.

Returning soldiers and war veterans often suffer the adversity of guilt from combat. In their line of work, innocent young children are sometimes killed in the crossfire. Clinically, doctors diagnose them with Post-Traumatic Stress Disorder as they struggle with the guilt that they have hurt or killed a fellow human. Despite the knowledge that it is not of their own free will to harm others and that they were doing their duty, they eventually suffer the consequences of their actions. They bear the agony of remorse and couldn't easily adjust back to society. Many turn to drugs and commit crimes.

Extreme guilt and shame can lead to the most tragic outcome: attempted or actual suicide. In 2014, an average of 70 Japanese people took their own lives daily.[13] Driven by the traditional core values of honor, the guilty or shamed Samurais committed "seppuku" by stabbing themselves with a short sword until they die. Today, some Japanese working men jump in front of an express train because they were bypassed in a recent job promotion.

Suicide and drug overdose are related. Many people consider death as the last remedy because they could not take distresses any longer. The WHO reports that:

> Worldwide, about 0.5 million deaths are attributable to drug use. More than 70% of these deaths are related to opioids, with more than 30% of those deaths caused by overdose. According to WHO estimates, approximately 115 000 people died of opioid overdose in 2017. Opioid overdoses that do not lead to death are several times more common than fatal overdoses.[14]

In recent history, Robin Williams, Michael Jackson, and Anthony Bourdain took their own lives due to addiction and depressing emotions. Because Whitney Houston's voice was severely damaged by drugs, people walked out of her comeback concert in London in 2010. Drugs, guilt, and shame could have driven her to take her life in a hotel room.

OVERCOMING REJECTION

> *If the world hates you, keep in mind that it hated me first.*
> **—John 15:18**

People suffer from rejection, at least at one point in their lives. We feel rejected when we fail in school, our job application is declined, or our marriage proposal is turned down by our fiancée. Rejection means deep pain and misery.

Jesus Christ suffered the most extreme form of rejection in history. The Jews claimed that Jesus was the false Messiah who preached erroneous beliefs and teachings. He endured all the humiliation and disgrace from the public until his painful crucifixion and death at Calvary.

Drug addicts and alcoholics experience the same rejection suffered by the lepers in the Bible. People shun away from them. As social outcasts, their consciences are besieged with the condemnation that they have crossed God and other people. They feel reviled that they have abandoned their faith, lost their jobs, neglected their families, and committed many sorts of disgraceful acts and crimes.

At the MRC, many of the young residents dread going back to a class filled with students much younger than them. Their former classmates have leapfrogged them in school. Many able-bodied men avoid going back to their jobs and mingle with sober people because of shame.

More frequently, they feel more shame about the consequences of addiction rather than the use of the drug itself. A person may feel greater shame because he stole his neighbor's motorcycle or manipulated a friend for drugs. In his mind, he couldn't possibly do these outrageous acts when sober. However, when they are drunk or high, many addicts are like beasts that do not feel any semblance of guilt and shame. Sin has hardened their hearts, and chemicals have fried their brains from many years of drug use.

Their destiny is destruction, their god is their stomach,
and their glory is in their shame. Their mind is set on
earthly things.
—Philippians 3:19

Shame is also borne out of rejection. Many drug addicts and alcoholics are denounced by their families and driven out of their houses. Scandal in the family heightens when a drug-crazed son assaults people in the streets or goes on a drunken rampage in the neighborhood. Drug addicts also suffer the same rejection in their workplaces. The feeling of accusation can be so harsh that the only way to gain a sense of belonging and safety is to take drugs again.

Guilt and shame also thrive in the family home. Many parents and siblings feel they are responsible for the addiction of a family member. They also blame themselves for being enablers and supporters of that dependency. The feelings of remorse can also be overwhelming when the addiction has led to terrible outcomes such as family separation or drug overdose. Because of guilt, the whole family suffers the social shame that also leads to denial. Guilt, shame, and rejection are parasites that rob the joy of the family home.

Sin: The Source of Guilt and Shame

I heard you in the garden, and I was afraid because I was naked; so I hid.
—Genesis 3:10

At the beginning of creation, "Adam and Eve were both naked, and they felt no shame" (Genesis 2:25). One day, the Devil tempted them to eat the forbidden fruit at the Garden of Eden. They later realized that they were naked and covered themselves with fig leaves (Genesis 3:7). When they heard the Lord walking in the garden, they felt afraid and hid among the trees (v.8). The sin of our first parents resulted in the fall of humankind, which gave birth to crippling guilt, shame, and rejection.

At a later time, Judas Iscariot betrayed Jesus Christ, selling Him out for thirty pieces of silver (Matthew 26:15). Besieged with remorse, he tried to return the silver but failed (Matthew 27:3-4). Unable to bear the guilt and shame, he threw the money away and hanged himself (v.5).

Like Adam, Eve, and Judas, sinful addicts and alcoholics feel unworthy and embarrassed because of their actions. They usually know they have done wrong—that they have hurt God, other people, and themselves. The guilt and shame of addiction carry with them tragic consequences. Losing a job, quitting from school, and family separation cause a heavy burden of brokenness that makes recovery a daunting task.

Family members also reinforce guilt and shame when they shield the addiction of a loved one from friends, neighbors, and coworkers. They turn into willing accomplices of a family cover-up. The family feels defeated if the society learns that a son or sibling is an addict.

Recovering addicts dread facing their sober friends and coworkers, and experience ridicule and silent judgment. Sometimes the degree of humiliation from the shameful consequences of addiction exceeds the burden of guilt from taking drugs.

When sober, addicts suffer more from these emotional wounds. In most cases, taking drugs is the sure remedy to numb away any feelings of remorse and disgrace. As soon as the highs of drugs wear off, negative emotions again surface. Addiction becomes a perpetual cycle of unresolved sin, guilt, and shame.

Addictive substances and lusts of the flesh are closely related. First John 2:16 says: "For everything in the world—the lust of the flesh, the lust of the eyes, and the pride of life—comes not from the Father but from the world." Because drugs and alcohol erase inhibitions and heighten the sexual experience, many users fall into adultery and promiscuity. Shocked, they later realize that they have borne multiple families.

At the MRC, many residents grapple with guilt and shame. They wrestle with how to reconcile themselves with their wives, numerous life partners, and children belonging to different mothers. Upon release, the heavy burden of facing reality, deciding which home to return to, and taking steps towards repentance and resolution make recovery difficult. Relapse becomes a natural consequence. The guilt and shame often become so severe that they isolate themselves or go to extreme lengths by using more drugs, hurting themselves, or taking away their own lives.

Brothers and sisters, I do not consider myself yet to have taken hold of it. But one thing I do: Forgetting what is behind and straining toward what is ahead.
—Philippians 3:13

Holding on to negative feelings keeps us stuck in the past. Guilt and shame can paralyze us and affect our capability to move forward in life. Many residents of the MRC wrestle with memories of the past. They used to have a steady, decent income and a loving family until drugs broke everything in their lives. The agony from the guilt and shame may remain for many years if the proper resolutions are not addressed.

Guilt and shame can paralyze us and affect our capability to move forward in life.

Recovering addicts are often tormented by the Devil of their past, which keeps them away from the faith. After sincerely confessing to God, they still feel barraged by condemnations, conflicting them with the lie that they are not yet absolved by God. Recovery becomes elusive as they wander in an abject state of desolation and confusion. Desperate for relief, they take drugs again and all feelings of guilt and shame disappear.

I sought the LORD, and he answered me; he delivered me from all my fears. Those who look to him are radiant; their faces are never covered with shame.
—Psalm 34:4-5

On a particular day, a large number of believers and followers swarmed around Jesus on the road. A woman who had been bleeding for twelve years pushed herself through the crowd to get to Jesus (Luke 8:42-43). "She came up behind him and touched the edge of his cloak, and immediately her bleeding stopped" (v.44).

Under Jewish Law, the bleeding woman would be declared ceremonially unclean (Leviticus 15:25-27). Her condition meant that she could not enter the temple courts as anything or anyone she touches would become unclean as well. Because of her state, she didn't dare face the crowds and Jesus. She suffered the shame and social stigma of rejection for being unclean. Desperate for healing, the bleeding woman sought to hide in anonymity by just touching the edge of the cloak of Jesus.

Because of pride and fear of failure, drug dependents dread the shame that comes from their sins and mistakes in life. They go to extreme lengths in avoiding degradation by hiding their reprehensible acts and weaknesses. Unresolved shame makes them lose their trust in God, who can heal their innermost hurts and sins. As a result, strongholds are created by the Devil, which continually torments them for many years. C.S. Lewis once said, "We have a strange illusion that mere time cancels sin… But mere time does nothing either to the fact or to the guilt of a sin."

If sin is not confessed, and guilt and shame are not adequately dealt with, recovery becomes obscure. They cocoon themselves back into their caves of isolation and use drugs. Addicts prefer to wallow alone in their locked-up rooms or with their fellow users in drug dens while high, away from the scrutiny of the judging public. Satan steps up his deception in enticing the recovering addict to remain in his fold. He whispers, "Don't mind other people; they are just as bad. Go and take your drugs."

There are two types of guilt: conviction and condemnation. Conviction of sin comes from the Holy Spirit (John 16:8), producing godly sorrow that leads to repentance (2 Corinthians 7:10). The other kind of guilt, which is condemnation or repeated accusations, comes from Satan. Sin and guilt, when properly confronted and resolved, leads to healing. Guilt allows the admission of self-responsibility, accountability, and submission to God and other people.

Vanquishing Grief and Loss

*Brothers and sisters, I do not consider myself yet to
have taken hold of it. But one thing I do: Forgetting
what is behind and straining toward what is ahead,
I press on toward the goal to win the prize for which
God has called me heavenward in Christ Jesus.*
—Philippians 3:13-14

Born in Germany, Anne Frank was a young Dutch-Jewish diarist captured by the Nazis during World War II. Together with her family, she suffered one of the worst afflictions and grief experienced by people in the past century. The Holocaust victims were stripped of their humanity, identity, and possessions and dragged into concentration camps like animals. However, Anne Frank saw something different. Despite all the plight and sorrows, she learned to overcome her desperation and loss. She wrote in her famous *The Diary of a Young Girl*, "I don't think of all the misery, but of all the beauty that remains."

Like Anne Frank, drug addicts and drunkards suffer extreme anguish and loss in life. They lose the love and trust of their families and other people. In addition, they also lost their jobs, honor, finances, and possessions. At the MRC, many residents experience distress for selling their passenger tricycles, which they use to earn a living, to get drugs. Guilt and shame from loss keep them in addiction, unable to move on in life. Sometimes, they become insane and commit suicide because of drugs.

The weight of the past can be a heavy burden for a person in substance recovery. But we can't keep brooding forever. Ultimately, the time will come when we have to let go of the past for our own good. An Old Chinese proverb says, "You cannot prevent the birds of sorrow from flying over your head, but you can prevent them from building nests in your hair."

> *The weight of the past can be a heavy burden for a person in substance recovery.*

We must keep moving. Philippians 3:13-14 reads: "But one thing I do: Forgetting what is behind and straining toward what is ahead, I press on toward the goal to win the prize for which God has called me heavenward in Christ Jesus." Avoiding or postponing the needed changes at the right time would not foster full recovery and would not create the proper state and environment for sober living. Albert Einstein once said, "Life is like riding a bicycle. To keep your balance, you must keep moving."

Grief and loss open our hearts to love. In many instances, the parent has to let go of his addicted child. In Luke 15, the father didn't go looking for his prodigal son, even though the child perhaps wandered into dangerous places. Distinctly, the father allowed him to experience extreme pain and go rock bottom.

In numerous cases, "tough love" works. If we haven't known loss, we would not have the capability to love others and appreciate the better things in life. Loss breaks down pride and imparts humility to our selfish, uncaring hearts. Only in the darkness can we see the light.

God loves the sinful addict but despises sin. Despite the painful circumstances, we must reject evil, stand firm, and keep drugs out of our lives. The hardships we encounter can serve as a timely opportunity to know God, make amends with Him, and the people we've hurt. We can resolve to chart new directions in life, identify and fix all our flawed psychological issues, and learn to be content and happy without drugs. Persistence is key. Dr. Martin Luther King Jr. once said, "The ultimate measure of a man is not where he stands in moments of comfort and convenience, but where he stands at times of challenge and controversy."

All will experience loss at some point in their lives. Grief and loss are parts of our natural existence. Mark Twain once wrote, "Nothing that grieves us can be called little: by the external laws of proportion, a child's loss of a doll and a king's loss of a crown are events of the same size." Addicts are often consumed by grief because of their addiction and life situations that lead to rebellion, desolation, and death. But, Jesus Christ experienced suffering in His distressing moments at Gethsemane. He said, "My soul is crushed with grief to the point of death" (Mark 14:34, *NLT*).

However, God promises strength in times of adversity. "I have told you these things so that in me you may have peace. In this world, you will have trouble. But take heart! I have overcome the world" (John 16:33).

God is a beacon of hope. He delivers desperate addicts from the tyranny of deadly substances to a liberated life. When we reach true recovery, our temporal grief and loss are replaced by an irreplaceable joy from having an intimate relationship with Christ. As the Messiah, He also gives us eternal life.

Resisting the Enemy

The Temptations of Satan

Be alert and of sober mind. Your enemy the devil prowls around like a roaring lion looking for someone to devour.
—1 Peter 5:8

Robert (not his real name) jumped with joy. After six months of rehab at the MRC, he was filled with anticipation and excitement. At last, he could breathe the exhilarating air of freedom, the warm welcome of his loving family, and the comforts of home. Robert could also feast on his favorite dishes—a break from the rationed food inside rehab.

Outside the gates of the MRC lies a small store that sells snacks, drinks, and tobacco. Immediately after exiting the gates, he leaped toward the shop and bought a stick of cigarette. Craving for a nicotine rush, Robert lit the cigarette and inhaled the smoke so hard it probably filled all of his lungs. His mother, who escorted him out of the premises, didn't mind.

At home, the family greeted him with hugs, kisses, and a small feast. Everybody missed Robert. Food overflowed and beer was served on the side. As a welcome gesture, his rich uncle handed him a wad of pocket money. In the background, the television ran a stream of shows and commercials that showed a pleasurable life. One advertisement depicted scenes of an alluring woman serving whiskey to a group of ogling men.

With festive smiles, they believed that Robert was fit and ready to go back to normal life. Little did they know that deep inside, he still struggled with drug cravings. He often imagined the blissful highs of meth. However, he has not really decided to stop taking drugs. Robert thought, "Maybe, I can use drugs once in a while. Besides, I think I am already strong enough not to fall again to addiction."

He walked outside the house for a breath of fresh air and saw his lanky drug-addicted friends huddled on a street corner. He couldn't help approaching them and say, "Hello." They responded in a welcoming manner, but winked and suggested, "Maybe you can come by later and join us for some hits. It's free, a welcome gift." Robert declined the invitation and rushed back home because he felt the rush of strange sensations. The events after leaving rehab triggered his drug cravings. Satan was back, and Robert was ripe for a drug relapse.

Robert's story is a common account of many individuals after their release from rehab. Temptations to retake drugs arise as drug memories and triggers heighten cravings.

At home, enabling and codependency further pushes recovering addicts to drug use. Some parents give their loved ones large amounts of money or a small business as a prize for finishing rehab. Others offer a nice vacation or a brand-new car. These haphazard gestures are dangerous moves that only foster drug relapse.

It would only take a few sober days or weeks when recovering addicts succumb to the pressures of drug cravings and catapult back to meth, alcohol, or pills. One remarkable incident at the MRC involved the re-admission of an individual six hours after his discharge. He was released in the morning, got drunk, and sent back to rehab in the afternoon.

Many of the former residents are not surprised, even expectant when they fall into a drug relapse. Rehab is just a pit stop—a respite to appease the family's anger and disappointment for their addictive ways.

*And no wonder, for Satan himself masquerades as an
angel of light.*
—2 Corinthians 11:14

After his expulsion from the heavens, Satan started his conquest of humanity. The Devil tempted Adam and Eve at the Garden of Eden that led to our fall. The battle between good and evil had begun. Satan led David, captivated and seduced by Bathsheba's beauty, to commit murder and adultery. Satan tempted Jesus on the mountaintops. Like a "roaring lion," Satan's evil scheme has permeated into our lives since times past.

Today, the Devil lurks in our homes, places of work, and on street corners. Satan's primary weapon and strategy is deception. The Apostle Paul said, "And no wonder, for Satan himself masquerades as an angel of light. It is not surprising, then, if his servants also masquerade as servants of righteousness." (2 Corinthians 11:14-15). Controlled by unholy spirits, many addicts and drug dealers are used by Satan in pushing his chief aim of peddling pleasure and sin.

It would not take a long time before the Evil One breaks the frail sobriety of the recovering addict. Charlotte Kasl wrote, "Thoughts enter the mind as if from some alien force, seeming to take over. Learning to recognize the early stages of an addictive episode can help dramatically in preventing the addictive urge from overwhelming a person."[1]

Temptations, triggers, and cravings confront people in recovery every day. Inside rehab, they long for the exhilarating high of meth. These dark enticements become more profound and intense when they return to the comforts of their homes and are out on the streets.

> *Temptations, triggers, and cravings confront people in recovery every day.*

THE RETURN OF THE WICKED SPIRIT

When an impure spirit comes out of a person, it goes through arid places seeking rest and does not find it. Then it says, 'I will return to the house I left.' When it arrives, it finds the house swept clean and put in order. Then it goes and takes seven other spirits more wicked than itself, and they go in and live there. And the final condition of that person is worse than the first.
—Luke 11:24-26

The human body is the inherent abode of the Holy Spirit. First Corinthians 6:19 says: "Do you not know that your bodies are temples of the Holy Spirit, who is in you, whom you have received from God? You are not your own."

As the passages in Luke 11 suggest, the Devil can occupy a person if he is devoid of the Holy Spirit. The number of demonic spirits that can dwell in the body can be more than one. Jesus cast out seven demons from Mary Magdalene (Mark 16:9). In Luke 8, Jesus asked the name of the evil spirit inside the demon-possessed man in Gerasenes: "Legion... because many demons had gone into him" (v.30[b]).

After the demons of addiction have been driven out, the body is left bare and wiped clean. In recovery, a person usually experiences feelings of emptiness and aimlessness. Soon, ungodly spirits come back to reclaim him. In Matthew 12, evil spirits come in and out of people. Besides, these wicked spirits bring with them more other unholy spirits. The heavy assaults result in relapse, and the person's condition becomes worse. His addiction escalates as he pursues more dangerous things. Greater consequences come about as he lies, robs stores, mugs other people, and forsakes his family.

The constant coming and going of dark spirits cripple drug addicts and those in recovery. Unbelievers are usually unaware of the spiritual battle raging between God and demons over them. After rehab, the Devil blinds them and causes them to think that they are already well with their glowing faces and healthy bodies. On the contrary, Satan still rules their hearts. They harbor their unconfessed sins and entertain thoughts of drinking or using drugs again.

On the other hand, many of those who have sought God for healing affirm their fragility in recovery. They feel the tug of war between God and the Enemy in their rough journey toward recovery.

Because of wavering faith, relapse eventually occurs to many recovering addicts. However, many long-term, real recoveries often involve a series of small and significant portions of sobriety, drug slip, and relapse.

> When tempted, no one should say, "God is tempting me." For God cannot be tempted by evil, nor does he tempt anyone; but each person is tempted when they are dragged away by their own evil desire and enticed. Then, after desire has conceived, it gives birth to sin; and sin, when it is full-grown, gives birth to death.
> **—James 1:13-15**

The mind is a constant battleground between God and Satan. As long as we live in our earthly tent, we are all exposed to the daily vortex of good and evil. We can't always entirely blame the Devil if we are tempted and fall into sin.

With our free will and unholy desires, we are also responsible and accountable for the outcome of our actions. Eve blamed the serpent for her disobedience, yet God punished her and Adam (Genesis 3). Jesus Christ "has been tempted in every way, just as we are—yet he did not sin" (Hebrews 4:15[b]).

FACING THE ENEMY

*Submit yourselves, then, to God. Resist the devil, and
he will flee from you.*
—James 4:7

God is faithful to those who trust in Him. Because God understands the weaknesses of recovering addicts, He helps them in getting out of difficult situations. First Corinthians 10:13 says: "No temptation has overtaken you except what is common to mankind. And God is faithful; he will not let you be tempted beyond what you can bear. But when you are tempted, he will also provide a way out so that you can endure it."

God's Word gives us wisdom on how to deal with difficult tempting situations. Our daily prayers must be charged with pleas of protection from the Unseen Enemy. Matthew 6:13 reads: "Lead us not into temptation, but deliver us from the evil one."

The Scriptures also show practical ways to avoid the snares of Satan. Mark 14:38 exhorts: "Watch and pray so that you will not fall into temptation. The spirit is willing, but the flesh is weak." Proverbs 23:31-32 tells us to avoid staring at alcohol: "Do not gaze at wine when it is red, when it sparkles in the cup, when it goes down smoothly! In the end it bites like a snake and poisons like a viper." Recovering addicts should also avoid their addicted friends and drug dealers as, "Bad company corrupts good character" (1 Corinthians 15:33[b]).

Many recovering addicts embrace the dangerous mindset of complacency, pride, and overconfidence. With little faith, they feel they are well enough to resist any kind of temptation. However, these harmful and deceptive attitudes often lead them back to drugs. Instead, they need to continually seek the Holy Spirit to fortify them from the relentless thwarts of the Enemy.

*So I say, walk by the Spirit, and you will not gratify the
desires of the flesh.*
—Galatians 5:16

Recovery is like walking in a mine-field. A seemingly small temptation can lead to a full-blown relapse. Healing often involves a lengthy spiritual battle with the Enemy, who does not easily give up. Besides, the mind of an addict is inherently wired to defend and pursue addiction. Satan is disgusted with the notion that a minion has left his kingdom and pursues recovery through knowing Christ.

> *The mind of an addict is inherently wired to defend and pursue addiction.*

On the other hand, those who have remained steadfast and became more spiritual are the ones most likely to face ruthless temptations and vicious attacks. If the recovered addict can't be toppled by drugs or alcohol, the Devil will bring him down by other means. Satan is persistent and does not easily give up.

Recovering addicts intermittently face the varied enticements of Satan in winning them back. The Devil tempted Jesus three times in the desert and the high places. Unable to win during the day, the Devil attacks the recovering addicts in their dreams. They give in and groan, "And I know that nothing good lives in me, that is, in my sinful nature. I want to do what is right, but I can't. I want to do what is good, but I don't. I don't want to do what is wrong, but I do it anyway" (Romans 7:18-19, *NLT*).

Drug addiction is idolatry. The Devil also drives the addicts to multiple sins involving adultery, greed, manipulation, trickery, and crime. It takes a firm level of faith and offensive spiritual warfare to halt the intrusions of the Enemy. Like those who have been healed by Christ and through His apostles, we have to pursue faith and "sin no more." First Peter 5:9-10 says: "Resist him, standing firm in the faith, because you know that the family of believers throughout the world is undergoing the same kind of sufferings."

After deliverance, we need to implore the Holy Spirit to reside in us to ensure the sacred fruits of God are indwelling. This baptism finally seals off the body from the persistent incursion of demons. We acquire the divine comfort and protection that come with a personal relationship with Christ. By the bruises of war and wrestling with the Enemy, we learn how to deal with temptation and survive in shining glory.

TESTING AND TRIALS OF FAITH

Consider it pure joy, my brothers and sisters, whenever you face trials of many kinds, because you know that the testing of your faith produces perseverance. Let perseverance finish its work so that you may be mature and complete, not lacking anything.
—James 1:2-4

God tested Abraham, the "Father of All Nations," through his beloved son Isaac. In Genesis 22, The Lord told him to go to Moriah and sacrifice Isaac as a burnt offering on a mountain (v.2). Filled with faith, Abraham bound the young Isaac and motioned to slay his son with a knife (vv.9-10). However, the angel of the Lord appeared (v.11) and said, "Do not lay a hand on the boy…Do not do anything to him. Now I know that you fear God, because you have not withheld from me your son, your only son" (v.12).

Testing is not the same as temptation. Temptation comes from the Devil, but testing and trials come from or are allowed by God. Satan tempted Eve at the Garden of Eden. God allowed Satan to test Job. The Devil tempted and confronted Jesus in the highest places.

The tests we encounter reveal the inner state of our hearts. They are comparable to the painful and challenging trials experienced by the Israelites in the wilderness. Tests expose our weaknesses and failures. First Peter 4:12 *(ESV)* reads: "Beloved, do not be surprised at the fiery trial when it comes upon you to test you, as though something strange were happening to you."

However, these tests also magnify God's love. In like manner, trials give us the opportunity for spiritual conquest and growth. Like school examinations, we have to pass the tests in order to advance to maturity. Victory can only be achieved if there is a battle to be fought.

Tests and trials are parts of healing. Recovering addicts face various ordeals, which are allowed by God to strengthen them and build up their faith. Like Job, they go through punishing struggles—desperation, joblessness, isolation, and deep grief.

Relapse to drugs can be a form of testing. Many recovering addicts realize (which is a good sign) that they have sinned because they again took drugs or got drunk. Like a long-distance runner who stumbled on the tracks, they need to stand up and continue the race. Despite the relapse, they should firmly resolve to halt all drug use, pursue faith, and remain repentant.

Many successful recoveries are achieved by those who have experienced relapses but remained steadfast to God. After the Lord's testing, they soon reached the promised land of true recovery. Until faith has passed the torments of testing, it hasn't been proven. The result of trials is that, over time, we learn to value more the divinity of Jesus Christ. James 1:12 reads: "Blessed is the one who perseveres under trial because, having stood the test, that person will receive the crown of life that the Lord has promised to those who love him."

Like gold, which is polished by fire, trials and tests refine us. First Peter 1:7 reads: "These [trials] have come so that the proven genuineness of your faith—of greater worth than gold, which perishes even though refined by fire—may result in praise, glory and honor when Jesus Christ is revealed."

We must not wander around, but journey in the desert of our lives. Only through perseverance, faith, and sovereign grace can we enter the Kingdom of God.

The Lure and Trap of Cravings and Triggers

*We remember the fish we ate in Egypt at no cost—
also the cucumbers, melons, leeks, onions and garlic.
But now we have lost our appetite; we never see
anything but this manna!*
—Numbers 11:5-6

In the desert, the Israelites grumbled and craved for the onions and garlic they used to eat in Egypt. They often thought it would be better to become slaves again and suffer in Egypt rather than die under the sun without these exotic spices.

History records the paramount value of seasonings for humankind. Nations fought against each other, and countries were colonized to secure spices. European nations, including Spain, Portugal, England, and Holland, all fought for control over the Indonesian Spice Islands between the 15th and 17th centuries, lasting for about 200 years.

Like onions and garlic, drugs have become a precious global commodity to users, dealers, traffickers, and manufacturers. Wars are waged, and people are killed to gain control of this lucrative product.

Comparable to the dejected Israelites, drug addicts and alcoholics crave for addictive substances to spice up their lives. They are willing to cross boundaries and live in the rough desert of addiction with the kicks and highs of drugs.

Drug cravings are fundamentally strong memories embedded in the brain. When a former or recovering addict remembers a past exhilarating drug episode, which acts as a trigger, cravings develop. Imaging studies have revealed that powerful brain activation occurs when the same person is exposed to pictures of a drug and paraphernalia like cocaine or smoking pipes.

A drug craving can be comparable to extreme hunger. In 1972, a plane crashed on a snow-laden mountain carrying the

Uruguayan rugby team. Desperate for their lives, the survivors ate the raw flesh of the other passengers who perished. In like manner, drug cravings can be so intense that addicts are driven to extreme, ghastly acts of deception, manipulation, and crime to satisfy their burning desires. For many drug addicts, cravings can be a matter of life and death.

Cravings are usually most severe during the withdrawal stage. The body writhes in pain as it cries out for drugs or alcohol. They experience body tremors, gut-wrenching aches, restlessness, nervousness, anxiety, and many days without sleep. These symptoms arise as the body's reaction to eliminate or alleviate the aching and dreary withdrawal symptoms. Addicts typically don't know they are in withdrawal because their focus centers on satisfying their desires for drugs.

Drug dependents, alcoholics, and nicotine addicts usually experience the same nature of symptoms and manifestations of drug cravings and withdrawal. An addicted cigarette smoker suffers from multiple and successive cravings and withdrawal symptoms throughout the day. By taking the drug of choice, relief from symptoms is achieved and replaced by feelings of euphoria. Addiction is a constant cycle of triggers, cravings, drug use, and withdrawal.

> *Addiction is a constant cycle of triggers, cravings, drug use, and withdrawal.*

Watch and pray so that you will not fall into temptation. The spirit is willing, but the flesh is weak.
—Matthew 26:41

A whiff of cigarette smoke from a passerby on the street, the smell of beer on a restaurant, or a news clip on TV that depicts pictures of cocaine or meth may not be bothersome to many people. However, to addicts and people in recovery, these sensations of sight, sound, touch, taste, or smell often act as dangerous triggers that lead to cravings.

Triggers are internal, external, and sensory cues that emanate from mental, emotional, social, or environmental situations that remind individuals of their past drug or alcohol use. The triggering properties of memories are often deep-seated that do not easily go away.

Harold C. Urschell, III, MD wrote:

> When alcohol or drugs activate the dopamine system, the hippocampus "switches on," ensuring that you will remember everything about the experience very clearly—not only the high, but also the people, places, objects, smells, and tastes associated with it (your trigger)... When you later come across the people, places, things, or emotional states related to your drug or alcohol use, your hippocampus activates the dopamine system to let you know that you are about to experience a very good feeling. This can arouse thoughts about drinking or using and a very strong emotional urge to do so.[2]

Drug triggers are unpredictable and unavoidable that people may encounter five episodes one day and forty the next day. A drug trigger may generate a temperate yet manageable urge to use or drink. But the next one may produce an overwhelming craving.

Internal triggers are feelings or emotions that people have experienced before or during drinking or using drugs. Some people take drugs or drink when they feel angry, happy, lonely, or depressed. Like a thief in the night, triggers suddenly break into us in our quiet moments.

Stress, anxiety, and depression are significant triggers that lead to drinking and drug use. The death of a loved one, loss of a job, financial problem, family breakup, work-related stress, or plain boredom can cause a person to reach for a shot of liquor, or a puff of meth, or cocaine. Health problems such as physical distress and other illness can also cause a person to use and abuse dangerous drugs and alcohol.

On the other hand, positive life events such as job hiring, promotion, payday, or a family reconciliation may increase the urge to celebrate, which may lead to cravings and relapse.

External triggers, which are usually sensory, are places, objects, music, activities, and people that elicit cravings for drugs or alcohol. The sight or smell of actual drugs, rock concerts, alcohol, bars, and drug dens or its images or pictures in print or on TV can induce past thoughts of using or drinking. Being with friends or some people associated with their drug use leads to cravings, as well as specific days or holidays such as Friday nights, Christmas parties, or birthdays.

Triggers, in its natural state, are not necessarily detrimental to many people. The sensory feelings, thoughts, and emotions about drugs, alcohol, or tobacco do not necessarily affect them. But Satan can turn these innocent incidents into cravings or temptations, especially to those who are prone to addiction or who are recovering from addiction.

> *Therefore do not let sin reign in your mortal body so that you obey its evil desires.*
> **—Romans 6:12**

The road to recovery is long and treacherous. Dealing with temptations, cravings, and triggers is like walking on a tightrope. The Unseen Enemy always eagerly awaits our downfall. With a single wrong step, one will fall back into the dark ravine of addiction and despair.

However, we can achieve victory. With God, we gain higher ground over Satan and deflect his enticements, pursue recovery, and reach healing.

The addict or alcoholic becomes fully recovered the moment he ceases to be excited about drugs and alcohol. Pastor Tony Dela Paz of CCF remarks, "Recovery from addiction is the absence of any cravings from drugs." He is not scared, but wary of triggers and has learned how to deal with the resulting cravings. He can enjoy parties without these substances. Pictures or images about drugs on TV or other external stimuli suggestive of drugs do not affect him anymore.

Temptations, cravings, and triggers will remain in our midst as long as we live in our mortal bodies. Satan, the Prince of this World, will continue to lure, trap, and lead us into his kingdom of darkness.

However, God shields us from ungodly attacks. Jesus prayed to the Father, "My prayer is not that you take them out of the world but that you protect them from the evil one. They are not of the world, even as I am not of it" (John 17:15-16). As believers, heaven is our destiny, where darkness no longer exists.

Overcoming Temptations, Cravings, and Triggers

1. Repentance and Confession
   Repent, then, and turn to God, so that your sins may be wiped out, that times of refreshing may come from the Lord (Acts 3:19).

   Seeking forgiveness from God removes our sin. Repentance keeps us holy, which strengthens our spirit.

2. Build up your Faith
   Who is it that overcomes the world? Only the one who believes that Jesus is the Son of God (1 John 5:5).

   Faith is the primary source of power against Satan and evil spirits. The more we engage in prayer, Bible reading, worshiping God, and meeting in church, the more we become like Him.

3. Fast Regularly
   "Even now," declares the Lord, "return to me with all your heart, with fasting and weeping and mourning" (Joel 2:12).

Fasting is a spiritual activity that overpowers the desires of the flesh. It has proven to be most effective in dealing with severe temptations and drug cravings.

4. Engage in Spiritual Warfare
I have given you authority to trample on snakes and scorpions and to overcome all the power of the enemy; nothing will harm you (Luke 10:19).

Temptations and cravings come from Satan. We cannot confront the Devil with our mortal and weak self. We need to bring the battle into the heavens and equip ourselves with God's armor to gain victory.

5. Practice Total Abstinence
Rather, clothe yourselves with the Lord Jesus Christ, and do not think about how to gratify the desires of the flesh (Romans 13:14).

Moderation is dangerous. Taking drugs or drinking alcohol on occasion or a specific schedule increases temptation and cravings. Recovering addicts and alcoholics have better chances if they completely cut off drugs, alcohol, and tobacco. Total abstinence is the definite way to "unlearn" past drug memories and habits.

6. Watch Your Environment
Flee the evil desires of youth and pursue righteousness, faith, love and peace, along with those who call on the Lord out of a pure heart (2 Timothy 2:22).

Stay away from bars, drug dens, street corners, and alleys where drugs are sold. If you can't avoid parties or social gatherings where drugs or alcohol is served or is available, learn how to say "no" and drink iced tea or lime juice. Over time, you and everybody else will get used to it. Leave these gatherings at the earliest possible time. Don't work in a bar or in other places where temptations and triggers abound.

7. Avoid Drug-addicted and Alcoholic Friends
   Do not be misled: "Bad company corrupts good character"
   (1 Corinthians 15:33).

   Mingling with your addicted friends would only lead to temptation and relapse. You can socialize with them once you have achieved true recovery. Instead, cultivate new friends who practice sobriety.

8. Identify and Avoid your Triggers
   And lead us not into temptation, but deliver us from the evil one (Matthew 6:13).

   Triggers come from past drug experiences of a user. Each person has a unique trigger, although many triggers are common to all. Keep away from your triggers. Pray over the source of each craving and cast out the unholy spirits from the trigger.

9. Don't Reminisce Past Drug Use or Drinking
   But one thing I do: Forgetting what is behind and straining toward what is ahead, I press on toward the goal to win the prize for which God has called me heavenward in Christ Jesus (Philippians 3:13-14).

   Romanticizing the drug or drink weakens our willingness to remain sober. Instead, gather lovely and godly thoughts. Set your mind on the present and think of the glorious future that God has planned in our lives.

10. Don't be Scared of Temptations and Cravings
    The Lord is my light and my salvation—whom shall I fear? The Lord is the stronghold of my life—of whom shall I be afraid? (Psalm 27:1).

    Recognize any temptation and craving for drugs. We become more anxious if we become afraid of them. Control the experience and resist the temptation. Develop your techniques like deep breathing, talking to another person about your urges, and prayer.

11. Be Occupied

Whatever you do, work at it with all your heart, as working for the Lord, not for human masters (Colossians 3:23).

Idleness is dangerous. It invites dark spirits that lure us to cravings and temptations. Instead, pursue meaningful and productive activities. Devote yourself to God and concentrate on your job. Exercise and do housework. Volunteer in social or charity programs and get involved in ministry work. Read Christian books, listen to Christian songs, and watch faith-based movies in your spare time.

12. Handle your Finances Wisely

For the love of money is the root of all kinds of evil. Some people, eager for money, have wandered from the faith and pierced themselves with many grief (1 Timothy 6:10).

Money is a primary trigger for drug and alcohol cravings. Significant and bold life changes may be called for if money becomes an obstacle to recovery. Submit your financial matters to an accountability partner. Let a family member handle and manage your money. In many cases, it is better to take some time off from your job during the initial critical stage of recovery. This would give the right perspective about work and money.

13. Banish Enabling and Codependency

Have nothing to do with the fruitless deeds of darkness, but rather expose them (Ephesians 5:11).

Enablers and codependent family members directly or indirectly support addictive behavior. Tough love is better than hiding in obscurity and ignoring the real specter of addiction.

14. Join a Support Group

Carry each other's burdens, and in this way you will fulfill the law of Christ (Galatians 6:2).

There is a sense of safety and belongingness when a recovering addict or alcoholic enrolls in aftercare or support circles. They share secrets and techniques on how to overcome the pitfalls of temptations, cravings, and triggers that are common to them.

Gearing for Spiritual Battle

For our struggle is not against flesh and blood, but against the rulers, against the authorities, against the powers of this dark world and against the spiritual forces of evil in the heavenly realms.
—Ephesians 6:12

The time had come for Jesus to start His ministry of salvation for all of humankind. He knew he had to work hard and suffer in obedience to his Father's will. He also had to deal with the Devil, whose primary aim is to deceive and lure people into sin and darkness.

After His baptism by John the Baptist, Jesus fasted in the desert of Judaea for forty days and nights (Luke 4:1-2). He needed the empowerment of the Holy Spirit for the ensuing epic encounter with Satan.

In the wilderness, the Devil launched the first assault on the famished Jesus, "If you are the Son of God, tell this stone to become bread" (v.3). Jesus replied, "It is written: 'Man shall not live on bread alone'" (v.4).

After failing for the first time, the Devil led Jesus to a high place and showed Him the kingdoms of the earth (v.5). The Devil said, "I will give you all their authority and splendor; it has been given to me, and I can give it to anyone I want to. If you worship me, it will all be yours" (vv.6-7). However, Jesus replied, "It is written: 'Worship the Lord your God and serve him only'" (v.8).

On the last attempt, Satan led Jesus to the highest spot of the Jerusalem temple (v.9[a]). Knowing that angels would come to His rescue (vv.10-11), Satan dared Jesus, "If you are the Son of

God...throw yourself down from here" (v.9 [b]). Jesus replied, "It is said: 'Do not put the Lord your God to the test'" (v.12). After three unsuccessful attempts at tempting Jesus, the Devil "left him until an opportune time" (v.13 [b]).

The temptation of Jesus in the wilderness epitomized the vile aims of Satan in establishing his supremacy on earth. Ever since God banished him from the heavens because of his pride and desire to take God's place, Satan continues his onslaught in rebellion to God. He propagates evil and leads us to a myriad of sins. He continuously peddles the notion that material possessions, power, and pleasure are supreme.

Blinded by the Devil, people can achieve a sense of false gratification and twisted meaning through drugs. In many cases, a stronghold is established by Satan in the minds and souls of addicts. Many years of drug use, hedonism, and a multiplicity of sins fortified this fortress. Breaking down these strongholds requires the power of Christ more than secular methods like rehab or medicine.

Throughout history, Satan has utilized addictive substances in luring people into his fold. Alcohol has been a primary bait and predicament since biblical times. Generic substances such as opium, cocaine, and other mind-bending substance that come from plants have plagued people and altered the course of history. Behind the genocide of Nazism was the influence of drugs and Satan.

In the past, holy wars and battles were waged to take control of lands and people. Today, Satan darkens and conquers minds to enslave people on a global scale through drugs. He also uses digital technology and "mindshare" as new frontiers of shaping how we think and live.

Drugs are a primary weapon utilized by Satan in providing a pleasurable escape from a life of deepening degradation. No country on earth is immune from the wicked lash of addiction, both from generic substances and new exotic pharmaceutical concoctions. Heroin swamps the poor and developing nations while opioids captivate and inundate the rich and developed countries.

The confrontation between Jesus and Satan in the desert mirrors the spiritual battle that goes on in present times. We are fast approaching the end of our times as we struggle with new and cunning schemes of the Devil. First Timothy 4:1 reads: "The Spirit clearly says that in later times some will abandon the faith and follow deceiving spirits and things taught by demons."

The lure of temptations and drug cravings attacks us anytime and anywhere. The Devil attacks us in the quietness of our homes or a crowded train car. While doing paperwork in our offices or cutting lumber in a construction site, the Unseen Enemy sneaks. While asleep, the Devil assaults us in our dreams. We are often caught by surprise as our focus and attention are derailed by the intrusion of wicked spirits.

Satan is the master of deception. He "disguises himself as an angel of light" (2 Corinthians 11:14[b], *ESV*). As the Father of All Lies, he tricks people into believing that there is nothing wrong with taking drugs or getting drunk. Trampled with idolatry, addicts consider drug dealers as their savior who provides the only relief from their constant miseries and drug cravings.

Many addicts also believe that their blissful drug highs are "holy experiences" given by God. Some residents of MRC claim that they have had "third-eye" powers or "prophetic callings from high above." These illusions do not originate from God but are the influences of the Devil.

Chronic and severe addiction often involves the indwelling of unholy spirits. Many addicts and alcoholics, especially unbelievers, are not wary that they are held captive by Satan. They believe that their addiction is merely a chemical dependency that will go away in time. But the Bible tells otherwise. Second Timothy 3:13, (*NKJV*) reads: "But evil men and impostors will grow worse and worse, deceiving and being deceived."

Many people are doubtful that demons are behind the menace of addiction. However, drugs and alcohol have often been used by Satan to control humanity. The word "pharmacy" came from the Greek word *pharmakeia*, which means sorcery and witchcraft. Galatians 5:30 (*GW*) mentions "idolatry [and] drug use" when referring to acts of the flesh. Addicts dabble in polydrug use by taking a mixture of drugs to provide ecstatic, but vile highs and feelings. Demons inhabit the realms of addicts and alcoholics.

CASTING OUT EVIL SPIRITS

The casting out of demons is a biblical way of warding off unholy spirits. It is only by the name of Jesus Christ that we can drive the Devil away. In Capernaum, Jesus commanded an impure spirit from a demon-possessed man: "Come out of him!" (Mark 1:25[b]). In Acts 16:16-18, Paul ordered the wicked spirit from a fortuneteller to go away. He said, "In the name of Jesus Christ I command you to come out of her!" (v.18[b]).

Spiritual warfare means active confrontation and engagement with the Enemy.

When confronted with temptations that are difficult to deal with, we should not run away from the Devil. Instead, we have to shun fear, call upon God, and gather the courage to drive out evil spirits. We claim authority over Satan and all unholy spirits. Spiritual warfare means active confrontation and engagement with the Enemy.

However, many people, even the faithful, believe that addiction is not, in any way, influenced by evil. They attribute addiction solely to personality disorders or unfavorable life conditions such as poverty, family breakup, or mere boredom. It is ironic that they wholeheartedly believe in God, but half-heartedly acknowledge Satan's vile influence in their lives. They think that the casting out of demons is confined only in olden times or cases of satanic possession, as pictured in exorcism movies. However, as the Scriptures show us, addiction is a form of control by the Devil. Deep in bondage, addicts usually do things that they would not normally do when they are sober. By not recognizing the works of the Unseen Enemy and dealing with them, true recovery becomes elusive.

Deliverance from addiction through the casting out of demons takes more than faith. It requires an active proclamation of the mighty name of Jesus Christ. The truth sets us free. In deliverance, we need to stress the authority of Jesus Christ over all evil and the reality that Satan is the source of all lies. Neil T. Anderson wrote:

> *Freedom from spiritual conflicts and bondage is not a power encounter; it's a truth encounter. Satan is a deceiver and he will work undercover at all costs. But the truth of God's Word exposes him and his lie. His demons are like cockroaches that scurry for the shadows when the light comes on. Satan's power is in the lie, and when his lie is exposed by the truth, his plans are foiled.*[3]

Casting out unholy spirits within us may be daunting. The thought of ministering and deliverance to drug addicts and alcoholics is also usually intimidating for most Christians. But Christians are called by God to heal the sick and to liberate the oppressed. Many believe that a special type of training or expertise is required for this kind of ministry. While those are helpful, faith and the fervent proclamation of the Gospel of Jesus Christ remain to be the essential weapons and tools for healing.

Churches also perform deliverance to those who are enslaved by evil spirits. Christian rehabs or recovery homes like Penuel Home and Victory Outreach also carry out spontaneous and regular schedules for casting out of demons among their residents. A truly recovered individual who has reached a certain level of spiritual maturity can well drive out ungodly spirits because of his familiarity with drug demons and their methods of attacks.

*Put on the full armor of God, so that you can take your
stand against the devil's schemes.*
—Ephesians 6:11

Going to battle with the Unseen Enemy requires preparation, training, and equipment. A soldier spends years learning the art of warfare to prepare for war—how to use a rifle and engage in hand to hand combat. A combatant is also equipped with the tools of war—rifle, ammunition, clothing, gear, and helmet. Patience, discipline, training, and logistics are the cornerstones that make a good soldier.

The same fundamentals of good soldiering are comparable to spiritual warfare. Jesus Christ prepared for ministry, knowing He would always face the Devil in the streets, mountaintops, and in other places. As a young boy, he studied God's Word in Nazareth (Luke 4:16-17). At the age of twelve, Joseph and Mary found him at the temple courts listening and questioning with the teachers (Luke 2:43-46). When asked why He stayed in Jerusalem, Jesus replied, "Didn't you know I had to be in my Father's house?" (v.49[b]). At the age of thirty, Jesus was baptized at the Jordan River by John the Baptist and indwelled by the Holy Spirit. After this, He went to the wilderness, prayed, and fasted for forty days before his encounter with the Devil.

Effective spiritual warfare requires faith, training, preparation, prayer, and knowledge of Scriptures. The power and gift of deliverance are not confined only to pastors, priests, elders, or church officials. Any believer anchored on faith can cast out demons in the name of Jesus Christ. In Matthew 17, Jesus Christ healed a demon-possessed boy after the apostles failed to cast out the evil spirits. The disciples asked Jesus, "Why couldn't we drive it out?" (Matthew 17:19[b]). Jesus replied, "Because you have so little faith" (v.20[a]).

Driving out of demons also requires the indwelling of the Holy Spirit from whom the gifts of healing and deliverance emanate. In Acts 19, some vagabond Jews in Ephesus went around and tried to cast out demons by invoking the name of Jesus Christ (v.13). The city was overtaken by idolatry and sexual immorality. However, the Jews failed and the ungodly spirit even questioned them, "Jesus I know, and Paul I know about, but who are you?" (v.15). Instead, the "man who had the evil spirit jumped on them and overpowered them all. He gave them such a beating that they ran out of the house naked and bleeding" (v.16).

Beyond the tenets of training, preparation, and the baptism of repentance (water), the presence of the Holy Spirit empowers us with God's participation in overcoming severe bondage. Otherwise, the Devil would play tricks and cause us more trouble.

The casting out of demons, combined with prayer and fasting, is the most potent spiritual force in driving out wicked spirits. Polycarp, a Christian martyr in 110 A.D., urged the believers to fast so they could resist temptation.[4] Fasting overtakes and suppresses the bodily urges for food and the cravings for drugs. After breaking the fast, the desire for drugs usually goes away. If we fast regularly, drug cravings leave our lives for good.

In severe addiction and alcoholism, multiple evil spirits reside inside the addict, emanating from the diversity and number of sins. In Mark 9:29 *(KJV)*, Jesus also said to his disciples, "This kind can come forth by nothing but by prayer and fasting." The practice of regular prayer and fasting is essential in building up faith and resiliency in battling the Evil One.

War is waged every day over the souls of countless, addicted individuals all over the world. We are not to rest solely on our identity with Christ and His protection. We need a proactive, godly approach in facing the Enemy.

The Armor of God

1. *For our struggle is not against flesh and blood, but against the rulers, against the authorities, against the powers of this dark world and against the spiritual forces of evil in the heavenly realms (Ephesians 6:12).*

   We are up against an Unseen Enemy. It is not our parents, coworkers, neighbors, or ourselves who ultimately cause our negative life situations, including addiction, but Satan and his cohorts.

2. *Stand firm, then, with the belt of truth buckled around your waist (v.14[a]).*

   The Word of God ties the armor of the warrior. In any encounter with the Devil, we assert and affirm the truth that God is supreme and that the Devil is a liar.

3. *With the breastplate of righteousness in place (v.14[b]).*

   Having righteous, holy lives protects our body, heart, and mind from the attacks of the Enemy. A continuous increasing level of faith makes us stronger against the Devil.

4. *And with your feet fitted with the readiness that comes from the Gospel of peace (v.15).*

   Proclaim the Good News that Jesus Christ died to reconcile us to God. The battle with addiction has already been won through the cross.

5. *Take up the shield of faith, with which you can extinguish all the flaming arrows of the evil one (v.16[b]).*

   The shield of a soldier is the sturdiest part of his armor—and it is for a good reason: to defend himself from an enemy attack. Having doubts about God and His preeminent authority over evil makes us more vulnerable to Satan.

6. *Take the helmet of salvation (v.17[a]).*
   The assurance of salvation is our impregnable defense against all the assaults of the Enemy. Declaring that victory has already been won makes evil spirits surrender and flee.

7. *[Take] the sword of the Spirit, which is the word of God (v.17[b]).*
   The sword is used for both offense and defense. God's Word expels the Enemy or protects us from evil attacks. The Bible says that the Word of God is "Sharper than any double-edged sword, it penetrates even to dividing soul and spirit, joints and marrow" (Hebrews 4:12[b]).

8. *And pray in the Spirit on all occasions with all kinds of prayers and requests (v.18).*
   Seek the guidance of the Holy Spirit for empowerment in our petitions and prayers. Pray for specific circumstances or other people who are being used by the Devil to attack us. It makes the Enemy succumb to and depart from us.

Sober Living with God

Rehab: A Remedy for Chronic Addiction

Hilsy: Recovery After Three Rehabs

Hilsy squirmed inside the dormitory of the Marikina Rehabilitation Center. His belly ached, and all his nerves felt like coming out of his skin. Restless, his mind spun, and he thought he might throw up. He knew the experience. Again, he had to struggle with the punishing episodes of withdrawal from drugs. His mind swirled as he grasped his utter powerlessness over drugs. In 2010, Hilsy bravely volunteered for rehab for the third time.

As a 5'4" young man in his mid-twenties, he has a stocky but lean body. Despite his intimidating personal background and history, Hilsy exudes a warm and friendly personality. In rehab, everybody liked him.

In 2008, the court ordered him to go to rehab because of violence related to the use of meth. Hilsy was released after six months but backslid after a few weeks. In 2009, with no one to help him, he sought admission to the MRC, voluntarily, for the second time. As a repeat offender, he had to stay for around a year. After his release in 2010, he relapsed for the second time.

Hilsy first used drugs at the age of fifteen. Because of his involvement with drugs, gangs, and crime, a judge sentenced him to prison for robbery. As a minor, his jail time was waived and he was instead ordered to the Boys' Town in the province of La Union for correction. Hilsy spent around eighteen months of custody and training in this government facility.

Broken family, gangs, crime, prostitution, and extreme violence filled Hilsy's drug-laced life. He took pot, meth, cheap solvent, and alcohol. He also broke into homes and robbed things. Hilsy assaulted people on the streets for money. Once, he nearly killed a rival gang enemy in a melee by banging his opponent's head on a big stone. In addition, he pimped girls and freely patronized them. Drugs controlled Hilsy's life and he experienced the constant cycle of addiction, sobriety, and relapse.

Despite this desperation, a life-changing event happened to him in 2009 in rehab. In the quietness of the isolation room, God intervened in his wrecked life. For the first time in his life, he felt he was not alone and that God cared for him. Hilsy sensed reasons to continue living without drugs. *It's possible to have the right life with God*, he thought. With his newfound faith, he learned to pray and read the Bible. His trust in God began to take root, and he felt much better. After his release, he pursued his faith by attending church services.

But an unexpected event occurred. His drug cravings came back, which led him to another relapse. However, this time, he didn't resort to crime to support himself and his bad habits. Instead, he felt remorseful and convicted that he again sinned against God. He realized he needed more time to know God to make himself stronger. He needed spiritual resiliency to battle the temptations of the Devil. Despite the relapse, he still trusted God. For Hilsy, going back to rehab for the third time to recover and gain more profound healing was the right move. Besides, Hilsy thought he cannot be a continuing burden on his family.

In 2010, he volunteered to be admitted at the MRC for the third time. When his discharge date arrived, he refused to be released from rehab. His decision stunned the community as it runs contrary to what the other residents desire—the day of discharge.

With the lessons he had learned about the fragileness of recovery, he sought an extension of his stay. He needed more time for healing. The administration of the MRC, sympathizing with his predicament, agreed to his request.

The MRC became his home on a "re-entry status," allowing him to reside at the premises and attend its recovery program. The arrangement also permitted him to go out on pass and participate in activities outside of rehab that would support his sobriety.

Hilsy attended church services, Bible studies, and joined our drug ministry. He also enrolled in a Bible school just across the street from the MRC. After two years of three successive rehabs, ministry work, and immersion in faith-building activities, God transformed Hilsy into a new creation. Since 2010, he has been free from drugs and other addictive substances.

Today, Hilsy works as a guard in a security firm. With God's help, his life turned around. He bought a parcel of land and a motorbike. He speaks on television, in churches, and rehab about the healing power of our Lord Jesus Christ. Hilsy also plans to marry his long-time girlfriend.

My recovery must come first so that everything I love
in life doesn't have to come last.
—Anonymous

The mind of an addict is wired to defend and pursue his addiction. Rehab is a dreaded word. Drug dependents and alcoholics detest incarceration and lose their liberty, the pleasures of a carefree life, and access to drugs of their choice.

We often struggle with whether to commit ourselves or a loved one to a recovery facility. The mixed emotions of double-mindedness and fear brought about by guilt and public shame overshadow the urgent need for recovery. Rehab also means taking some time off from our jobs, families, and other pursuits in life. In addition, the time and effort needed to obligate ourselves or look after a loved one in rehab also poses a considerable challenge.

Because of our hesitation, the urgent need for rehab is delayed or ignored. Gene Heyman wrote, "Just 30% of those who met the criteria for dependence or drug abuse had ever brought their drug problems to the attention of a health specialist"[1]

However, rehab is not necessarily needed during the early stages of drug use. Pastor Tony Dela Paz of CCF and Penuel Home said, "Rehab is not necessary to overcome addiction. But it is a good tool." Most of the studies about addiction are based on those who are in treatment.

However, the majority of addicts are not in rehab but out on the streets. Yet, many get well without rehab or any outside treatment. We must also go beyond the models that entirely rely on outside help to achieve sobriety. Addicts can take primary responsibility for their recovery, go to rehab, or devise and combine recovery strategies. Counseling, CBT, home care, support groups, church care, and the professional advice of an addiction specialist are some of the alternate means of recovery.

However, the intervention of a drug rehabilitation facility becomes necessary when the drug dependent becomes irresponsible and is unable to control many aspects of his life. The addict needs confinement if he resorts to burglary, assaults people, and commits other crimes to satisfy his drug habits. Rehab also becomes necessary when his health is failing, money becomes a problem, work is affected, or when he could not quit on his own.

Deprived of the bliss from drugs, addicts experience many kinds of disturbances as they pursue recovery. Rehab and recovery specialists offer a much-needed personal connection, which brings a sense of safety and belongingness. Designed to help drug addicts and alcoholics salvage their messed-up lives, rehab serves as a safe refuge that provides the structure and services in correcting the vicious habits of addiction.

Rehab can be done either by forced admission or by voluntary submission of an addict. Caution is exercised in convincing the addict to submit willingly to a recovery facility. Forced rehab, in many instances, creates a rebellious attitude, which makes the addict uncooperative in the recovery process and program. The majority of addicts go to rehab, even if it is against their will just to appease their families and the outside world. They also put up a charade inside the rehab to please the staff, other residents, and their families to shorten or not extend their stay in rehab. In these cases, so much time, energy, and resources were wasted by all concerned parties. The aims of recovery are not achieved if their mindsets regarding drug use and life have not changed.

Total abstinence is pivotal in drug recovery. Rehab provides an environment where drugs are entirely not available, and the constant triggers and stresses that lead to relapse are taken away.

> *Rehab provides an environment where drugs are entirely not available, and the constant triggers and stresses that lead to relapse are taken away.*

The drug detoxification process, a critical point in recovery, is likewise safely supervised in the premises. In this stage, painful bodily aches are experienced with extreme psychological symptoms like trauma and hallucinations. Drug withdrawal can last for a few days or many months.

Psychiatrists, psychologists, and social workers are accessible to provide the needed lifestyle foundations to advance the residents' coping mechanism. These professionals also help deal with the residents' psychological drawbacks, like psychosis or having suicidal thoughts. The recovery facility also gives clinical services to address other health concerns of residents like HIV and tuberculosis.

Rehab can provide a temporary home where members become comfortable in a community of peers. Group and family therapy sessions help the addict and his relatives mutually hurdle addiction as a family problem. Occupational professionals also provide life skills training programs to equip residents with the required tools for a drug-free, productive life. Finally, faith ministers and volunteers impart spiritual guidance, not only to get away from drugs but also to have a godly, changed life.

Above all, the serenity and solitude in rehab can be a place to meditate and surrender to God. Detached from worldly cares and the hurts of life, the recovering addict has ample time to focus on knowing God, pray, repent, and study the Bible.

Many drug rehabilitation facilities also offer support and after-care services after rehab. As part of their commitment toward recovery and in compliance with the country's drug laws, recovering addicts are required to attend aftercare for monitoring. At Penuel Home, former residents regularly undergo scheduled drug tests to ensure their sobriety. Sanctions are employed if the recovering addict fails in the drug test, including a recommitment to rehab or the employment of other measures.

Rehab must be treated in the right perspective. Many families view rehab as the "last resort" for their son's addiction. On the contrary, rehab is often the first remedy in conquering drug addiction.

True recovery does not end in rehab. The real battle happens in the home and out on the streets where the recovering addict faces actual triggers, temptations, and struggles. If they fail to deal with these adversities properly, they backslide or remain in addiction. Many are also misled that going past the withdrawal or detoxification stage, where the gnawing physical pains are erased, means recovery has been achieved. Pastor Tony Dela Paz of CCF said, "Some parents view rehab as a 'car repair shop,' expecting their addicted son to be completely recovered when released." Real recovery is a lifetime commitment to sobriety.

When relapse after rehab happens, many parents refuse or hesitate to recommit their son back to a recovery facility. Because of sheer frustration and helplessness, they give up, lose faith in rehab, and eventually tolerate their son's addiction. Bringing them back to a facility seems futile and a waste of time.

Despite the drawbacks and failures, it is laudable not to give up and send our addicted son back to rehab. A famous Japanese proverb, "Fall seven times, stand up eight," indicates persistence in pursuing recovery.

Pastor Tony adds, "Successive rehabs are sometimes needed for purposes of removing the stimulus from the external environment of the addict that leads to chronic addiction and relapse." In sum, many successful long-term recoveries happen because of several rehabs or multiple recovery cycles.

THE ESSENTIAL AND RIGHT REHAB

Drug addiction progresses further in number, diversity, and complexity. Recovery requires continuous improvements in rehabilitation and therapy programs to treat upgraded levels or types of addiction. However, many rehab institutions are not coping with that demand and even employ erroneous strategies.

Many rehab institutions often serve mainly as withdrawal and detoxification centers. The primary tools for recovery, like personalized counseling and rigid monitoring of each resident, are often superficial or neglected. The right and active implementation of recovery programs fail to materialize because of the lack of personnel, budget, knowledge, and other resources.

Many rehabilitation facilities refer to drug addicts in their care as "patients." They unknowingly reinforce the controversial rationale that drug dependents are "sick." Under this scenario, the addict expects the outside world to "treat" them. This belief often falsely absolves the addicts from their responsibility and liability. I prefer to call them "residents" who need help.

The approach of many rehab communities, especially in developed countries that treats the addict like a guest in a five-star hotel, is repugnant. As a competitive marketing strategy, they boast of lavish rooms and amenities, including a daily spread of sumptuous buffets. There is nothing wrong with good food and comfort. However, the overindulgence of the senses may send the wrong signal and fortify the defective outlook of addicts that pleasure is supreme. Our delight springs from the Lord, not from the world (Psalm 37:4). Rehab should not be peddled as an extended luxurious vacation but must be designed as a place for healing, meditation, and bare reflection.

While rehab accomplishes the primary aims of weaning the addict from drugs and leading him to a recovered life, true deliverance is often not achieved. The need for spiritual healing is often relegated to secondary importance. Some rehabs publicly proclaim the inclusion of spirituality or faith-based teachings in their program but are not practicing them. Some facilities include spiritual content in their approach but neglect or barely touch essential doctrines that address the deep-seated, biblical roots of addiction.

The Bible is not against doctors or medicine. As the author of all creation, God has included medical and secular methods of recovery as parts of His healing design. Science helps multitudes of people all over the world. Without these God-given gifts, humanity would not have conquered smallpox, the bubonic plague, cholera, and other diseases, which had wiped out millions of people on this planet.

God allows us to seek help from physicians. In Mark 2:17[a], Jesus said: "It is not the healthy who needs a doctor, but the sick." Paul also affirmed Luke in Colossians 4:14: "Luke, the beloved physician, and Demas, greet you." God heals our souls, cures the body, and changes our lifestyle through the care of physicians, social workers, and faith ministers.

However, real long-term recovery requires divine intervention. Pastor Tony remarked, "Doctors give temporary relief to the symptoms of addiction, but true recovery will not happen without God." King Asa of Judah, once a good ruler, caught a terrible disease on his feet. He lost trust in the Lord, and despite the severity of his illness, "He did not seek help from the Lord, but only from the physicians" (2 Chronicles 16:12).

There is nothing wrong with seeking human help. But, recovery from addiction also means repentance and the seeking of forgiveness from God. Drug addicts are usually mired in sins of many kinds. Bruce Epperly wrote, "Healing of body, mind, and spirit may occur unexpectedly and in virtually any context and by virtually any modality, be it laying on of hands, prayer, surgery and medications, herbal remedies, or non-Western medicine."[2]

The ideal rehab facility espouses the right treatment strategies and puts great emphasis on spirituality. Daily prayers, Bible studies, and worship are the cornerstones of healing. The building up of faith shreds the idolatrous love of self and pleasure that reside in the corrupt souls of drug addicts.

The proclamation of Jesus Christ as the Great Physician is the centerpiece of any recovery program that enhances holistic healing. Bruce Epperly further adds, "I believe that a Christian is called to use any form of health care, provided that it does not explicitly deny the witness of God present in Jesus Christ."[3] Rehab facilities that offer a faith-based program in its methods produce better chances of true recovery.

Recovery need not be a lifelong process. When God has healed and renewed us, there is nothing more to recover. The ultimate aim of divine healing is not only the removal of addictive substances from the lives of drug dependents and alcoholics but also the transformation of depraved sinners to new, holy creations in Christ.

Support Groups

My command is this: Love each other as
I have loved you.
—John 15:12

Support is the backbone of recovery. After rehab, support groups provide the needed environment, input, and encouragement for the recovering addict to keep track and advance his recovery. As a stand-alone recourse, support groups can be an alternative for rehab if the residential option is not available or required, especially during the early stages of addiction. The government also mandates support groups by sending drug offenders to rehab or after-care facilities. In the United States, drunk drivers are posted by a judge to AA for treatment.

Real recovery often happens outside and after rehab. Many individuals are mistaken when they say they have achieved sobriety and ready to face real life after rehab because they felt cleaner and stronger. But a drug relapse is like lightning that suddenly and unexpectedly strikes out of nowhere.

Joining a support group reduces the chances of relapse.

Joining a support group reduces the chances of relapse. In the book, *Free from Addiction*, Morteza Kaleghi Ph.D., who also runs Creative Care, wrote that 60 percent of their patients who enrolled in after-care support groups could maintain long-term sobriety. In contrast, between 30 and 40 percent of their patients who don't commit to aftercare succumb to repeated relapses.[4]

An addiction recovery support group is mainly composed of peers of drug dependents. The support process is the mutual giving and receiving of non-professional, non-clinical assistance from fellow drug dependents or alcoholics.

While support groups are mostly lay entities that do not give formal clinical treatment and recovery methods, they are often recommended by physicians to aid in a person's recovery. Some groups, however, are led by professionals (psychotherapists, addiction counselors, social workers, and others) with a more rigid and defined treatment plan. These meetings are usually called psychotherapy or group therapy.

A support circle can be the popular groups like AA, NA, or its similar groups and variations. Some churches have also established support groups or programs that cater specifically to those undergoing deep-seated hurts, trauma, and different types of addiction. CCF, for example, conducts a regular healing seminar called *Glorious Hope*, which is open to the public, free of charge.

Peer support groups are more casual and informal. Membership comes from all ages, gender, races, and religious affiliations. Meetings are free, and donations are accepted to pay for some expenses like snacks and some materials. The sharing of stories and advice is confidential and does not go out of the support circle.

A small number of peers can voluntarily form their support group that would address their specific needs and environment. There are also resources and downloadable data regarding support groups that can serve as a guide. Because they have a common goal of sobriety, members are encouraged to share their status, experiences, and perspectives about recovery. Everybody gives a sympathetic ear to one another, including advice and emotional support.

Members observe the biblical doctrine of confession and the sharing of defeats and victories. James 5:16[a] says, "Therefore confess your sins to each other and pray for each other so that you may be healed." The support group becomes the second family of the recovering addict. The church is also an excellent support group where addicted sinners or recovering addicts can seek refuge and healing.

New members are inspired and would be encouraged to learn from other senior members who have earned milestones in their recovery. Advanced coping strategy skills are acquired to deal with cravings and triggers.

Support groups resolve the problem of isolation commonly experienced by recovering addicts. Members realize that they need not be alone and can connect to others without fear, guilt, and shame. They usually exchange phone numbers so troubled members can immediately call the others for immediate help, especially to combat drug cravings. The existence of a common goal encourages a member to remain stronger, knowing that somebody else is depending on him as well.

These groups also give out "sobriety chips," indicating periodic milestones in the addict's recovery. Once a person backslides, he starts all over again, without fear of rejection and shame.

Accountability is an essential element in support groups, and confrontation is discouraged. Despite the more stabilized recovery status of a member, everybody is considered in danger of relapse. They are not judged for their actions and backslides because most members encounter similar incidents.

Support groups work. A study revealed that a recovering addict or alcoholic who completes treatment, complies with regular monitoring like urine testing, and attend regular recovery meetings would have a 90% chance of staying sober five years later.[5]

Because there are many established support groups, we must exercise care in choosing the right and suitable support circle. Enrollees must scrutinize the methods and aims of the group. They must focus on their healing and not be beholden to their leaders or sponsors. Support groups that proclaim Jesus Christ as the Great Healer and highest power provide the best environment for healing.

The church is also one of the best support groups. Pastor Christian Wilson said, "Addicts who choose to go to the Recovery Home at the start of the recovery process grow three times faster spiritually than those who choose to just attend church services every weekend."

HALFWAY HOMES

A halfway house is a good alternative for in-house rehabs if the addict is showing control, not violent or troublesome, and not committing criminal acts. As a residential facility, these homes provide the environment for treatment and healing, without the requirement of quitting one's job and other meaningful pursuits. The halfway house may be ideal for some drug dependents, as it does not impose mandatory confinement and rigid standards. A halfway home also serves as a support group.

Resembling a family home, everybody in the facility is treated as a family member, supervised by house parents. Also called "sober living homes" or "extended care facilities," halfway houses can be a good transition between residential rehab and full recovery. Residents typically stay in halfway houses for one to six months and up to a year. Sober living homes provide the option for people to stay longer for a more gradual adjustment.

These homes impose specific essential rules. Schedules and daily activities are monitored, including the mandatory overnight stay and attendance to key checkpoint meetings and events. As a Christian family home, daily prayers, Bible study, sharing, and fellowship are practiced as keys to active recovery. In addition, regular medical and psychological evaluations are conducted, including schedules of drug tests.

Halfway houses impose their own distinct rules. As a small organization, everybody helps in the expenses of the home. Contributions of fees are fixed, voluntary, or in some other forms. Responsibility and accountability are necessary virtues that must be espoused by everybody at the home.

Churches are one of the best proponents of halfway houses, as the facility also serves as a vehicle for ministry. As a place for divine healing, members are trained to become faithful disciples of Jesus Christ. Essentially, the halfway home becomes a church.

Volunteer groups also offer halfway home facilities. In the absence of such homes, a group of recovering peers can set up their own. For example, a person can volunteer the use of his own home or they can opt to rent a house. These homes can work well in a small environment, maybe from three to fifteen members. Local government units can also setup recovery houses as part of their community drug addiction treatment and related efforts and program.

The Family Home: The Bedrock of Recovery and Healing

The Salvadors (not their real names) is a typical Filipino family. Renting in a small apartment, the household of five members belongs to the lower-middle-class group. The husband works as an office clerk in a distant city while the wife sews part-time in a garment factory. She also takes care of the household chores—cooking, laundry, and cleaning. Their three children are studying in a public school in the neighborhood.

The Salvadors barely see each other as a family. The father goes to work around 5 a.m. while the children are still asleep and arrives home at around 10 p.m. with the children again on their sleep. He spends about six hours a day in traffic.

After school, the two sons scurry to an internet shop to bask in social media and play ferocious online games. The youngest daughter buries herself in her cell phone, spending many hours chatting with school friends and viewing the latest trending videos. Soon, the siblings are bound to experiment with tobacco, alcohol, and marijuana with their adventurous friends.

The family is complete at home on Sundays. But the father spends most mornings sleeping to recover from the many long hours of lost sleep. In the afternoon, he goes to the town cockpit to gamble. Later, he joins his neighbors in drinking beer and talking about politics and the hardness of life. The mother does more household chores in the morning and later indulges in senseless chatter and gossip with friends. Again, the children spend more time with their digital devices or indulge in useless and unsafe carousing with friends. The family seldom goes to church, pray, and spend quality time together.

The Lord's curse is on the house of the wicked, but he blesses the dwelling of the righteous.
—Proverbs 3:33, *ESV*

Many Filipino homes are rigged for addiction.

Many Filipino homes are rigged for addiction. The harsh realities of life, immoral lifestyle, wrong parenting, and lack of the Word of God lead to moral and spiritual decay. Not surprisingly, the Salvador children will later find themselves thrown out of school and end up in addiction or teen pregnancy. There is also a big chance that the father may engage in extramarital relationships or the mother runs off with another man. It is also not startling if the couple ends up with drug addiction and alcoholism. Evil thrives in homes where sin exists. The Salvador family is spiritually broken at the beginning.

Every home is a target or prey to the drug contagion. The inevitable specter of addiction erupts at an unexpected time. Addiction intrudes into the family home and creates chaos and desperation in the family. Buffeted by blows of drug abuse and alcoholism, the family suffers in deep sorrow, fear, and misery.

Drug addiction affects the family on many levels: emotional, financial, social, and spiritual. As a family problem, drug dependency undermines the love and trust among its members. It may force children into a parental role because their addicted parents could no longer function as heads of the family.

Deception, lies, and trickery consume the household. Money becomes a problem as the whole family spirals down into financial ruin and spiritual decay. Satan is bent on holding hostage our hearts, minds, and homes through all sorts of sins and bondage.

Many families view addiction and substance abuse as a daunting problem that they would rather conceal. Denial, guilt, and shame put a toll on family life. The existence of denial within the family reinforces the false belief that the addicted child is not really in danger because he just "used once" and would most probably not take drugs again. They trust that drugs couldn't break their stable family. They force themselves to believe that a problem does not exist and the drug incidents are just passing episodes that are "normal" parts of their loved ones growing up. In their earlier years, they too also smoked marijuana and drank too much. The parents think, *There is no danger at all.*

The fear of shame exacerbates the denial of addiction. Families dread the social stigma attached to an addicted home and its repercussions on the cultural pride of a model family. Rehab is often out of the question as it reveals the actual state of their broken family—that is, they are vulnerable and victims of a social malady.

When addiction strikes, everyone is affected or hurt. Statistics reveal a significant probability that addiction or alcoholism will infringe the family home. In the United States, the combined 2009 to 2014 National Surveys on Drug Use and Health show that about 1 in 8 children (8.7 million) aged 17 or younger lived in households with at least one parent who had a substance use disorder in the past year.[6]

Generational addiction occurs when children are put at risk of developing drug habits because of a parent or sibling who uses drugs. In some instances, the father and his son are both in rehab at the same time. Children exposed to these conditions are more likely to experience child abuse.

> *The Lord is close to the brokenhearted and saves*
> *those who are crushed in spirit.*
> **—Psalm 34:18**

We all came from a broken family. Our first parents, Adam and Eve, fell into sin, expelled from the Garden of Eden, and ruined God's original plan for humankind. Their offspring Cain murdered his brother Abel because of jealousy. Desperate for a child, Abraham took his slave Hagar as his mistress and had an illegitimate heir. Jacob married Leah but loved and married her sister Rachel. David committed adultery with Bathsheba and then killed her husband, Uriah. Polygamy, adultery, divorce, and crime that pervaded in biblical times still exist today.

Broken family relationships also lead to unbelief. In his paper, "The Psychology of Atheism," Paul Vitz noted, based on the studies of Sigmund Freud, that "once a child or youth is disappointed in and loses his or her respect for their earthly father, then belief in their heavenly Father becomes impossible."[7]

Broken homes are also on the rise. Data from the Philippine Statistics Authority (PSA) reveal that one out of five married couples in the country is headed for separation.[8] The Philippines and the Vatican are the only two countries on earth where divorce is not legal. Marriage is also losing its sanctity. According to the PSA, "In a span of 10 years, the reported number of marriages decreased by 14.4% from 2007 to 2016."[9] Consequently, cohabitation is fast becoming popular in our country and many parts of the world.

Many children are also headed for a dismal life. According to the United Nations Children's Rights & Emergency Relief Organization, around 1.8 million children in the Philippines are abandoned or neglected.[10] In the United Kingdom, "Nearly one child in three is living without their father or mother."[11]

In the Philippines, the Overseas Filipino Workers (OFW) are often considered gallant heroes for bringing good tidings to many deprived families and lifting the country's economy. There are around 2.3 million OFWs in 2018.[12] But, in many cases, their separation from the household also spells disaster, extramarital relationships, child neglect, and brokenness.

A perfect family is an illusion. Even the most morally and spiritually fortified walls of our homes cannot always protect us from the daunting thwarts of the Unseen Enemy. The poor and depraved are highly vulnerable to substance abuse. The rich, highly educated, and godly families also fall prey to drugs and alcohol. Like the COVID-19 virus, addiction knows no boundaries or limits.

Unbelief and estrangement from God result in broken families. Our families become divided morally, spiritually, and physically when we remove God from the center of our lives. Households that downgrade God and His commands as top priority are bound to experience hardship and breakup.

How good and pleasant it is when God's people live together in unity!
—Psalm 133:1

Jesus Christ emphasized the value of family in the society. The same Bible also teaches us to obey our parents, to love each other, and to cherish our children. Because we are His children and part of His family, God exacts our faith and obedience. In Matthew 10:37-39, Jesus exhorted the disciples of placing God first in their lives.

Faith in God in the family home is essential for healing. In Mark 9, Jesus healed a demon-possessed boy since birth after his father reversed his doubt about Jesus and exclaimed, "I do believe; help me overcome my unbelief!" (v.24[b]).

> *The family home is the first line of defense against addiction.*

The family home is the first line of defense against addiction. As the famous saying goes, "Prevention is better than cure." Parents bear the primary responsibility of teaching their children about the ills of drug use. Their godly teaching and living exemplify the right character to children from an early age. Proverbs 22:3 reads: "Train up a child in the way he should go: and when he is old, he will not depart from it." The home environment must also be conducive to a drug-free life. We must temper the use of digital media and check the social life of the child, such as his friends and classmates in school. Parents need to set an excellent example of sober living by not indulging in drugs, alcohol, and tobacco.

DEALING WITH ENABLING AND CODEPENDENCY

If an addict is happy with you, you're probably enabling him. If an addict is mad at you, you're probably helping him.
—Anonymous

Gerome is a handsome young man who belongs to an upright family. His father is a supervisor of a construction firm while his mother works part-time as a teacher. They also have a small tutorial school for children at home as a side business. Gerome usually gets what he wanted in life. As a result, he fell into addiction.

His parents, out of fear and confusion, supported him in the wrong ways.

Gerome was admitted to the MRC four times in a span of nine years because of chronic addiction to meth. In one of his drug-induced outbursts, he threatened his parents with a gun if they get in the way of his drug habit. Because of sheer fear and the dismay of Gerome's past unsuccessful rehabs, the father and mother opted to take the easy way out. They sustained his addiction by freely giving him money for meth and allowed him to take the substance at home. The parents of Gerome exemplified an extreme form of enabling.

I also have a neighbor whose son was addicted to meth. She spent most of her time guarding the house because their things and personal belongings often went missing. Her son stole money, cell phones, and small appliances inside the home to get drug fixes. Because of public shame and pity for her son, she refused to send his son to a recovery facility. She later admitted to being an enabler and codependent by continuously postponing his son's apparent need for intervention.

There are millions of drug dependents in the world and their addictions are often brought about by dysfunctional family living. Enabling and codependency are two of the most misunderstood practices that prevail in the family home. Many parents and siblings do not know that they play a significant influence that causes, perpetuates, and worsens the addiction of their loved ones.

Because of shame or ignorance about addiction, family members often turn into supporters of addiction. Enablers are persons (frequently siblings or parents) who provide the addict with the means, opportunity, and authority to continue his or her habit. Most of the time, they are at a loss on how to cope and manage the drug problem. Enabling and codependency shield the addict from knowing his or her accountability and responsibility. Morteza Kaleghi Ph.D. wrote, "In most cases, family members enable the addict through denial because the truth hurts."[13]

Enablers organize their lives around the addict at the expense of their principles. They continuously evade the crisis for fear of social rejection, shame, and difficulties that will arise when they take the proper actions to help their loved ones. Tolerating the addiction, unnecessarily giving money to the addict, and the refusal or delay for rehab are examples of enabling.

Codependency occurs when a spouse or another family member controls the behavior of the alcoholic or drug user. Codependents like to rescue alcoholics and addicts. They are obsessed with managing the circumstances of the user. Taking care of household chores of the addict, paying his bills, or telling lies to cover the user's mistakes are some examples of codependent behavior.

Parents also allow their addicted children to smoke tobacco and drink alcohol, thinking that these are legal and not dangerous if taken in moderation. However, these substances are a tripwire to other dangerous illegal drugs, especially for those prone to addiction and people in drug recovery. The Devil dances in the living room of the addicted family home.

Despite the difficulties, we must investigate our dysfunctional attributes and deal with them. Dr. John Vawter, general editor of the book *Hit by a Ton of Bricks* wrote, "We must stop enabling because although our motives in doing so may be pure, the effect denies the [drug] abusers the responsibility of seeing the error of their ways." [14]

"Tough Love" must be enforced to counter chronic enabling and codependency. Proverbs 13:24 *(ESV)* says: "Whoever spares the rod hates his son, but he who loves him is diligent to discipline him." Stern measures are sometimes required to help the addicted child in the long term. For example, parents must supervise money matters for the addict. Pampering and spoiling a child only add injury to the addiction. If necessary, the son must be sent to rehab. Parents should not pity their son and themselves if they are separated for six months or a year. They must also be willing to bear and overcome the social stigma attached to rehab. We need all the necessary measures to begin recovery.

> *He heals the brokenhearted and binds up their*
> *wounds.*
> **—Psalm 147:3**

Satan does not easily give up. We fall into sin and addiction because of our fragile human nature. Viewing addiction primarily as sin gives us the right perspective in dealing with drug abuse. We bring God into the problem and solicit divine healing.

In addiction recovery, the family home can be the best place for healing. Unless the addict is gravely uncontrollable, the home can provide a safe refuge for recuperation. If the proper family dynamics exist, rehab is often unnecessary, especially during the early stages of drug use. With faith and mutual cooperation, we can achieve real, lasting recovery at home.

The primary advantage of home recovery is that the addict gets more attention from parents and siblings in an environment where he feels secure and comfortable. It removes the dreary feeling of being locked up in a remote rehab with total strangers.

Recovery in addiction is not achieved alone. A big fallacy about drug addiction is that only the addicted child goes through rehabilitation. Substance abuse is sometimes called a "family disease." Enablers and codependent members of the family also suffer some extreme forms of anxiety, depression, denial, and social stigma brought about by the drug use of a child.

Home recovery requires the commitment of all family members and the willingness to put in place all the relationship adjustments and changes in the environment. The home is where we live and spend most of our time. As a place of comfort, trust, and love, we share our joys, hurts, and everything else in the safety of our homes. Most importantly, it is also the place where we pray, say grace over meals, and exalt God.

The family is deeply involved in the formation of an addicted person; thus, the family is also a primary influence in recovery. When godly values replace the wrong dynamics of family living, the prospects of healing significantly increase.

Some residents of the MRC face barriers in their willingness to pursue faith in God. For example, they find it awkward to pray alone before meals while the rest of the family members skip it.

Family members must be oriented and trained about addiction and recovery and not entirely rely on their perception and approaches to the problem. They have to watch out and learn how to deal with their child's mood swings, manipulation, episodes of depression, anxiety, drug cravings, and difficulty coping with stress. They should not hesitate to seek counsel and assistance.

In addition, the family should know about drug withdrawal and learn how to help the addict ease them. In severe cases, they can consult a doctor or a specialist for this critical stage. The majority of detoxification cases, however, are not damaging. The unwanted physical symptoms of addiction usually go away after detoxification.

In home recovery, it is essential to outline a precise treatment and recovery plan. Because all the members of the family are involved in the recovery process, it is crucial that they also participate in related family counseling and therapy. Rehab, support groups, and other support circles hold meetings that touch on the recovery issues of the child and that of the family. They must learn the dynamics of enabling and codependency and learn how not to practice them. At Penuel Home, family members of the addicted child are required to attend the regular family meetings after rehab.

Family members must also change their mindsets and ways. The attributes of a dysfunctional home environment, such as fear, secrecy, and conflicts, must be resolved. In an environment of recovery, it is vital to identify and take out specific triggers that lead to drug cravings. Parents should, at least, refrain from drinking and smoking in the presence of an addicted or alcoholic child. They should remove cursing and bad language from their confines. Children cursed by their parents end in addiction because of damaged identities. Love and respect must prevail while they enforce responsibility and accountability.

On the other hand, the recovering addict must also comply with the detailed recovery plan mapped out by the family. He is also held accountable to share distressing drug cravings and confess each slip or relapse. Ephesians 5:21 reads: "Submit to one another out of reverence for Christ."

The family can adopt a system of monitoring with regular drug tests at home. With the consent of the addict, the family can impose sanctions for failures, such as forced rehab or the forfeiture of money and other personal privileges. Success depends on the faithful commitment and compliance of both the implementer (parent or sibling) and the addicted family member.

Home confinement is ideal during the early stages of home recovery. Under quarantine, the addict is willing not to go out of the house for a certain period, say several weeks or months. Cell phones should be surrendered to remove the addict from any further contact from people he should avoid. The home shields him from his addicted friends and drug dealers. The recovering addict may be allowed to go out (going to church, watching a movie, or taking a walk in the park is helpful) only with a responsible family member.

> *A dysfunctional family, which is not God-centered,*
> *makes a person prone to addiction.*
> **—Pastor Tony Dela Paz**

Drug addiction is a sin. Along with any form of addiction, such as gambling, adultery, alcoholism, sexual immorality, we must banish any wrongdoing from the four walls of the house. The family home must be spiritually and morally strengthened against the internal and external attacks of the Enemy.

The brokenness of a family home can begin with a single addiction in the family. Since addiction is a family problem, all members must repent and seek God's grace. When the family approaches God in humility and asks His forgiveness and mercy, healing follows.

The addicted family home is a battleground. Intense prayer and spiritual warfare are primary tools in conquering the Enemy. Prayer and fasting are among the best remedies given by God to overcome addiction. With meditation and Bible reading, prayer and fasting are effective ways of surrendering our sinful flesh to our Almighty God for healing.

God often uses the deliverance of an addicted child as a gateway in transforming the whole family into disciples of Jesus Christ. Many unbelieving families become followers of Jesus Christ because of the liberation of a child, sibling, or parent from addiction. We must go beyond the family and seek the Kingdom of God, where our true and eternal family resides.

Church: A Refuge for Addicted Sinners

And I tell you that you are Peter, and on this rock I will build my church, and the gates of Hades will not overcome it.
—Matthew 16:18

Victory Outreach: A Christian Recovery Home

After taking their lunch, around fifteen people settled around the porch of a large old house. They read the Bible, wrote notes on their journals, and prayed in a silent manner. Some gathered around a table preparing and piling rice puddings and fried bananas on sticks, which they cooked earlier in the morning. On most days, they would sell these snacks in the city streets later in the afternoon. As part of their recovery program, the small business forms part of their training on the value of responsibility and accountability. The sales would also augment the costs of living in the home.

These male individuals are residents of the Victory Outreach Recovery Home in San Pedro, Laguna. Coming from different parts of the Philippines, even as far as Mindanao, they are former drug dependents, criminals, and abandoned street kids. They volunteered to enter the Recovery Home to reach out to God, know Him, and plead for divine healing from all their hurts, addictions, and wounds.

About an hour and a half away from Metro Manila, the undersized city exudes a provincial air of quietness and solitude. Despite its ongoing transformation as a modern hub, the countryside atmosphere makes it conducive for healing and recovery.

Victory Outreach is a worldwide church and ministry organization, which was started by Pastor Sonny Arguinzoni in 1967 in California, U.S.A. After God delivered him from heroin addiction, he opened his house to the homeless and hurting drug addicts from the troubled areas of East L.A. Most of the residents were engaged in drugs, prostitution, or gang-related activities in the inner-city streets.

The primary mission statement reads: "Victory Outreach is an international, church-oriented Christian ministry called to the task of evangelizing and discipling the hurting people of the world, with the message of hope and plan of Jesus Christ."

From these humble beginnings, God's message of salvation has transformed many addicted lost people into faithful disciples of the Lord all over the world. Today, Victory Outreach has around 500 churches located in significant parts of the globe, and approximately 80 percent maintain a Recovery Home as a ministry.

Victory Outreach Philippines, established in 1995, has exemplified an active role in pursuing the Great Commission. It has a church in Metro Manila. The church building in Laguna is on the main street in the city while the 2,000 square meter Recovery Home is approximately 500 meters away.

As a church ministry, the Recovery Home requires no payment, only the residents' sincere commitment and dedication to its discipleship program. Displaced people in the society, including drug dependents, homeless people, and troubled juveniles, are welcomed to the ministry after passing an intake review.

There is no fixed term as the residents can leave anytime at their discretion. But Victory Outreach expects them to complete at least a year of faith-building activities and life skills training. Some graduates who can't find any job are assigned as leaders of the home or referred to the city government for work as traffic aides or office clerks.

The positive outcome of recovery has led many former residents to relocate to San Pedro with their families. Some have also set up their small businesses. They preferred the safety of being near Victory Outreach than stay in their home community where temptations abound and the possibility of relapse is high. Besides, they could continue to foster their recovery by attending church services and getting involved in after-care programs.

Pastor Christian Wilson of Victory Outreach said, "Most successful long-term sobrieties happen when the recovering addicts continue to remain active in the church. Many graduates who go back to their distant homes and leave the faith usually end in relapse as they still can't cope with their life issues and problems."

For where two or three gather in my name, there am I
with them.
—Matthew 18:20

The church is where we find the feet and hands of Jesus Christ. It is not defined by the four walls of a temple or building, but by the congregation of faithful believers. Jesus established and commissioned the church to be the sanctuary and hope of the people.

People gather as a church to praise and worship God, hear God's Word, seek healing, and have fellowship with one another. God plants and grows our faith through His Word. Romans 10:17

says: "Consequently, faith comes from hearing the message, and the message is heard through the word about Christ."

Drug addicts and alcoholics live in abject loneliness. When dry from drugs, they hesitate to mingle with sober people because their minds are focused on getting high, and their bodies are wrestling with drug cravings. When high or drunk, they also cannot relate well to society. They live in a world of their own, sustained by artificial bliss and passing relief. Consumed with idolatry, they consider drugs and alcohol as most important—bringing temporary escape from the hard realities of life.

When they finally decide to become sober, they realize that they have lost the love and trust of their families and other people. They also long for the warmth of a loving home and the company of good friends. They also begin to accept the need for God and the healing He alone can provide.

But pursuing godly recovery at home sometimes seems meaningless, especially if the household is mired with unbelief and sin. Suspicion from the family also shrouds the sincere intentions of an addict who is seeking recovery.

This is where the church becomes a family of God. People in recovery need to break away from sinful drug addicts and dealers and connect with the right people. Ephesians 2:19 says: "Consequently, you are no longer foreigners and strangers, but fellow citizens with God's people and also members of his household." There is also a big chance that they can meet a fellow recovering addict with whom they can freely share their hurts and progress.

It is a common fallacy among addicts or recovering people that they must be free from addiction before they can go to church. Many feel guilty, saying that they don't have the right to enter the holiness of the church while under drugs. When I first attended church, I thought I was an addicted outcast who doesn't deserve the right to be with righteous people. However, I later found out that some members were former or struggling drug addicts and alcoholics, gamblers, adulterers, and criminals. I was in the company of sinners, searching for God and deliverance from many kinds of sins and tyranny.

Faith is intrinsic in man. A study by the Pew Research Center of more than 230 countries and territories revealed that 84% of the 2010 world population identify with a religious group.[15] Faith also directly correlates with drug addiction and alcoholism. A study of the National Center on Addiction and Substance Abuse (CASA) of Columbia University reveals that:

> *Adults who do not consider religious beliefs important are more than one and one-half times likelier to use alcohol and cigarettes, more than three times likelier to binge drink, almost four times likelier to use an illicit drug other than marijuana and more than six times likelier to use pot than adults who strongly believe that religion is important.*[16]

The church is a sanctuary of sinners. A famous saying goes, "The church is a hospital for sinners, not a museum for saints." God designed His church for the sick, hurting people, sinners, addicts, and alcoholics. When we soak ourselves with God's Word and fellowship with the Holy Spirit and other believers, the Devil flees.

Jesus commanded us to gather always as the Body of Christ. Hebrews 10:24-25 reads: "And let us consider how we may spur one another on toward love and good deeds, not giving up meeting together, as some are in the habit of doing, but encouraging one another—and all the more as you see the Day approaching."

Church attendance also has a direct influence on substance abuse. The same study of CASA also discloses that:

> *Adults who never attend religious services are almost twice as likely to drink, three times likelier to smoke, more than five times likelier to have used an illicit drug other than marijuana, almost seven times likelier to binge drink and almost eight times likelier to use pot than those who attend religious services at least weekly.*[17]

The church is the place where our faith grows. First Corinthians 3:6-7 says: "I planted the seed, Apollos watered it, but God has been making it grow. So neither the one who plants nor the one who waters is anything, but only God, who makes things grow." The apostle emphasized that church members have different roles to fulfill in building each other's faith. God, however, ultimately increases our confidence. He further stressed that we are God's house and farm, and all are His coworkers in building His kingdom (v.9). The church is the place where addicted sinners can make whole the scattered debris of their broken lives.

> Is anyone among you sick? Let them call the elders of the church to pray over them and anoint them with oil in the name of the Lord. And the prayer offered in faith will make the sick person well; the Lord will raise them up. If they have sinned, they will be forgiven.
> **—James 5:14-15**

One day in a house in Capernaum, a multitude of people, Pharisees, and teachers of the Law from Galilee, Judea, and Jerusalem gathered around Jesus to hear Him preach. Because of the crowd, four desperate believers made a hole on the roof and lowered a paralyzed man to the ground in a mat so he can be brought to Jesus (Mark 22:2-4). Because of their faith, Jesus forgave the sins of the paralyzed man (v.5) and made him walk (v.12).

As the Body of Christ, believers will pray for addicts, hear their troubles, give advice, and help them in all kinds of need. The church serves as a vehicle for healing, casting out demons, and the laying of hands for the sick and troubled. Because of their liberation from sin and oppression, the recovering addicts are much willing to share God's healing power with others.

Public confession is also integral in healing. James 5:16 says: "Therefore confess your sins to each other and pray for each other so that you may be healed. The prayer of a righteous person is powerful and effective." By sharing our lives and iniquities, we are bringing darkness into light. Specific prayers for forgiveness and repentance are pleaded to God by the church for spiritual conciliation and healing.

Church members help in the recovery of an addict by bringing him closer to God. An accountability partner will guide the recovering addict in his spiritual journey and recovery. This partner should be a mature Christian who has also preferably gone through the travails of drug addiction or alcoholism. He is a brother who will not condemn but instead empathize and guide the addict back on track. Also, the accountability partner serves as the ideal partner in prayer.

In response, the recovering addict must confide openly about his hang-ups, shameful sins, and secrets for specific prayers and proper guidance. He should also disclose and confess incidents of backsliding. There should be no censure if there is a continued willingness on the addict's part to start again and continue the faith.

The Scriptures illustrate the direct correlation between sin, faith, and healing. Secular studies reveal the relation between faith and health. Belief in God or a higher power, whether in the Christian or other denominational faiths, results in better physical and emotional conditions and longer life. Dr. Jeff Levin wrote, "People who regularly attend church services have lower rates of illness and death than do infrequent or non-attendees. For each of the three leading causes of death in the United States—heart disease, cancer, and hypertension—people who report a religious affiliation have lower rates of illness."[18]

Each of you should use whatever gift you have received to serve others, as faithful stewards of God's grace in its various forms.
—1 Peter 4:10

The church is the best support group for recovering drug dependents. Enlisting in or starting a drug ministry is an excellent service to God and other hurting addicted people. Not only can former or recovering addicts relate to other drug users, their faith increases as well. Proverbs 27:17 (*ESV*) reads: "Iron sharpens iron, and one man sharpens another." They can also put into full use their experience in helping other people in recovery.

Every recovered or recovering addict is the best witness and testimony to other addicts who need healing. Pastor Christian Wilson said, "Deliverance happens when God takes away from the addict the addiction. But it takes discipleship for healing to take place."

Some churches have an active addiction recovery ministry or healing circle. Many recovering addicts also find joining a church ministry a fulfilling endeavor in warding off temptations and drug cravings. Joining a music group or participating in evangelistic work is always a joyful act in our expression of our love for Him. A sense of belonging and responsibility from being part of a ministry team is a big exercise towards recovery.

Because of the increasing number of addiction in our ranks, there is a dire need for more churches to engage in drug ministries. Christianity is the best vehicle in bringing sinful addicts closer to God. Pastor Christian Wilson further said, "Churches need to be more active in the drug ministry by becoming more familiar with the addiction problem and its underlying issues. It will take a lot of hard work; you need to get into the lives of each addicted person. The discipleship program or process must be more intense." He added, "Churches who want to help addicts but don't have its own recovery home can arrange a working arrangement with rehabs, allowing them to hold discipleship programs."

The church is a beacon of hope, empowerment, and healing. We need not be alone in our quest for a liberated life. In the church, we can find the magnified presence of God in the company of saints who love and care for us. In the process, we also find greater joy and fulfillment when we love and care for others.

> *In the church, we can find the magnified presence of God in the company of saints who love and care for us.*

The Road to Recovery

The best thing about the future is that it comes one day at a time.
—Abraham Lincoln, former U.S. president

Not long after they left Egypt, the Israelites grumbled in the desert. They complained to Moses and Aaron, "If only we had died by the Lord's hand in Egypt! There we sat around pots of meat and ate all the food we wanted, but you have brought us out into this desert to starve this entire assembly to death" (Exodus 16:3). The Lord responded by raining down bread each morning for six days from heaven (v.4) and sent quails in the evening (vv.12-13).

God instructed them to gather manna enough for the day. Whenever they collected more than the day's needs, the extra food rotted (v.20). The Lord also told them to double their harvest on the sixth day so that they can rest on the next day, which is the Sabbath. On the seventh day, the manna did not decay (v.24).

Later, Jesus said: "Do not store up for yourselves treasures on earth, where moths and rust destroy, and where thieves break in and steal. But store up for yourselves treasures in heaven, where moths and rust do not destroy, and where thieves do not break in and steal" (Matthew 6:19-20).

For forty years in the desert, God taught the Israelites to live "one day at a time" and stressed the virtue of contentment and gratefulness. Above all, God established the attributes of His kingdom and preeminent authority on earth.

LIVING ONE DAY AT A TIME

Therefore do not worry about tomorrow, for tomorrow will worry about itself. Each day has enough trouble of its own.
—Matthew 6:34

Plagued by their addicted wandering minds, recovering addicts find difficulty in focusing on the present day. They become prone to romanticizing the past and daydreaming of the uncertain future. Beneath their addiction, they know that they don't have an ideal life—living under bondage and rejected by society as outcasts. However, drugs are the only refuge they know that provides an ecstatic escape from the pains of the past and the uncertainty of the future.

But, like the disgruntled Israelites, they need to focus on today, not be dragged by the past, and let God take care of the future. Life is too short to worry about tomorrow and too precious to wail or reminisce about yesterday.

Recovery is difficult and does not happen overnight. At the start of the recovery, and with the added torment of drug withdrawal, each day can be an excruciating episode of adjustment back to reality. However, a single day of sobriety is a golden moment of victory that merits celebration. Soon, sober days will turn into months, and sober months will turn into years.

The Lord's Prayer explicitly illustrates God's command to live for today: "Give us today our daily bread" (Matthew 6:11). Hebrews 3:13 also reads, "But encourage one another daily, as long as it is called 'Today,' so that none of you may be hardened by sin's deceitfulness." Thanking God for our lives, being contented with what we have, and putting our hearts into whatever work we are doing today are essential keys to healing. The more we can keep ourselves in the *now*, our recovery will start to get easier.

Today is the first day of the rest of your life.
—American proverb

Living one day at a time is the secret to a happy and contented life. Every baby step toward recovery means a giant leap of triumph. The folks at AA put great emphasis on the value of counting each period of sobriety by giving out chips to mark individual milestones in recovery. In contrast,

Living one day at a time is the secret to a happy and contented life. Every baby step toward recovery means a giant leap of triumph.

most residents of the MRC meticulously count with anticipation the days left before their release from rehab, not minding or being grateful for each day of sobriety. They fail or refuse to recognize the truth that they can live and survive without drugs. Instead, they focus on going back home and return to their old, addicted ways.

Recovering addicts are overly concerned about the many aspects of their life. Instead of keeping a close watch over their recovery, they consider their sobriety as a low priority. Many residents of the MRC often proclaim the need to fix things first when they get out of rehab. Yet, their minds get boggled by the heap of mundane tasks ahead of them.

Many recovering addicts stress the urgency of going back to work to bring food to the family table. However, these intentions are often ploys of fake recovery to deceive the outside world and use their wages to get drugs. Some residents clamor for a "needed leisurely vacation" after the ordeals of rehab. Oddly, enabling parents succumb to their child's absurd requests.

Repentance, faith, prayer, and bare reflection are most important in healing after rehab. Pastor Tony Dela Paz adds, "It is important for the person to have a godly purpose and vision upon release from rehab."

While most of their goals are commendable and need to be addressed as early as possible, every move must be examined if it truly fosters sobriety. Recovery is fragile and does not end in rehab. Half-baked in recovery, many recklessly plunge back into the real world without God and soon fall back into relapse.

Jesus Christ told us not to worry about our life, what to eat or drink, and even the clothes we are to wear (Matthew 6:25). Only the pagans run after these worldly things (v.32). Instead, he said, "But seek first his kingdom and his righteousness, and all these things will be given to you as well" (v.33). As the Great Provider, God will use other people and circumstances to help sincere recovering addicts in times of need.

He also instructed us to be still and meditate on God: "Be still, and know that I am God; I will be exalted among the nations, I will be exalted in the earth" (Psalm 46:10). In divine healing, we need to entrust our worldly cares to the Lord. Having faith in God is paramount in our daily recovery.

To cherish life daily, we have to put God in the center of our lives. The steadfast daily acts of prayer, Bible reading, spiritual pursuits, and the seeking of the Holy Spirit enable us to rise above our worries. Philippians 2:12-13 reads: "Continue to work out your salvation with fear and trembling, for it is God who works in you to will and to act in order to fulfill his good purpose." A part of the Serenity Prayer also says, "Living one day at a time; enjoying one moment at a time." Meditating on the holiness and the beauty of God's creation is a constant act of worship. In recovery, we need God on our side every day in whatever we do.

PUTTING ORDER IN OUR LIVES

Finally, brothers and sisters, whatever is true, whatever is noble, whatever is right, whatever is pure, whatever is lovely, whatever is admirable—if anything is excellent or praiseworthy—think about such things. Whatever you have learned or received or heard from me, or seen in me—put it into practice. And the God of peace will be with you.
—Philippians 4:8-9

The wrath of addiction has scathed our character and wrecked many areas of our lives. We have to rid ourselves of our twisted personalities and manners—drug talk, foul grooming, cursing, perverted ways, and immorality.

Sobriety means a change of behavior. Gerald May wrote, "Every sincere battle with addiction begins with an attempt to change addictive behavior. Literally, we try to reform our behavior, substituting constructive actions for destructive ones."[20] True recovery also means the removal of all addictions in our lives.

A recovered drug addict may turn to gambling, which becomes his newfound source of refuge and joy. Pastor Tony remarked, "Without God, a 'recovered addict' merely switches the object of his addiction."

Young kids need to go back to school, and able men and women should look for a job or take care of the home. However, work should foster sobriety, not support an addiction. There is fulfillment in work. Whether one is a stockbroker, homemaker, or a street sweeper, our occupation must be satisfying, not only for the provision it brings but for the greater glory of God. At home, washing the dishes, taking care of the laundry, and cooking for the family are daily toils that advance sobriety and healing. Pastor Tony said, "It is better for the person to get back to work after rehab in order to be productive." Being occupied with work and other positive pursuits also prevent temptations and drug cravings.

Bringing order in our lives means we have to settle our debts. We also need to repair our broken roofs or see the dentist, which we ignored for ten years. Besides, we have to take care of our health (nutrition, exercise, and proper sleep), which was ravaged by addiction.

Most importantly, we have to mend broken relationships and seek forgiveness from those we have wronged and hurt. A major challenge that faces people in recovery is the reparation or healing of a broken family.

Recovery often means a total change of lifestyle.

At the MRC, many residents remain desperate and lost on how to go about their lives without their families. Their wives have left them, their children are living with a distant relative, or their parents have thrown them out of the house.

Drug addiction leads to promiscuity and adultery. As a result, many residents have produced several families. They are perplexed about where to settle and live, and how to resolve conflicts with their disgruntled wives and other partners. In addition, they also have to contend with the daunting task of reconciling with their many children from different mothers.

While some of these aims may seem irrelevant regarding recovery, addicts must eventually face and tackle them. They need to fix things in their lives, which they alone can resolve. Recovery often means a total change of lifestyle.

Getting sober is a big job. Overwhelming ourselves with many mundane tasks when we're not ready is a dangerous road to relapse. Ecclesiastes 3:1 reads: "There is a time for everything, and a season for every activity under the heavens." We will become ready to tackle things according to the level of our faith, sobriety, and resiliency.

Fasting: Breaking the Severe Bondage

"Even now," declares the LORD, "return to me with all
your heart, with fasting and weeping and mourning."
—Joel 2:12

The skies were still dark at four in the morning. Inside a large building, believers from different church congregations assembled on the ground floor. They wore sweaters and jackets to ward off the gusts of cold winds blowing down from the mountains.

The gentle strums of the guitar broke the solemn silence, ascending to a slow cadence of a song of worship. Moments later, the light of dawn ushered a refreshing sight to the community of God's people. The Dawn Watch marked the culmination of an overnight dedication of prayer, fasting, and worship.

Touch of Glory Prayer Mountain located in Antipolo City is an open, public place for spiritual gatherings. A facility of the Bread of Life Ministries - Philippines, it has provided a sanctuary for the faithful to pray, fast, and seek guidance from God.

The complex includes a large auditorium, bathrooms, and a cafeteria. Private and group dormitories are available on the second floor for those who want to sleep and stay overnight. Single-person meditation rooms, where one can pray and cry out to God in seclusion, also dot the sloped mountain area.

Church groups formed their circles and sat on plastic chairs or flat on the floor. They prayed, spoke in tongues, and chanted their distinct forms of devotion. Collectively, the chorus of diverse sounds created a heavenly hymn of worship.

In these hallowed grounds, the Lord is exalted—an embodiment of the life Jesus wants us to foster—prayer, worship, meditating on God's Word, and fasting.

This is the verdict: Light has come into the world, but people loved darkness instead of light because their deeds were evil.
—John 3:19

Fasting radically alters our deep-seated love of the self and reverts us to the primary purpose of our existence—that is, to worship our Divine Creator.

Humanity is under the grip of Satan. Abortion, same-sex marriage, gender change, gene mutation, and the patronage of deadly substances are some of the unbiblical and wicked ways that have become acceptable tenets in our society. The sins, which brought fire from the wrath of God upon the idols of our biblical ancestors, still prevail today in more vicious forms.

The progress of our civilization—democracy, education, infrastructure, food, sanitation, and technology—has brought increasing comfort and blessings in our lives. But, despite these gifts from God, humankind forsakes the Almighty One who gives us life and everything that we need. We have lost the sacred art of gratitude, remain dissatisfied, and complain we should have more of everything.

Addiction has mutated into a variety of ugly forms. It mirrors Satan's control over the lives of many people who are dominated by chronic discontent. Greed, money, possessions, digital space, and addictive substances rule the lives of millions of people around the world.

In Japan, "internet fasting camps" are being introduced to deal with the roughly 500,000 kids addicted to video games, the web, and social media. Akifumi Sekine, a spokesman for the education ministry, said, "It's becoming more and more of a problem. We estimate this affects around 518,000 children at middle and high schools across Japan, but that figure is rising, and there could be far more cases because we don't know about them all."[1]

Addictive substances inundate street corners and alleys. Opioids flood the West, alcohol abuse is widespread, and tobacco can be purchased at corner stores. Heroin, cocaine, and meth can also easily be obtained in bars, by mail, and on online black market sites. Satan lures humanity into falling into sin and break away from God.

Addiction is a global crisis, and recovery from addiction is elusive. We have tried numerous methods to deliver ourselves from addiction. Multiple rehabs, support groups, and moving to another place or country to avoid our drug dealers and addicted friends didn't work. We also prayed and sought diverse spiritual circles to remove ourselves from the bondage of drugs. But still, recovery is elusive.

In Isaiah 58, the prophet declared in bold detail the essence, purposes, and benefits of fasting. But, throughout the history of humanity, true fasting has been distorted and permuted by individuals, communities, tribes, and nations for purposes other than God's original design and intention. Today, many people fast for the wrong reasons. For example, health advocates label the abstinence of food to lose weight as "fasting" instead of "dieting."

Fasting brings us back to the altar of God. It purifies our bodies, minds, and souls. Fasting radically alters our deep-seated love of the self and reverts us to the primary purpose of our existence—that is, to worship our Divine Creator.

The Sacred Power of Fasting

Is not this the kind of fasting I have chosen: to lose the chains of injustice and untie the cords of the yoke, to set the oppressed free and break every yoke? Is it not

> to share your food with the hungry and to provide the
> poor wanderer with shelter—when you see the naked,
> to clothe them, and not to turn away from your own
> flesh and blood? Then your light will break forth like
> the dawn, and your healing will quickly appear; then
> your righteousness will go before you, and the glory of
> the LORD will be your rear guard. Then you will call,
> and the LORD will answer; you will cry for help, and
> he will say: Here am I.
> **—Isaiah 58:6-9**

One historic day, God sent the runaway prophet Jonah to the great but decadent, sinful city of Nineveh to warn its people of their impending doom (Jonah 3). As an arch-enemy of the Israelites, the Ninevites were known for their idolatry, witchcraft, sorcery, and cruelty in war. After emerging victorious from their battles, they brought the severed head of the opposing king for display in their banquets and the chopped-up parts of the generals to be distributed all over the kingdom as souvenirs.

Fearful of God's wrath, "The Ninevites believed God. A fast was proclaimed, and all of them, from the greatest to the least, put on sackcloth" (v.5). The king ordered that the whole household, including their animals, to abstain from food and water and wear sack clothes as a sign of repentance (vv.7-8). The king also told them to call upon God and "give up their evil ways and their violence" (v.8[b]). Because of their sincere acts, God relented and spared them from destruction (v.10). However, the Lord eventually destroyed them because of their unceasing barbaric paganism and hatred for His chosen people.

The Israelites fasted for various reasons: repentance, mourning, supplication, obedience, a form of prayer, plea, and as an act of ceremonial public worship. Later in the New Testament, Jesus Christ commended the Ninevites for their repentance (Matthew 12:41), while denouncing the Jewish leaders for defying Him as the Messiah and for not believing in the coming Kingdom of God.

When you fasted and mourned in the fifth and seventh
months for the past seventy years, was it really for me
that you fasted?
—Zechariah 7:5[b]

Fasting is the ultimate form of worship. The old prophetess Anna waited for Jesus for many years and "never left the temple but worshiped night and day, fasting and praying" (Luke 2:37[b]). Like prayer, fasting for the sole benefit of the self runs contrary to the true nature of fasting. We show our utmost reverence to God by denying our sinful flesh.

The Israelites also fasted as an act of confession and repentance to God. As cupbearer to king Antaxerses of Persia, Nehemiah was instrumental in the rebuilding of the walls of Jerusalem. He and Ezra led the spiritual revival of the people from their sins against God and their political and religious restoration from Babylonian captivity.

Nehemiah 9:1 states: "On the twenty-fourth day of the same month, the Israelites gathered together, fasting and wearing sackcloth and putting dust on their heads." They confessed their sins, read the Scriptures, and worshiped the Lord (vv.2-3). He also admitted his wrongdoings and that of his family before God (Nehemiah 1:6).

For three days he was blind, and did not eat or drink
anything.
—Acts 9:9

God struck Saul of Tarsus because he persecuted Christians. He was not only without natural sight, but he also had no hint about what happened. God revealed Himself to Paul (Saul's converted name) and said, "Saul, Saul, why do you persecute me?" (Acts 9:4). "I am Jesus, whom you are persecuting" (v.5).

After fasting and praying for three days, Paul met Ananias, who was sent by the Lord to restore his eyesight and be filled by the Holy Spirit (v.17). Paul became one of the great leaders of the first-century Christians who led the evangelization of the Gentiles.

The Israelites also fasted when they sought God's will because they conflicted with the tribe of Benjamin. "Then all the Israelites, the whole army, went up to Bethel, and there they sat weeping before the Lord. They fasted that day until evening and presented burnt offerings and fellowship offerings to the Lord" (Judges 20:26).

Fasting is an avenue for God to reveal Himself and His will to a person or a community of faithful believers. Arthur Wallis wrote:

> *Without a doubt there is a very close connection between the practice of fasting and the receiving of spiritual revelation. Many non-Christian religions such as Buddhism, Hinduism, Confucianism and Islam also practice fasting because they know its power to detach one's mind from the world of sense, and to sharpen one's sensibility to the world of spirit.[2]*

Searching for God's revelation regarding any major decision in life (marriage, career, education, and others) can be realized through fasting. When faced with difficult choices and directions, individuals, churches, families, and the community can fast and pray for His will.

A fast is also practiced to bless and help other people in need. Fasting makes us realize the abundance of our food and possessions and the necessity to share with others in need. The Great Commandment means loving and helping others. In the Church of the Latter-day Saints, members undertake a fast offering on a Fast Sunday. They are encouraged to fast at least once a month and give the money they saved by skipping meals to the church to provide food, clothing, shelter, and medical help to the needy.

Jesus Christ often fasted and prayed. He emphasized its importance in seeking humility and the indwelling of the Holy Spirit. The disciples emulated the Master by fasting. After they worshiped God and fasted (Acts 13:1-3), the Holy Spirit said, "Set apart for me Barnabas and Saul [Paul] for the work to which I have called them" (v.2). Fasting is mentioned in both Old and New Testaments over fifty times.

Fasting was an integral practice of Jesus and his followers so they can be empowered by the Holy Spirit in the pursuit of the Great Commission. They preached the Good News, healed the sick, and drove out unholy spirits.

Today, fasting is part of the Christian life. Whether for personal, church, or broader intentions, fasting breaks the Enemy and cleanses our sinful, trampled souls. A multitude of believers all over the world fast and pray to worship God and seek His divine will. In 2018, Open Doors (a worldwide organization for persecuted Christians), called for 24 hours of prayer and fasting on behalf of the 300,000 Christians persecuted in North Korea.[3]

Healthy churches fast regularly for specific reasons, to plea for restoration, revival, and help in ministries and missions. Arthur Wallis declares, "We shall rediscover one of the lost secrets of the early church: the power that is released through the truly biblical practice of fasting unto God."[4]

> *Go, gather together all the Jews who are in Susa, and fast for me. Do not eat or drink for three days, night or day. I and my attendants will fast as you do.*
> **—Esther 4:16[a]**

In the Book of Esther, the Jews faced a threat of mass destruction during the reign of King Xerxes. Haman, the highest advisor of the king, was an enemy of the Jews. Esther, the Jewish Queen of Xerxes, asked the Jews to fast and ask God to spare them from destruction (c.4). She interceded and asked the king to put a stop to the planned killing (c.7). God finally delivered the Jews from the crisis as King Xerxes put a stop to the planned killing (c.8).

In 2 Chronicles 20, King Jehosaphat declared a fast for all the people of Judah, which faced destruction from their enemies.

One of the most striking acts of supernatural deliverance happened after the fast, as God wiped out the armies of invading nations.

Fasting on a community or national level is not defunct. God hears the plea of His people. In the book, *Fasting for Spiritual Breakthrough*, Elmer Towns wrote, "A private problem requires a private fast. A group problem requires the group to fast with you. Even when the circle of concern becomes national, the circle of fasting should be as large as the circle of concern."[5]

In a national or global crisis, like the COVID- 19 pandemic, Christians could fast and petition God for intervention and rescue. Manesh Chavda adds, "The enemy knows that you can change the shape and the destiny of your city and even your nation by joining God's end-time army of men and women who are committed to fasting and prayer."[6]

Fasting of the body is food for the soul.
—Saint John Chrysostom, archbishop

Our ancestors fasted for a variety of reasons. Abstaining from food for spiritual reasons was a primary component of the fabric of ancient cultures. However, they also fasted for natural reasons. Because of their austere lifestyle, the sourcing and preparation of food took a significant amount of time. The storage of food was limited and confined to natural means of preservation. They did not possess refrigerators, ovens, and electric or gas-powered cooking appliances that could preserve or cook food in an instant. Besides that, they had to spend time looking for prey and produce.

Breakfast, as we know it, was probably nonexistent. Women collected grains, roots, fruits, nuts, and vegetables. Men hunted for fish and meat using sharpened sticks, nets, harpoons, spears, and bows and arrows.

After a successful and long hunt, the preparation and cooking of food also took many hours. After dinner, they slept early since electricity, TV, and other amenities didn't exist. Their lifestyle made their periods of fast longer. The long hours of fasting promoted therapeutic healing and cleansing enjoyed by our fore-fathers. They naturally fasted.

Breakfast did not exist for a long time in history. Food historian Caroline Yeldham reported that the Romans usually consumed only one meal a day at around noon. She said, "The Romans believed it was healthier to eat only one meal a day...They were obsessed with digestion, and eating more than one meal was considered a form of gluttony. This thinking impacted on the way people ate for a very long time."[7]

The word *fast* came from the word *tsom* in Hebrew and *nesteia* in Greek, which means voluntary abstinence from food. Personal and communal fasting publicly emerged later in various religious groups as part of their doctrines or rituals.

The dominant faith groups and religions in the world practice fasting: Christianity, Islam, Judaism, Hinduism, and Buddhism. Fasting is a central doctrine in the Christian faith to develop a deeper personal relationship with God. It is the most profound form of worship that encompasses knowing and loving God, repentance, guidance, healing, spiritual warfare, seeking His will, love for others, and divine intervention.

John Piper wrote in his book *Hunger for God*: "Christian fasting, at its root, is the hunger of a homesickness for God... [it] is not only the spontaneous effect of superior satisfaction in God, it is also a chosen weapon against every force in the world that would take that satisfaction away."[8]

The Jews observe Yom Kippur or the Day of Atonement by fasting. Leviticus 34 reads, "This is to be a lasting ordinance for you: Atonement is to be made once a year for all the sins of the Israelites." They spend most of the day in the synagogue with around 25 hours of fasting and intensive prayer, confession, and repentance. There is complete abstinence from food and drink from sunset on the previous evening until the first three stars show up at the end of the day. They also refrain from brushing their teeth to avoid unintentionally swallowing water. Because of their strict observance of Yom Kippur, some Jews in Nazi concentration camps during World War II, despite their hunger, gave up their small portions in obedience to their faith.

For Muslims, fasting is integral to worship. As one of the "The Five Pillars of Islam," the fast (*sawm*) is the fourth obligation they need to perform in obedience to Allah. They fast during Ramadan, which is held on the ninth month of the Islamic calendar when Mohammed revealed the Koran. They pray, read the Koran, and hear sermons, including reminders to help the poor and feed the hungry. Adult Muslims are prohibited from eating, drinking, smoking, or even swallowing their saliva. The fast begins at daybreak and ends until sundown. Fasting and feasting is a hallmark of the Muslim faith during Ramadan.

Fasting in Hinduism is a pronouncement of faith and decision to foster a person's character, power, and cleanliness. It creates a bond with the Absolute (omnipresent, eternal, and spiritual source of the universe) by establishing harmony between body and soul. Fasting means the denial of the body's physical needs to achieve spiritual gains.

Buddhist monks eat their last meal before noon and take no food until the next day. However, they generally regard this practice as a form of discipline rather than fasting. According to the Vinayas (Buddhist texts on discipline), Buddhists should utilize the abstinence period as a time for meditation and sutra chanting. Pious laypersons also follow this regimen during particular days of religious ceremonies.

Native American Indians fast as part of their traditions, for purification, and in preparation for war. Practiced both in private and as a tribe, fasting means abstinence from food and water. At the age of puberty, a young man is sent to a special place to fast and pray alone for up to four days or longer. A tribal fast is sometimes called by the leader to evade threats of crisis or disaster.

In 1620, The English Puritans, also known as the Pilgrims, fasted the day before disembarking from the English ship Mayflower to reach North America and set up a mission colony.

England designated February 6, 1756, as a day of solemn fasting and prayer in remembering its war with France in the Americas. President Abraham Lincoln also declared a national day of fasting and prayer during the Civil War. The victories of England and the northern states of the United States were considered as godly interventions by the believers who fasted and prayed. Political leaders have also proclaimed prayer and fasting during World War II.[9]

At present times, the Telegraph reports, "Many German hospitals now run fasting weeks, funded by health insurance programmes, to help manage obesity, while fasting holidays at centres and spas throughout Europe, include Hungary, the Czech Republic, and Austria, are growing in popularity."[10]

The town of Geneva, Switzerland, holds the *Jeûne genevois* or "Fast of Geneva," which is a public holiday and day of fasting in the Canton of Geneva in September. The holiday originated during the Middle Ages, wherein some days were officially decided to be fasting days as penitence after calamities such as wars, epidemics, or the plague.

Fasting is usually a religious act. However, abstinence from food is also used for other purposes. In ancient Ireland, a person could fast against a man who had injured him. The victim goes to the wrongdoer's house and sits outside from dawn to dusk and declines to eat. This practice is believed to bring bad luck to his enemy. The perpetrator has two options: he could either admit his mistake or wrongdoing or make remedies for the fasting to stop and to restore harmony. The perpetrator could also counter fast to remove the curse.[11]

GREAT SPIRITUAL AND WORLD LEADERS PRACTICED FASTING

The great men of history fasted. In 210 A. D., Tertullian, an early Christian author, defended fasting as a better aid to religion than feasting.[12] Polycarp, a second-century Christian bishop, advocated fasting as a powerful weapon against temptation and lusts of the flesh.[13]

Zoroaster, the Persian prophet, practiced and taught fasting around 4,000 years ago. The great philosophers Aristotle, Socrates, and Plato also fasted. Plato said, "I fast for greater physical and mental efficiency." Confucius, China's great philosopher and teacher, included fasting in his teachings.

The Prophet Muhammad, the founder of Islam, fasted, prayed, and bowed prostrate. He said, "Whoever observes fasts during the month of Ramadan out of sincere faith, and hoping to attain God's rewards, then all his past sins will be forgiven."[14] His famous quote reads, "Prayer brings us halfway to God, fasting takes us to the gateway of heaven."

Siddhartha Gautama, or the Buddha, fasted. Mahatma Gandhi exemplified one of the greatest modern-day fastings when he fasted and led India to gain freedom from the British Empire through nonviolent means.

The early physicians of our time fasted. Paracelsus, one of the three fathers of Western medicine, said, "Fasting is the greatest remedy—the physician within." Hippocrates, the "Father of Medicine," considered fasting as a great natural healer. He claimed, "Everyone has a doctor in him; we just have to help him in his work. The natural healing force within each one of us is the greatest force in getting well....to eat when you are sick, is to feed your sickness."

The great leaders of the Christian Reformation fasted. As a monk for nearly 20 years, Martin Luther practiced fasting starting at 3 a.m. with confession, prayer, and reading of the Scriptures.[15] He translated the Bible into the German language while fasting.[16] John Calvin also fasted regularly and lived to witness the conversion of almost a whole city. Calvin said, "Therefore, let us say something of fasting; because many, for want of knowing its usefulness, undervalue its necessity, and some reject it as almost superfluous, while, on the other hand, where the use of it is not well understood, it easily degenerates into superstition."[17] In Scotland, John Knox fasted and prayed so much that Queen Mary said she feared his prayers more than all the armies of Scotland.[18] John Wesley, the founder of Methodism, fasted twice weekly from sunrise until late afternoon.

The genius inventor, painter, and sculptor Leonardo da Vinci practiced and advocated fasting. The Rev. Dr. Martin Luther King, the leader of the Civil Rights Movement, also regularly fasted.

World leaders of recent history fasted. Some of the U.S. Presidents who advocated or practiced fasting are George Washington, John Adams, Abraham Lincoln, and Barack Obama.

Our biblical ancestors and leaders of the early Christian church fasted. Moses fasted for 40 days and 40 nights without food and water when God instructed him to write the Ten Commandments on the tablets of stone at Mt. Sinai. David, Nehemiah, Esther, Daniel, Elijah, Hannah, and Anna fasted. The apostles and disciples fasted (see Acts 13:1-3; Acts 14: 21-23; Acts: 9:9).

Our Messiah, Jesus Christ, fasted for 40 days and 40 nights in preparation for His ministry on earth (Matthew 4:2).

TYPES OF FASTING

God's chosen fast, then, is that which He has appointed; that which is set apart for Him, to minister to Him, to honor and glorify Him; that which is designed to accomplish His sovereign will.
—Arthur Wallis, Bible teacher

REGULAR FAST

The regular fast involves abstaining from all forms of food and commonly lasts 24 hours. Judges 20:26 reads: "Then the Israelites, all the people, went up to Bethel, and there they sat weeping before the Lord. They fasted that day until evening and presented burnt offerings and fellowship offerings to the Lord."

According to the Foods and Nutrition Encyclopedia, "For healthy individuals, no harm results from short-term fasting."[19] The average healthy person can survive without food between 21 and 40 or more days before the body starves or disposes of vital tissue.

TOTAL, ABSOLUTE, OR COMPLETE FAST

The absolute fast allows no food and water and should be short. In the Bible, this fast lasts mostly not over three days. Ezra "ate no food and drank no water, because he continued to mourn over the unfaithfulness of the exiles" (Ezra 10:6). Queen Esther instructed all the Jews to gather and not to eat or drink for three days and nights (Esther 4:16). Saul of Tarsus (later Paul) was struck blind with an encounter with the risen Christ. Acts 9:9 reads: "For three days he was blind, and did not eat or drink anything." Today, the Jewish people take no food or water for 24 hours during Yom Kippur—the Day of Atonement.

Absolute fasting is God's tool for severe chronic drug dependency. Pastor-evangelist Manesh Chavda wrote, "The complete fast is a fast of desperation, a fast of all-out hunger and urgency for the presence of God to come on the scene."[20] Arthur Wallis adds, "We conclude that the absolute fast is an exceptional measure for an exceptional situation. It is something usually reserved for spiritual emergencies. One knows of extreme cases of need which have not yielded to normal prayer and fasting, but which have responded when the intercessor was led by God to fast absolutely. This is especially true in cases of powerful possession by evil spirits."[21]

PARTIAL FAST

The partial fast, like eating only fresh vegetables, omits certain foods during the fasting period. Daniel, with his three friends, only took vegetables and water when they were taken captives by the Babylonians (Daniel 1:12). Daniel 10:2-3 reads: "At that time I, Daniel, mourned for three weeks. I ate no choice food; no meat or wine touched my lips; and I used no lotions at all until the three weeks were over." Daniel also avoided these foods because they could probably have been offered to idols (Daniel 1:8). John Wesley ate only bread (whole grain) and water for many days during his fast. A partial fast also means abstaining from food and water for less than 24 hours. It includes omitting one or two meals a day.

SUPERNATURAL FAST

A supernatural fast means abstaining from eating and drinking for a more significant period. It is called 'supernatural' because it would be medically impossible to survive for so long without God's intervention. Moses fasted for forty days and nights without food and water at Mount Sinai (Exodus 34:28).

HEALING BENEFITS OF FASTING

The best of all medicines is resting and fasting.
—Benjamin Franklin, one of the founding fathers of the United States

Mahatma Gandhi, a fragile and bald-headed man, often sat cross-legged on prison cells or the busy streets of Delhi. With his small and skinny frame, he could be mistaken as an old, malnourished, and impoverished beggar in this vastly populated city. However, on closer look, Gandhi was an enigmatic, wise leader with a sharp mind and a body brimming with excellent health. He led the peaceful revolution movement that liberated hundreds of million people in India from British rule.

Gandhi frequently fasted as part of his nonviolent movement to help India gain independence from Great Britain. On May 18, 1933, one of Gandhi's physicians attended to him on the tenth day in one of his fasting periods. The doctor said, "Despite his 64 years, from a physiological point of view, the Indian leader was as healthy as a man of forty."[22] Gandhi once said, "All the vitality and energy I have comes to me because my body is purified by fasting."

Today, many people have often misunderstood fasting. They mistakenly believe that abstaining from food and water for a particular time is detrimental to one's health and well-being. Skipping breakfast, for example, would cripple the start of a busy day of the average working man. Those involved with hard labor would claim it would be impossible to work if there's no amount of food in their stomachs. Many sectors of society also claim, "Breakfast is the most important meal of the day." The food industry, driven by profits, massively advertises TV cereals, milk, hotdogs, and other products. Our obsession with food leads us to "live to eat," not "eat to live."

Humanity has been trapped by tradition that having "three square meals" is essential for healthy living. Nothing is farther from the truth. Our obsession with food has brought us illness and disease. Fuhrman wrote, "The primary cause of illness can be summed up in one word: toxicosis. The self-pollution that destroys our bodies from the inside out, from wrong living and wrong eating, is a dangerous lifestyle to continue."[23]

There is a time to eat, and there is a time to abstain from food for digestion and healing. Our bodily system requires energy to digest and transform food for our nourishment. Our digestive system and related organs also need sufficient time to rest and recuperate.

In 2016, Japanese cell biologist Yoshinori Ohsumi won the Nobel Prize in Medicine for his study on autophagy—the cellular self-cleansing process that breaks down, recycles, and renews damaged molecules and cells in our bodies. Fasting activates autophagy, which slows down the process of aging and has a positive influence on cell renewal.[24]

Fasting is for everyone. Dr. Herbert Shelton (1895-1985), the author of *The Science and Fine Art of Fasting*, supervised the fasts of over 40,000 people in the United States. He wrote, "[Fasting] must be recognized as a fundamental and radical process that is older than any other mode of caring for the sick organism, for it is employed on the plane of instinct and has been so employed since life was first introduced upon the earth."[25]

Fasting is therapeutically beneficial to drug addicts and alcoholics. Drug addiction brings havoc to a person's body and mind. Tuberculosis, liver disease, hypertension, cancer, and other deadly diseases come as a result of drug

> *Fasting is therapeutically beneficial to drug addicts and alcoholics.*

and alcohol use. Addiction also causes depression, anxiety, and other mental disorders such as neurosis, paranoia, and psychosis.

Elmer Towns wrote, "God has placed within every physical body the ability to heal itself. Technically, doctors, surgical procedures, and medicine do not heal people. In the study of pathology, we see that disease and germs cause illness in the human body. When the doctor, surgery, or medicine removes the cause of the disease, then the body will heal itself."[26] Shelton adds, "After the fast has cleared away the accumulations and the devitalized cells, stronger, more vital and healthy tissue is built to take the place of that which was cast away. Regeneration of the body is brought about by the daily renewal of its cells and tissues, and fasting hastens this renewal."[27]

> *How can the guests of the bridegroom mourn while he is with them? The time will come when the bridegroom will be taken from them; then they will fast.*
> **—Matthew 9:15 [b]**

The time to fast is now. Today, many people, including Christians, consider fasting and the works of evil spirits as typical only during the biblical period. As we approach the return of The Bridegroom, Satan's deception upon humankind continues to become bolder. First Peter 5:8 reads: "Your enemy the devil prowls around like a roaring lion looking for someone to devour." Satan uses drugs to hold people captive in his kingdom of darkness.

In the book, *God's Chosen Fast*, Arthur Wallis wrote, "The fast of this age is not merely an act of mourning for Christ's absence, but an act of preparation for His return."[28] The holy practice of fasting is not solely confined during ancient times but also very applicable in our present age.

The benefits of fasting must be underscored. Christians fast not only for its innate biblical goals but also for health and therapeutic purposes. Mark Twain once said, "A little starvation can really do more for the average sick man than can the best medicines and the best doctors. I do not mean a restricted diet; I mean total abstinence from food. I speak from experience; starvation has been my cold and fever doctor for 15 years, and has accomplished a cure in all instances."

In the Philippines, many people fast and repent in the wrong ways. During Holy Week, some people permute the essence of fasting by abstaining only from meat, flagellate themselves by getting their backs whipped with cords, or by being nailed on a cross. They believe that by undergoing what Jesus went through, they will earn back God's graces and rewards.

Fasting is safe. According to Joel Fuhrman, M.D., in his book *Fasting and Eating for Health*, "Fasting is such a safe therapeutic intervention that many laypeople argue that daily supervision by a physician is not necessary. Although it is true that fasting is both natural and safe, all prolonged fasts must be supervised by a physician with expertise and knowledge."[29]

Fasting is also not uncomfortable. One of the biggest myths of fasting is that it causes pain, discomfort, and distress. People who regularly fast do not complain about these symptoms. Fuhrman explains, "These individuals, who exhibit uncomfortable signs early in the fast, are in greatest need of a fast. Headaches and other discomforts brought on by not eating are signs that the body has begun to withdraw from and detoxify waste products retained in body tissues."[30]

The COVID-19 pandemic has shown humanity's sheer helplessness on things unseen. These small viruses have radically changed our ways of life. But the crisis also made us realize our need to go back to God's good and eternal goals in our lives. As a result, the lockdowns made us closer to Him and our families. Like our ancestors, we need to fast, repent, and plead God to remove the deadly scourge.

The biblical doctrine of fasting and feasting is revealed and clarified when a person regularly fasts with the right motives. Fasting is the diminution of self before God by denying our flesh. Feasting comes about as a joyful celebration of God and His goodness.

Legalism and a lack of knowledge of the Scriptures have concealed the powerful biblical doctrine of fasting. We must strip away its deception and mystery and seek the excellent tool in getting near to God and achieve healing.

> *However, this kind does not go out except by prayer and fasting.*
> **—Matthew 17:21, *NKJV***

When Jesus and his disciples came into a crowd, a man approached Jesus, knelt before Him, and said, "Lord, have mercy on my son…He has seizures and is suffering greatly. He often falls into the fire or into the water. I brought him to your disciples, but they could not heal him" (vv.15-16). Jesus rebuked the demon, and the boy got healed (v.18). The disciples asked Jesus, "Why couldn't we drive it out?" (v.19). Jesus replied, "However, this kind does not go out except by prayer and fasting" (v.21, *NKJV*).

Jesus Christ emphasized the overriding value of prayer and fasting in healing and deliverance. In extreme cases such as demon-possession, deadly diseases, and chronic drug addiction and alcoholism, faith alone is sometimes not sufficient in gaining freedom from bondage. Prayer and fasting are two ultimate biblical weapons in casting out diseases, addictions, and vile spirits. Pastor Christian Wilson of Victory Outreach adds, "Fasting is vital in divine healing. Starving the flesh makes you realize more our sinful nature. It also gives you the ability to resist temptations of many kinds." Fasting works both ways—for the person undertaking the fast and to the person who is the subject of the fast. Robert Shelton adds, "Nothing enables the alcoholic, the drug fiend, the tobacco addict, to overcome his 'desire' for his accustomed poison and to return to a state of good health, as does fasting."[31]

THE LEGACY OF PASTOR HSI

Around 1851 in Shangxi, China, a lawyer and Confucian scholar named Xi Zizhi gained popularity in his village. Against the backdrop of the country's turmoil and poverty, the people came to him for mediation in lawsuits, quarrels, and other conflicts.

Despite his relative success, Xi harbored doubts about many things. He questioned life and sought answers from Confucianism, Buddhism, and Taoism. But, Xi was not satisfied. He also held a deep distrust of foreigners and Christian missionaries.

Because of his failing health and disillusionment, Xi tried smoking opium to alleviate his weakness and depression. The drug was legal in China, and his newfound habit turned into a full-blown addiction for ten years.

Xi later met David Hill, a Christian missionary, who asked him for some help in scholarly work. Despite his indifference to foreigners, Xi agreed. He then found a New Testament at Mr. Hill's home, and he became interested in Jesus and his teachings. Xi fell on his knees, wept, and accepted Jesus Christ as Lord and Savior. He heard Him cry, "My soul is exceedingly sorrowful, even unto death [and yet I realized] … He loved me and gave Himself for me."[32]

As a believer, it dawned upon him to rid himself of opium. He also realized the physical torment of withdrawal from the drug and stopped using the drug. He sacrificed and "For seven days and nights he scarcely tasted food, and was quite unable to sleep."[33]

With fasting, God delivered him from addiction. His wife also got sick, writhing in convulsions that resembled epilepsy and seemed possessed by dark spirits. Xi called for fasting and prayer in his household for three days.[34] Mrs. Xi was also healed, and her deliverance produced amazement among the villagers on what the new faith had done. She also became a Christian and helped Xi in God's work.

From the time of his conversion, Xi changed his name to Hsi Sheng-mo, meaning "conqueror of demons." Hsi called the people to follow Christ, and they gathered in Sunday services.

God called Hsi to service and started an Opium Refugee Project for opium addicts where thousands were delivered. He also treated them with his own concocted medicine. Above all, Pastor Hsi ministered them to Christianity.

Mrs. Howard Taylor wrote, "There was nothing of the ascetic about him, and yet he [Pastor Hsi] constantly resorted to fasting. This was not with any idea of mortifying the flesh, but simply with a view to the furtherance of the Gospel. He found that in times of difficulty, his prayers were more in the power of the Spirit, and more effectual, when he was fasting than otherwise."[35] Prayer and fasting were the cornerstones of Pastor Hsi's recovery and in his discipleship ministry.

> *The weapons we fight with are not the weapons of the world. On the contrary, they have divine power to demolish strongholds.*
> **—2 Corinthians 10:4**

Drug addiction is a besetting sin. Trapped in idolatry and the love of the self, drug addicts become powerless on their own. Philippians 3:19 reads: "Their destiny is destruction, their god is their stomach, and their glory is in their shame. Their mind is set on earthly things." Satan uses drugs and addictive substances to gain control of people. Addiction establishes a stronghold as the Devil constructs walled fortifications around people's hearts and minds.

A stronghold is a high and inaccessible place built for defense purposes. In Medieval times, a towering castle serves as a fortress not quickly overtaken by enemies. An addicted individual is similar to a sturdy structure not easily toppled by conventional warfare or techniques.

Battling the Enemy on our own will lead us nowhere. We need faith, willpower, and special weapons to overcome Satan's strongholds. Prayer and fasting are our ultimate weapons in demolishing Satan. The Scriptures maintain that fasting not only treats the mind and body but also delivers our trampled souls from sin and bondage. Fasting brings the issues of the drug dependent into captivity to Christ.

Most recovering meth addicts are adamant about fasting to gain recovery. They quickly complain that they wouldn't be able to bear the hunger and thirst required for fasting. Yet, they could last for days or weeks with barely enough food, water, and sleep when loaded with successive intakes of meth. The substance causes extreme highs that suppress appetite and impede sleep.

Fasting wards off temptations and cravings for drugs that could otherwise lead to relapse. First Corinthians 10:13 reads: "No temptation has overtaken you except what is common to mankind. And God is faithful; he will not let you be tempted beyond what you can bear. But when you are tempted, he will also provide a way out so that you can endure it." Fasting provides an escape hatch for drug cravings.

In addiction recovery, fasting has been proven effective in quickly wiping out addictions with its symptoms. Fasting eases, relieves, and bypasses aches and adverse symptoms of drug withdrawal. These episodes include gut-wrenching anxiety and extreme nervousness. Fasting also removes hallucinations and other adverse physical and psychological reactions during detoxification. In many cases, fasting cancels out the need for rehab.

With prayer and fasting, God can deliver addicts and alcoholics not only in the confines of a rehab or hospital, but also in their own homes. Outside of secular treatment institutions, the church plays a vital role in overseeing the physical and spiritual rejuvenation of addicts through its ministries.

In an article, "The Benefits of Fasting," Alan Goldhamer, D.C., wrote, "Addictions to drugs such as alcohol, cocaine, nicotine, and caffeine are examples where fasting can dramatically reduce the often-protracted withdrawal symptoms that prevent many people from becoming drug-free. Most people are surprised at how easy it is to quit smoking or drinking with the help of fasting."[36]

Many drug addicts and alcoholics feel condemned for wrecking their lives and that of their families. They think and declare that they are most sinful and unworthy of forgiveness. However, the message in the Book of Jonah reveals that God forgives the wicked people if they repent and surrender their unholy ways. Even their sheer momentary faith in God saved them from God's wrath on that occasion. The account of the Ninevites highlights fasting to obtain mercy and grace from God.

Addicts and alcoholics have devastated their minds and bodies brought about by the unabated use of addictive substances. Long-term users and alcoholics have compromised the vital parts and organs of their bodies—brain, heart, liver, lungs, kidneys, nerves, bones, teeth, and others.

Aside from the primary benefit of deliverance from bondage to addictive substances, fasting also cures ailments brought about by alcoholism and drug addiction. It also wards off psychological effects, like neurosis, psychosis, and paranoia.

Faith in God and the help of the Holy Spirit is essential before, during, and after a fast to unleash divine healing and deliverance. Pastor Tony Dela Paz of CCF and Penuel Homes fasts for six to seven days as part of church ministry. He said, "Fasting is a good way to be intimate with God. But you need the Holy Spirit in fasting to achieve true healing."

Addicts should repeatedly fast until a breakthrough is achieved. Fasting should be a lifetime habit of recovering or recovered addicts and alcoholics. Pastor Christian Wilson of Victory Outreach, at the height of his recovery, used to fast regularly from three days to a week with water only. Today he still fasts.

Fasting and prayer are the most potent weapons in dealing with extreme forms of spiritual and demonic tyranny. In the book

The Hidden Power of Prayer and Fasting, Manesh Chavda wrote, "Psychologists cannot help them, nor can psychiatrists. God's Word says that this kind won't even come out by a simple command in the name of Jesus Christ—they do not come out except through prayer and fasting."[37]

Many people give up when medicines and professionals fail in the treatment of addiction, sickness, or mental condition. They are unaware of fasting or hesitant to pursue this God-given remedy. But fasting is an ultimate relief for bondage, illness, and disease.

Guidelines for Recovery Fasting

PLANNING THE FAST

1. Fast for the right motives. Fasting is undertaken primarily for spiritual reasons and deliverance. It involves utmost faith in God as our Creator and Divine Healer.

2. Plan a fasting schedule. For first-time fasters, a one- to two-week fasting period is ideal for recovery. The type of fast depends on individual circumstances. Herbert Shelton wrote, "There are patients who do not need a complete fast and those who should not have a complete fast, as well as those who do not get well without a complete fast."[38]

3. The biblical doctrine of absolute fasting (without food and water) is best for healing. A person can initially undergo an absolute fast and then take on a partial fast. Thus, the two-week fast involves a combination of complete fasts, partial fasts, and intermittent breaks for food and water.

   In urgent cases, immediate fasting can be ideal for putting a sudden stop to an ongoing drug binge or drug and alcohol relapse.

4. Share your fasting intentions with your pastor, church leader, friend, or family. The primary purpose of telling somebody else is that he or she can pray and intercede for you during the fast. Informing your family about your fast would also allow them to support and guide you, which includes not expecting that you would be around them during meals. If you are working and have decided to fast for the first time or an extended period, seek a leave of absence.

5. Prepare a conducive place where there are no distractions to quiet fasting, prayer, and meditation. The home, a retreat house, or rehab is an excellent place to hold your fast.

6. Consult a medical professional if you have doubts about fasting because of specific ailments.

DURING THE FAST

1. For first-time fasters, start small by fasting for around twelve hours. The hours of fasting include hours spent while sleeping. Depending on your circumstances, you can increase the hours of fast for optimum recovery. As a whole, the fasting plan is an intermittent cycle of fasting and breaking.

2. Worship, confess, and pray to God. Seeking forgiveness from God for our addictions and sins fosters the aims of fasting. Prayer and fasting are two powerful weapons to conquer the strongholds of the Unseen Enemy. Most spiritual warfare and encounters happen during a fast.

3. Read the Bible and Christian literature. The indwelling of the Holy Spirit often manifests in times of fasting. You can also listen to Christian music during the fast.

4. If needed, rest your body or sleep during the fast.

5. Fasting during church services, ministry, or social work is encouraged. It amplifies the essence of ministry by honoring Him and helping other people.

6. Don't complain or boast about your fast, and avoid talking about it. Matthew 6:16 reads, "When you fast, do not look somber as the hypocrites do, for they disfigure their faces to show others they are fasting."

Breaking the Fast

1. The time to break the fast depends on the fasting plan and the condition of the body.

2. Break the fast into small and gradual portions. After an absolute fast, take water, juice, or some soft food. Slowly add solid food as you see fit.

3. Break the fast with praise and celebration.

Make Fasting a Regular Habit

1. Regular fasting promotes long-term healing and recovery. Depending on your circumstances, you can fast daily, once a week, or once a month. Elmer Towns wrote, "The greater the spiritual attack, the more often or the longer you should fast."[39]

2. Congregational fasting differs from personal fasting. Some churches call for fasts to all its members for individual, church, community, or national intentions.

3. Regular personal fasting means frequent intimacy with God. Like prayer, the habit of periodic fasting also fosters Christian character. It keeps in check temptations, cravings, and drug triggers that surround us every day.

4. Regular fasting promotes good physical health and enhances a positive mental outlook.

God's Covenant of Healing

The Parable of the Lost Son

*The pattern of the prodigal is: rebellion, ruin,
repentance, reconciliation, restoration.*
—Edwin Louis Cole, psychologist

In Luke 15, a young man asked his father one day, "Father, give me my share of the estate" (v.12[a]). The father agreed and divided his property between the two sons (v.12[b]).

The younger son went to a distant country, and there wasted his wealth in "wild living" (v.13[b]). After exhausting all of his money, he worked as a servant feeding pods to pigs. Desperate for food, he craved the animal feeds that the pigs were eating. Alone and depressed, he experienced starvation as no one gave him food (v.16).

He finally came to his senses and realized that there was plenty of food at home. With a repentant heart, he went back to his family. His father saw his son arriving, ran towards him, embraced, and kissed him (v.20). The son confessed, "Father, I have sinned against heaven and against you. I am no longer worthy to be called your son" (v.21).

Filled with compassion, the father ordered the servants to clothe him with the best robe, put a ring on his finger, and give him sandals (v.22). They also celebrated with a fattened calf (v.23).

The older brother heard the revelry and became angry. He asked his father, "Look! All these years I've been slaving for you and never disobeyed your orders. Yet you never gave me even a young goat so I could celebrate with my friends. But when this son of yours who has squandered your property with prostitutes comes home, you kill the fattened calf for him!" (vv.29-30).

The father replied, "You are always with me, and everything I have is yours. But we have to celebrate and be glad, because this brother of yours was dead and is alive again; he was lost and is found" (vv.31-32).

> *For everything in the world—the lust of the flesh, the lust of the eyes, and the pride of life—comes not from the Father but from the world.*
> **—1 John 2:16**

Today, a multitude of prodigal people inhabit the earth. They bear the mark of rebellion characterized by Cain and the Israelites. They go against God, family, and society by prioritizing their self-serving and vile rules of living. Drug addiction, alcoholism, promiscuity, gambling, and self-centeredness mirror humanity's departure from God's intention.

Blinded by Satan's enticements, they choose to satisfy the sinful desires of the flesh instead of pursuing a righteous and holy life. They also place more value on money, possessions, and the things of this world over God and other people.

Satan reigns supreme in many family homes. Since times past, his primary mission is to peddle sin and break apart a beautiful and loving family. He pushes Jesus Christ away from our hearts and the center of our lives.

CHRISTIAN WILSON: FROM ADDICTION TO GOD'S MISSIONS

At a young age of four in California, U.S.A., Christian first experienced the reality of pain in life. His parents were both using drugs and later got divorced. When he reached the age of seven, he began to use marijuana and alcohol because of brokenness in the home. Staying with his mother, he witnessed her openly taking meth at the house. His mother knew he was also into drugs and advised him to take them at home rather than on the streets.

During his teenage years, Christian's drug use soon graduated to meth, LSD, and other heavy substances. Because of the bruising hurt he had experienced since childhood, he questioned the existence of God. In one drug session with his friends, he was puzzled why they were reading the Bible. As a self-proclaimed atheist, he remarked, "Why bother? There is no God."

From the age of twenty-one, he was jailed several times for drug possession and crimes to satisfy his habits. He was married at the time of his arrests and had a three-year-old daughter. In jail, Christian noticed that his daughter could not cope with the family visits. She couldn't bear seeing his father locked-up. Consumed with guilt, he knew he needed to change.

At his last arrest, he befriended a drug dealer who was in his fifties and was beginning to be touched by God. Unable to read, he'd asked Christian to read the Bible for him. The older man had broken into tears. For the first time in his life, Christian had also felt God's touch in his heart.

One day, Christian attended a Bible study on the jail premises and heard a moving testimony from someone who had been with Victory Outreach Recovery Home. Frustrated with his life, he said, "Okay, God. I need help. Prove to me that you are real!"

At that moment, Christian received Jesus Christ as Lord and Savior. He became a new creation. Since then, he took no drug and alcohol, except the few times he smoked some cigarettes. The judge allowed him to visit and attend services at the Victory Outreach Church and the Recovery Home.

After his release in 1995, he went to the Recovery Home to build up his newfound faith in God. At this time, his wife divorced him because of problems in their relationship.

However, the added torments in Christian's life prodded him to go deeper into his belief in God. He steadfastly prayed, examined the Bible, and learned the rudiments of witnessing for the Lord. He also fasted for divine healing. After a year, the Lord confirmed he should serve through missions. Christian served the Lord through Victory Outreach Church and Recovery Homes.

In 1996, he went to Ireland for his first mission trip to open a Recovery Home. He also heard the good news that his meth-addicted mother had received Jesus Christ as Lord at Victory Outreach in California. She had been sober ever since.

In 1999, Victory Outreach assigned Christian to Manila for a two-year stint where he served with his fiancée—also a missionary who he'd met in the United States. Troubled by the thoughts of his daughter, he visited her and told her she loved her. With his pastor's approval, he went to the United States and adequately reconciled with his former wife and daughter.

In 2002, he married his fiancée and Victory Outreach sent them both for missions in South Africa and Indonesia. However, due to specific reasons and the pregnancy of his wife, they were re-assigned to the Philippines. In 2003, Victory Outreach ordained Christian as a pastor in San Pedro, Laguna.

Today, he serves the Lord in the Philippines. His wife remains active in the ministry and church. Their sixteen-year-old daughter is about to enter senior high school in the city. She also speaks fluent Tagalog and serves in the music ministry.

With unswerving faith in God, Pastor Christian Wilson now oversees the whole church and home recovery operations in the Philippines. He also preaches at the San Pedro church and is always within reach of the people in the community. Compassionate to the faithful and the lost, many of the city folks call Pastor Christian as their "Big Brother."

Pastor Christian Wilson has traversed the desert of loss, addiction, and desperation. But God found and transformed him into a faithful and loyal servant.

Rejoice with me; I have found my lost sheep.
—Luke 15:6[b]

A drug addict is comparable to a missing sheep that has wandered away from the shepherd's flock. Separation from God and the family also goes beyond the physical parting of the relationship. The addict may be living with his family but exists in a world of his

> *A drug addict is comparable to a missing sheep that has wandered away from the shepherd's flock.*

own. Many teenagers often consider their friends closer than their families. Kids are lost in cyberspace, spending more time in digital games and senseless social media chatter than on their studies. Drug addicts and alcoholics prefer to wallow and lose themselves in an artificial realm of bliss than face the hard realities of life.

Hedonism rules the lives of drug dependents. They become irresponsible and lose control over their lives. Driven by idolatry, they place more value on getting high or drunk than God, family, and work. Addiction soon takes its toll on their lives as they suffer the consequences of their actions for years or decades. They forfeit the love and trust of their families. They also lose their possessions, sobriety, and sanity.

Drug dependents realize the futility of continuing the addiction when they have reached rock bottom. Their besetting sins drive them to repentance as they seek the rescue and loving embrace of God and their families. Psalm 40:2 reads: "He lifted me out of the slimy pit, out of the mud and mire; he set my feet on a rock and gave me a firm place to stand."

Society also exacerbates addiction and the feeling of isolation by casting a sweeping accusation that addicts are depraved outcasts. Many people believe drug users and alcoholics are beyond rescue and reform. A famous saying goes, "Once an addict, always an addict." Because of the extreme pains addiction brings and the many failures at rehab or recovery, the family gives up and ceases all efforts and concerns for their addicted child.

Sin, brokenness, and addiction can happen to anyone and any family. Romans 3:22-23 reads: "There is no difference between Jew and Gentile, for all have sinned and fall short of the glory of God." Treating addiction as sin is the first step towards recovery.

God loves us. Jesus Christ is our God of second, third, and many chances. Despite our insurgent ways and stubbornness, God always wants us back. First John 1:9 reads: "If we confess our sins, he is faithful and just and will forgive us our sins and purify us from all unrighteousness."

His mercy abounds in grace. First Peter 5:10 reads: "And the God of all grace, who called you to his eternal glory in Christ, after you have suffered a little while, will himself restore you and make you strong, firm and steadfast." Grace is God's undeserved love for all sinners. Jesus Christ gave up His life on the cross for our sins as an ultimate display of His love for us.

Despite their rebellion, the Israelites received God's grace. Gerald May M.D. wrote:

> The desert is a laboratory where one learns something about addiction and grace. In more fullness, it is a testing ground where faith and love are tried by fire. And with grace, the desert can become a furnace of real repentance and purification where pride, complacency, and even some of the power of attachment itself can be burned away, and where the rain of God's love can bring conversion: life to the seeds of freedom.[1]

While repentance and forgiveness are the key lessons in the Parable of the Prodigal Son, the overriding message reveals the grace of God. When the son came home, the father openly stretched his arms to welcome the son without the latter asking yet for forgiveness. As the Great Shepherd, Jesus finally intervenes and breaks the yoke of addiction of a repentant addict. Second Corinthians 2:19[a] says: "My grace is sufficient for you, for my power is made perfect in weakness."

The story of the prodigal son teaches about forgiveness. Matthew 6:14-15 reads: "For if you forgive other people when they sin against you, your heavenly Father will also forgive you. But if you do not forgive others their sins, your Father will not forgive your sins." Parents must not harden their hearts because of the pain from the chronic addiction of a child. With God's grace, time will eventually come when our lost son comes back to our embrace.

Likewise, in the Parable of the Lost Sheep, Jesus Christ illustrated that heaven celebrates when a sinner repents despite the unrighteous ninety-nine others who did not repent (Luke 15:7). God often lets us roam in desolation and reach rock bottom as an excellent learning experience to reach out to Him.

The Assurance of Complete Healing

If my people, who are called by my name, will humble themselves and pray and seek my face and turn from their wicked ways, then I will hear from heaven, and I will forgive their sin and will heal their land.
—2 Chronicles 7:14

On a beautiful day, the Israelites gathered to dedicate the temple of the Lord. Led by Solomon, gladness filled their hearts. As a fitting tribute to God's supremacy, the Ark of the Covenant has finally found a permanent and magnificent structure that eluded the Israelites for many years.

After King Solomon finished praying, "fire came down from heaven and consumed the burnt offering and the sacrifices, and the glory of the Lord filled the temple" (v.1). When the Israelites saw the fire striking down, they knelt and worshipped God and said, "He is good; His love endures forever" (v.3).

The Israelites also gave tributes to the Lord. King Solomon "offered a sacrifice of twenty-two thousand heads of cattle and a hundred and twenty thousand sheep and goats" (v.5[a]).

Despite the people's idolatry and rebellion, the Lord appeared to Solomon and expressed His abounding forgiveness and healing.

God has always used fire to mark His presence and to purify His people. God spoke to Moses through a burning bush (Exodus 3). The Lord consumed the altar built by Elijah to show His preeminence over Baal, which the idolatrous Israelites worshiped (1 Kings 18). On the day of the Pentecost, the Holy Spirit appeared to the disciples in "tongues of fire" (Acts 2).

From the fall of Adam and Eve, the rebellion of our ancestors, to the multiplicity of sins in our everyday modern lives, Satan has reigned on the earthly throne. Humankind has often found itself caught up in idolatry, disobedience, war, pestilence, and sickness. But God always forgave and healed us after we repented. Jeremiah 30:17[a] reads: "But I will restore you to health and heal your wounds."

We live in dangerous times. Today the perpetuation of evil through the killing of unborn babies, the rise of occultism, the breakdown of morality exemplified by widespread promiscuity and same-sex marriage, and the scourge of addiction point to Satan. He lies, manipulates, and destroys.

Second Timothy 3:1-5 reads:

> *But mark this: There will be terrible times in the last days. People will be lovers of themselves, lovers of money, boastful, proud, abusive, disobedient to their parents, ungrateful, unholy, without love, unforgiving, slanderous, without self-control, brutal, not lovers of the good, treacherous, rash, conceited, lovers of pleasure rather than lovers of God— having a form of godliness but denying its power.*

But God never abandoned us. When God called the Israelites out of Egypt, He made a promise—a covenant of protection and healing. He said, "If you listen carefully to the Lord your God and do what is right in his eyes, if you pay attention to his commands and keep all his decrees, I will not bring on you any of the diseases

I brought on the Egyptians, for I am the Lord, who heals you" (Exodus 15:26).

God's message to the Israelites lingers today to all of human-kind. His fiery presence exhibits His hatred of people turning away from Him and seeking truth and identification from drugs. Edward Welch wrote, "We desire something in creation more than we desire the Creator."[2] God detests making addictive substances as our source of joy and contentment.

His promise remains. If we humble ourselves, seek sobriety, and repent of our sins, God would deliver us from the oppression of addiction. Nations besieged with the addiction menace can repent of its ways. In Jonah 3, the king removed his robes, wore sackcloth, and sat in ashes. The Assyrians responded to Jonah's warning, repented, and God spared them. The COVID-19 pandemic is a strong reminder that no one is safe and only God saves.

The fire of God purifies our hardened hearts and darkened souls when we turn away from our addicted and wicked ways. Throughout the passages of the Bible, faithfulness was rewarded, and betrayal was judged. Repentance, faith, and humility are hallmarks of true recovery. Pastor Christian Wilson

> *The fire of God purifies our hardened hearts and darkened souls when we turn away from our addicted and wicked ways.*

explained, "You can recover without God but only from addiction itself. But you need God for the healing of all the mistakes, issues, and pains arising out from the addiction."

The New Testament sustained the covenant of healing in the Old Testament. About 2,700 years ago, Isaiah prophesied that God would come and make the blind see, the deaf hear, the mute speak, and the crippled leap (Isaiah 35:5-6). Jesus fulfilled the prophecy of the coming of the Messiah and Divine Healer (Matthew 11:5). Isaiah 53:5 (*KJV*) foretells about divine healing: "But he was wounded for our transgressions, he was bruised for our iniquities: the chastisement of our peace was upon him; and with his stripes we are healed." We were proclaimed emancipated by the death of Jesus Christ at Calvary. From a dark realm, drug dependents can cross to the promised land of sobriety with God.

THE INDWELLING OF THE HOLY SPIRIT

But you will receive power when the Holy Spirit comes on you.
—Acts 1:8[a]

When Jesus Christ ascended into heaven, he left a band of nervous tax collectors and fishermen to carry on His message to the world. The Lord said to them, "Therefore go and make disciples of all nations, baptizing them in the name of the Father and of the Son and of the Holy Spirit, and teaching them to obey everything I have commanded you. And surely I am with you always, to the very end of the age (Matthew 28:19-20)."

The task seemed overwhelming to the apostles. How can they—a few and a meek number of lowly people make the rest of the unbelieving world turn to Christ for salvation?

God promised them a Helper. In Acts 2, the Holy Spirit arrived in glory and dwelled in them on the day of the Pentecost. God's power manifested in them. Filled with awe, they spoke in tongues (v.4) and performed many wonders and signs (v.43). The Holy Spirit enabled them for the Great Commission—the evangelization and discipleship of the world, which is the primary mission of Christians.

We need the Holy Spirit to sanctify and empower us in surmounting the challenges and hurts of life. Facing recovery on our own is difficult and complicated. The road to sobriety is filled with dangers, traps, and overwhelming challenges that make sobriety a seemingly impossible task. Godly healing means a total change of our character and ways of living. We also have to contend with the Enemy with his bag of tricks and temptations to keep us away from God's grace. Pastor Deo Salgado remarked, "The Holy Spirit rejects sinful addictive substances like drugs and alcohol."

God is spirit and truth who delivers us from sin. John 8:31 reads: "Then you will know the truth, and the truth will set you free." Rebecca DeYoung adds, "The more we understand the dynamics of sin [addiction] and the deep network of its combined forces in us, however, the more amazing we will find the grace and power promised to us to help us change."[3]

The Holy Spirit also produces in us the attributes of God and character for righteous living. Galatians 5:22-23 reads: "But the fruit of the Spirit is love, joy, peace, forbearance, kindness, goodness, faithfulness, gentleness, and self-control. Against such things there is no law." The Holy Spirit equips us to live for Christ, take charge of our lives, and expel the intrusions of Satan.

Therefore, if anyone is in Christ, the new creation has come: The old has gone, the new is here!
—2 Corinthians 5:17

The Apostle Paul epitomized one of the most significant life changes in history, going blind at the time of his conversion. As a high-ranking Roman officer, Paul led the killing of many Jews. But God called and changed him for a purpose. He became the foremost evangelist to the Gentiles and the many parts of the world. God restored his sight and his name was later changed from Saul to Paul.

We must be born again to receive the Holy Spirit. Jesus Christ emphasized in His encounter with the Pharisee Nicodemus that one must be born again with "water and spirit" to enter the Kingdom of God (v.5). John 3:3 reiterates: "Very truly I tell you, no one can see the kingdom of God unless they are born again." Water baptism signifies true repentance while the indwelling of the Holy Spirit confirms our transformation as a new creation in Christ.

Most drug addicts and alcoholics are idolaters and sinners who need God's deliverance. Scarred by many years of drug abuse, they need the anointing of the Holy Spirit to expel the vile nature of the flesh.

The Holy Spirit transforms our lives and helps us denounce our old, selfish, and sinful ways of living. Galatians 5:16 says: "So I say, walk by the Spirit, and you will not gratify the desires of the flesh." As a new creation in Christ, we also depart from worldly ways. Romans 12:2 reads: "Do not conform to the pattern of this world, but be transformed by the renewing of your mind. Then you will be able to test and approve what God's will is—his good, pleasing and perfect will." Drug dependents need to plead the Holy Spirit to purify their souls and soothe their guilt-tormented lives.

FROM BONDAGE TO HOLINESS

Be holy, because I am holy.
—1 Peter 1:16

We are called to be holy because God is holy. The word holiness came from the Hebrew word *kadash* meaning "to separate" or to "set apart." Despite our struggles and imperfections in our recovery, God wants us to aim for sanctification. By removing the power and growth of sin in our lives, sanctification leads us to a life designed by God.

We are also justified when God removed the penalty and guilt of our sins. He reversed our ungodly nature of addiction to righteousness through the atoning sacrifice of Jesus Christ. Justification happens the moment we trust Jesus as our Lord and Savior. Justification declares the addict righteous, while sanctification makes him upright. We are washed clean by the blood of Christ.

Sobriety and recovery will not make us perfect and do not make us immune from pain in life. Sometimes we fall into relapse and sin. The hallmark of recovery is to stand the moment we fall. Like a long-distance runner, we should not stay fallen on the ground for a long time. Instead, we must immediately stand and join the race. Relapse does not necessarily mean total failure. Winston Churchill once said, "Success consists of going from failure to failure without loss of enthusiasm."

Maintaining a steady walk with Christ is one of the most challenging tests addicts face in sobriety. Paved with potholes, stop signs, and dangerous curves, the recovery road is hard to traverse without God. The Enemy still roams around like a roaring lion, ready to entrap us (1 Peter 5:8). We need to call on God for resiliency and guidance every day.

Despite the frailty of our sobriety, we must trust God amid all the circumstances around us. Romans 8:28 reads: "And we know that in all things God works for the good of those who love him, who have been called according to his purpose"

God calls us to lead lives of purity and holiness because He calls us into a relationship with Him. Virtue is not necessarily a life of asceticism where we deprive ourselves of pleasure designed and provided by God. But we should reject sin, addiction, deception, and vile desires that come from the Enemy. Holiness is a life of joy and righteous living in Christ.

Our joy is complete when we know that God is in control. Freedom is achieved when we are liberated from past hurts and become untroubled with past sins. Recovery means keeping our feet on the ground as our minds are focused on eternity.

Jesus Christ: The Great Healer and Messiah

Jesus went through all the towns and villages, teaching in their synagogues, proclaiming the good news of the kingdom and healing every disease and sickness.
—Matthew 9:35

The roads led to Jericho. Its balmy climate, palm trees, and clean water springs made the city the home of the rich. As a strategic crossroad of ancient Palestine, many traders, pilgrims, and armies passed through this vital route. Jericho was a natural oasis for beggars.

Bartimaeus, a blind man, belonged to this group of destitute and hopeless crowd. When he heard that Jesus was leaving the city with the disciples, he shouted, "Son of David, have mercy on me!" (Mark 10:47-48). Jesus called him and said, "Your faith has healed you" (v.52[a]). Immediately the blind man received his sight and followed Jesus (v.52[b]).

As the Messiah, Jesus Christ proclaimed the Kingdom of God and advanced the Gospel through divine healing, miracles, and wonders. The Bible has always shown that God graciously healed lepers, the blind, the sick, and the demon-possessed. As a fitting testimony to His godly attribute, Jesus also raised Lazarus from the dead (John 11:38-44) and turned water into wine (John 2:1-10). Divine healing is a miraculous gift from God and a reminder of God's promise of the most important things to come in His reign.

The era of miracles is not over. The coming of the rains, the birth of an anticipated baby, and the turning of a hardened drug addict into a Christian are miracles that happen every day. The change of a fallen addict or alcoholic to a holy creature is an astonishing affirmation of God's power. If Jesus Christ was able to make Bartimaeus and many others see, He could also liberate drug dependents and alcoholics from the yoke of addiction.

Divine restoration is a supernatural act from our Almighty God. Gerald May, M.D. wrote, "Humanity's struggle with addiction is a journey through the wilderness of idolatry where temptations, trials, and deprivations abound, but where God's grace is always available to guide, protect, empower, and transform us."[4]

Jesus Christ stressed repentance and faith as the two pillars of divine healing. Faith obliterates God's wrath while repentance earns back His grace. Author Betty Dvorak writes, "Healing is part of our birthright when we receive Jesus Christ as our Lord and Savior."[5] His incarnation on earth was to free humanity from the condemnation of sin, save our souls, and give us eternal life. All can conquer illness, addiction, and death because Jesus shed His blood for humankind.

I consider that our present sufferings are not worth comparing with the glory that will be revealed in us.
—Romans 8:18

Sickness, disease, and death primarily came into the world through the fall of the human race (Genesis 3). Romans 5:12 reads, "Therefore, just as sin entered the world through one man, and death through sin, and in this way, death came to all people, because all sinned." Dr. Allen Ross, a university professor, wrote, "In sum, the Scripture teaches that all sickness, disease, pain, contamination, pollution, and death is the result of the presence of sin in the world."[6]

The bondage to addictive substances is but one of the many symptoms and consequences of our fallen, sinful state. As long as we live under our earthly tents, addiction and sin will never be wiped out from the face of the world. Drug dependency is an arena where Satan continues to challenge the preeminent authority of God. He uses drugs as primary baits in deceiving us on a massive scale.

Comparable to the Israelites and the prophets of ancient times, God lets us loose in the wilderness of pain, degradation, and addiction. God uses trials and sufferings to remind us of our mortality and innate need for God. Romans 5:3-4 reads: "Not only so, but we also glory in our sufferings, because we know that suffering produces perseverance; perseverance, character; and character, hope."

He will wipe every tear from their eyes. There will be no more death or mourning or crying or pain, for the old order of things has passed away.
—Revelation 21:4

The world is careening towards Armageddon and self-destruction. People are tearing down the environment, pursuing obscene wealth, engaging in genetic manipulation, and other immoral, ungodly pursuits that violate God's will and purpose in our lives.

The glorification of the self and the constant goal of satisfying one's appetites and bellies have become the daily object of everyday living. We live in a modern-day Sodom and Gomorrah where God is abandoned, and the pursuit of pleasure is a constant aim. Our thirst for God has diminished as the Judeo-Christian ethics that guided our daily lives for centuries have loosened. Strange, vile ways and habits consume our daily lives. We spend more time in selfish pursuits of escapism through drugs and digital space than spending more time with our families. Many people glamorize addiction and degrade God and His Word. We abuse our bodies with drugs—the temple of the Holy Spirit—in utter disregard of God's holy design.

Many people use drugs and alcohol to seek artificial pleasure and distort the truth. Augustine once said, "My sin was this, that I looked for pleasure, beauty, and truth not in [God] but in myself and his other creatures, and the search led me instead to pain, confusion, and error." Drug dependents look at the world as one big pharmacy where a pill is available to relieve any ailment—physical, mental, and spiritual. An anonymous quote reads, "In the 1960s, people took acid [LSD] to make the world weird. Now the world is weird, and people take Prozac [an antidepressant] to make it normal."

Hurts and grief are part of our lives. Mindful of our mortality, we will all soon depart from this life. But with God, we can find joy and contentment on earth. Guilty of spiritual blindness, drug dependents can finally find freedom in Christ. Pastor Tony Dela Paz remarked, "Addicts need Jesus to fill the void and the lack of purpose in their lives." We need to pant for God as the deer pants for water.

Jesus Christ will return, but at this time, for good and all eternity. As the promised Messiah, Jesus showed us the way to eternal life and the meaning of the cross and resurrection. After saving humanity from eternal damnation and bearing the sins of all humanity, He will come back to restore Paradise and remove all the pain, suffering, and death. Ephesians 2:8-9 reads: "For it is by grace you have been saved, through faith—and this is not from yourselves, it is the gift of God—not by works, so that no one can boast." As the Last Adam, Jesus is to become our Sovereign Ruler in the promised Kingdom of Heaven.

I am the Lord that healeth thee.
—Exodus 15:26[b]

Similar to the lepers in the Bible, drug addicts and alcoholics are outcasts in the modern world. They have lost their honor, possessions, jobs, health, and the love and trust of their families and society. However, Jesus Christ is our God of hope and many chances in life.

The Bible debunks the popular notion that recovery from addiction is impossible. In the recovery movement, there is a groundswell of support that God heals, and faith is essential for lasting sobriety.

God is always willing to heal. A leper approached Jesus, fell on the ground, and begged Jesus, "Lord, if you are willing, you can make me clean" (Luke 5:12). Jesus touched the man and replied, "I am willing" (v.13[a]). The disease immediately left the man (v.13[b]). Despite our idolatry, rebellion, sins, and addiction, God loves us.

The question is: Are we eager to be healed? No amount of rehab or any intervention can help us change if we are not willing to leave drugs. Recovery is an utmost effort and willingness to remove addiction from our lives by changing our deviant lifestyle and behavior. Redemption, on the other hand, involves the transformation of our old and addicted self to a new creation, made in the image of God. Divine healing is a collaboration between God and man.

Redemption is more than recovery. While recovery can be achieved in rehab, a facility of choice, at home, or with the help of a support group, redemption only happens in the inner sanctum of the soul. Ephesians 1:7 reads: "In Him we have redemption through his blood, the forgiveness of sins, in accordance with the riches of God's grace."

Jesus Christ is our Good Shepherd. He keeps us away from evil, delivers us from sin, and leads us to liberation. The pains of the past remain in our memories. However, they no longer cause us to shed a tear or bring anguish in the present. God's promise in Ezekiel 36:26 reads: "I will give you a new heart and put a new spirit in you; I will remove from you your heart of stone and give you a heart of flesh." Instead, we are always filled with joy and hope. If we remain faithful, Jesus also promised an abundant life (John 10:10).

Taking drugs for mind-altering purposes defeats God's intent and design for His creation. We are made to be content with God. Seeking joy from substances is an abominable and massive deception by Satan. We ought to worship the Creator rather than His creation.

The baffling transformation of an addict into a new, holy creation of Christ is an unyielding testimony that God is our Great Healer. Divine deliverance means the banishment of idolatry and wickedness in our hearts and giving way to our Sovereign Master, who crowns us with a renewed and victorious life.

The road to recovery and redemption is long and rough. But with God, we're on the right path.

Endnotes

Chapter 1

[1]   Edward T. Welch, *Addictions: A Banquet in the Grave* (New Jersey: P&R Publishing Company, 2001). p. 35.

[2]   "Lexicon of alcohol and drug terms," Management of Substance Abuse. World Health Organization, Accessed May 5, 2017, http://www.who.int/substance_abuse/terminology/who_lexicon/en/.

[3]   "Letters of Edgar Allan Poe," Eapoe.org, Accessed April 5, 2016, https://www.eapoe.org/works/letters/p4811030.htm.

[4]   Barbara Brown Taylor, *Home by Another Way,* (Cambridge MA: Cowley Publications), p.67.

[5]   Paramabandhu Groves and Roger Farmer, "Buddhism and Addictions," Harwood Academic Publishers Gmbh, 1994, Accessed March 5, 2018, http://www.sbu.net/uploads/files/Buddhism%20and%20addictions.pdf.

[6]   Maya Angelou, "BrainyQuote," BrainyQuote.com, Accessed July 14, 2016, http://www.brainyquote.com/quotes/quotes/m/mayaangelo634519.html.

[7]   Ruben Castaneda, U.S. News and World Report, April, 2017. https://health.usnews.com/wellness/articles/2017-04-24/why-do-alcoholics-and-addicts-relapse-so-often.

[8]   Brenda Vallarta, "PNP data shows number of crimes down 10 percent," GMA News Online, June 30, Accessed February 28, 2018, http://www.gmanetwork.com/news/news/nation/616449/pnp-data-shows-number-of-crimes-down-10-percent/story/.

[9]   "Criminal Justice Drug Facts," National Institute on Drug Abuse, Accessed February 7,2020, https://www.drugabuse.gov/publications/drugfacts/criminal-justice.

[10]   Charlotte Davis Kasl, *Many Roads, One Journey.* (New York: Harper Collins Publishers, 1992).

[11]   "What is Nicotine Withdrawal?" Accessed May 1, 2017, https://www.webmd.com/smoking-cessation/understanding-nicotine-withdrawal-symptoms#2.

[12]   Nikki Seay, "Robin Williams Dead from Apparent Suicide," Rehabs.com, August 12, 2014, Accessed February 20, 2018, https://www.rehabs.com/tragedy-strikes-robin-williams-dead-from-apparent-suicide.

[13]   "Fact Sheet," Media Center, World Health Organization, accessed February 14, 2020, https://www.who.int/news-room/fact-sheets/detail/tobacco.

14 "What's In a Cigarette?" American Lung Association, August 20, 2019, Accessed February 24, 2018, https://www.lung.org/quit-smoking/smoking-facts/whats-in-a-cigarette.

15 "Cigarettes 'cut life by 11 minutes," BBC News, December 31, 1999, Accessed March 13, 2018, http://news.bbc.co.uk/2/hi/health/583722.stm.

16 "Alcohol," World Health Organization, 2018, Accessed August 26, 2020,https://www.who.int/news-room/fact-sheets/detail/alcohol

17 James R. Milam and Katherine Ketcham, *Under the Influence: A Guide to the Myths and Realities of Alcoholism*,(New York: Madrona Publishers, 1981), p.4..

18 "Understanding the Epidemic," Centers for Disease Control and Prevention, March 2020, Accessed October 4, 2020, https://www.cdc.gov/drugoverdose/epidemic/index.html.

19 "The drugs found in Michael Jackson's body after he died," BBC Newsbeat, November 8, 2011, accessed December 16, 2016, http://www.bbc.co.uk/newsbeat/article/15634083/the-drugs-found-in-michael-jacksons-body-after-he-died.

20 Ralph Ellis and Sara Sidner, "Prince died of accidental overdose of opioid fentanyl, medical examiner says," CNN Health, updated June 3, 2016, Accessed February 14, 2020, https://edition.cnn.com/2016/06/02/health/prince-death-opioid-overdose/index.html.

21 World Drug Report, Executive Summary, (Vienna: United Nations Office on Drugs and Crime), p.19.

22 Rebecca A. Clay, "Substance Abuse & Suicide: White Paper Explores Connection," Samhsa News, January-February 2009, Accessed February 20, 2018, https://archive.samhsa.gov/samhsaNewsletter/Volume_17_Number_1/SubstanceAbuseAndSuicide.aspx.

23 *World Drug Report*, United Nations Office on Drugs and Crime, Accessed August 26, 2020, https://www.unodc.org/unodc/en/frontpage/2019/June/world-drug-report-2019_-35-million-people-worldwide-suffer-from-drug-use-disorders-while-only-1-in-7-people-receive-treatment.html.

24 "Global Overview of Drug Demand and Supply," United Nations Office on Drugs and Crime, p.21, Accessed March 13, 2018, https://www.unodc.org/wdr2017/field/Booklet_2_HEALTH.pdf.

25 2019 World Drug Report, Global Overview of Drug Demand and Supply, p.19, Accessed August 26, 2020.

26 Global Study on Homicide, Executive Summary, (Vienna: United Nations Office on Drug and Crime, p.29).

27 Euan McKirdy, "Life inside the Philippines' most overcrowded jail," CNN International, August 23, 2016, Accessed August 27, 2016, http://edition.cnn.com/2016/08/21/asia/philippines-overcrowded-jail-quezon-city/.

28 Republic of the Philippines, "Republic Act 9165 Dangerous Drugs Act, Section 11," 2002.

29 Joe Donatelli, "The World's Scariest Places to be Busted For Drugs," The Fix, April 11, 2011, Accessed November 15, 2016, https://www.thefix.com/content/worst-places-be-caught-drugs?page=all.

30 Marvin Perry, *A History of the World: Revised Edition*, (Boston: Mifflin Company, p.569).

31 Welch, *Addictions: A Banquet in the Grave*, p. 53.

32 Alfred W. Tozer, *The Pursuit of God*, (Massachusetts: Wyath North Publishing LLC).

Chapter Two

1 Josephine Vivaldo, "Anthony Hopkins Talks about Finding God, Alcohol Addiction," The Christian Post, February 7, 2011, Accessed December 5, 2017, https://www.christianpost.com/news/anthony-hopkins-talks-about-finding-god-alcohol-addiction-48873/.

2 *World Drug Report 2019* - Booklet 2, (Vienna: United Nations Office on Drugs and Crime, p.11), accessed February 14, 2020, https://wdr.unodc.org/wdr2019/en/drug-demand-and-supply.html

3 "Marijuana Drug Facts." National Institute on Drug Abuse, drugabuse.gov, February 2018 (revised), Accessed February 21, 2018, https://www.drugabuse.gov/publications/drugfacts/marijuana

4 Robert DuPont, "Marijuana Has Proven to Be a Gateway Drug," The New York Times, updated April 26, 2016, Accessed January 23, 2018, https://www.nytimes.com/roomfordebate/2016/04/26/is-marijuana-a-gateway-drug/marijuana-has-proven-to-be-a-gateway-drug.

5 2019 *World Drug Report 2019*, Booklet 2, p.13, Accessed October 6, 2020. https://wdr.unodc.org/wdr2019/prelaunch/WDR19_Booklet_2_DRUG_DEMAND.pdf.

6 "History of Cocaine and Crack Use," intheknowzone.com, Education Specialty Publishing, Accessed February 20, 2018, http://www.intheknowzone.com/substance-abuse-topics/cocaine/history.html.

7 "History of Coca," Drug Enforcement Agency, Accessed December 8, 2015, https://www.deamuseum.org/ccp/coca/history.html.

8 "History of opium," Drug Enforcement Agency, Accessed August 8, 2015, https://www.deamuseum.org/ccp/opium/history.html.

9 "World Drug Report 2020, Booklet 2, p. 15. Accessed October 7, 2020 https://wdr.unodc.org/wdr2020/field/WDR20_Booklet_2.pdf.

[10] "Synthetic Drugs in East and South-East Asia," United Nations Office on Drugs and Crime, Accessed August 26, 2020, p. 1 https://www.unodc.org/documents/southeastasiaandpacific/Publications/2019/2019_The_Challenge_of_Synthetic_Drugs_in_East_and_SEA.pdf.

[11] *Ibid.* P. 3.

[12] History of Meth, August 2018, Accessed August 26, 2020, https://www.history.com/topics/crime/history-of-meth.

[13] "History of Methamphetamine," Foundation for a Drug Free World, Accessed March 13, 2018, http://www.drugfreeworld.org/drugfacts/crystalmeth/history-of-methamphetamine.html.

[14] World Drug Report 2020, Booklet 2, p. 15. Accessed October 7, 2020 https://wdr.unodc.org/wdr2020/field/WDR20_Booklet_2.pdf

[15] Barry Meier, "In Guilty Plea, OxyContin Maker to Pay $600 Million," The New York Times, May 10, 2007, Accessed March 13, 2018, http://www.nytimes.com/2007/05/10/business/11drug-web.html.

[16] Neil T. Anderson, *The Bondage Breaker*, (Oregon: Harvest House Publishers, 1990), p.9.

[17] "Hitler the drug addict: How he used a cocktail of drugs including cocaine to make him a 'Nazi superman'" Mail Online, August 24, 2013, Accessed February 6, 2018, http://www.dailymail.co.uk/news/article-2401242/Hitler-drug-addict-Fuhrer-used-cocktail-drugs-make-Nazi-superman.html.

[18] 2019 World Drug Report, Executive Summary, (Vienna: United Nations Office on Drugs and Crime), pp.7-8.

[19] Welch, *Addictions: A Banquet in the Grave*, p. 55.

Chapter Three

[1] Charles Colson with Ellen Vaughn, *Against the Night: Living in the New Dark Ages*, (Michigan: Servant, 1991).

[2] Neil T. Anderson, *Victory over the Darkness*, (California: Regal Books, 1990), p.196.

[3] Rebecca Konyndyk DeYoung, *Glittering Vices*, (Grand Rapids, MI: Brazos Press), p.21.

[4] Al J. Mooney, M.D., Arlene Eisenberg, and Howard Eisenberg, *The Recovery Book*, (New York: Workman Publishing, 1992), pp.311-312.

[5] John White, *Money Isn't God*, (Illinois: Intervarsity Press, 1993), p.192.

[6] "The Federal Response to the Opioid Crisis," Center for Disease Prevention and Control, October 5, 2017, Accessed February 14, 2020, https://www.cdc.gov/washington/testimony/2017/t20171005.htm.

Chapter Four

[1] Harriet Sherwood, "Non-believers turn to prayer in a crisis," The Guardian, January 14, 2018, Accessed February 14, 2020, https://www.theguardian.com/world/2018/jan/14/half-of-non-believers-pray-says-poll.

[2] Ed Stetzer, "Idolatry is Alive Today," Christianity Today, October 8, 2014, Accessed February 8, 2020, https://www.christianitytoday.com/edstetzer/2014/october/idolatry-is-alive-today-why-modern-church-leaders-still-fig.html.

[3] Anderson, *Victory Over the Darkness*, p. 112.

[4] Dale Matthews, M.D. with Connie Clark, *The Faith Factor*, (London: Penguin Books, 1998), p. 27.

[5] "Believers consume fewer drugs than atheists," ScienceDaily, October 3, 2013, Accessed February 14, 2020, https://www.sciencedaily.com/releases/2013/10/131003093041.htm.

[6] Lee Strobel, *The Case for Faith*, (Michigan: Zondervan, 2000), p. 12.

[7] *Ibid.*, p.315

Chapter Five

[1] Kara Gavin, "Spirituality Increases as Alcoholics Recover," The University of Michigan News Service, Accessed February 22, 2019, http://ur.umich.edu/0607/Mar19_07/06.shtml.

[2] Gerald May, M.D., *Addiction and Grace*, HarperCollins e-books, p. 131.

[3] Charles Stanley, *Enter His Gates,* (Nashville: Thomas Nelson, Inc., 2002), p.50.

[4] Michael Lipka, "5 Facts About Prayer," Pew Research Center, Accessed February 27, 2019, http://www.pewresearch.org/fact-tank/2016/05/04/5-facts-about-prayer/.

[5] Jeff Levin, PhD, *God, Faith, and Health*, (New York: John Wiley & Sons, Inc., 2001), p.77.

[6] Anderson, *The Bondage Breaker*, p. 22.

[7] "Duke Study: Attending Religious Service May Improve Immune Status," Duke Health, Updated January 2016, Accessed August 30, 2020, https://corporate.dukehealth.org/news-listing/duke-study-attending-religious-service-may-improve-immune-status.

[8] Levin, *God, Faith, and Health*, p.89

[9] *Ibid.*, p. 90

[10] Anderson, *Victory Over the Darkness*, p. 110

Chapter Six

[1] Ruben Castaneda, U.S. News and World Report, Accessed February 15, 2020, https://health.usnews.com/wellness/articles/2017-04-24/why-do-alcoholics-and-addicts-relapse-so-often.

[2] "Is Addiction Just a Matter of Choice?" ABC News, January 7, 2006, Accessed February 15, 2020 https://abcnews.go.com/US/story?id=90688&page=1.

[3] Viktor Frankl, *Man's Search for Meaning*, (Boston: Beacon Press, 1992), p.75.

[4] Christopher Ringwald, *The Soul of Recovery*, (New York: Oxford University Press, 2002), p.162.

[5] Marc Lewis, Ph.D, *The Biology of Desire*, (New York: Public Affairs, Perseus Books Group, 2015), p.21.

[6] Carl Hart, "As With Other Problems, Class Affects Addiction," The New York Times, Accessed October 4, 2016, http://www.nytimes.com/roomforde-bate/2014/02/10/what-is-addiction/as-with-other-problems-class-affects-ad-diction.

[7] DeYoung, *Glittering Vices*, p. 81.

[8] May, *Addiction and Grace*, p. 47.

[9] Tim Hansel, *Holy Sweat*, (Dallas: Word Publishing, 1987), p.73.

[10] Bruce Epperly, *God's Touch*, (Kentucky: Westminster John Knox Press, 2001), p.145.

[11] "Mental Health and Substance Use Disorders," March 22, 2019, Accessed August 8, 2019, https://www.mentalhealth.gov/what-to-look-for/mental-health-substance-use-disorders.

[12] Andrew Newberg, M.D. and Mark Robert Waldman, *How God Changes Your Brain*, (New York: Ballantine Books, 2009), p.4.

[13] Marc Lewis, *The Biology of Desire*, (New York: Public Affairs, 2015), p.10.

[14] DeYoung, *Glittering Vices*, p.15.

[15] Michael Kuhar, Ph.D., *The Addicted Brain*, (New Jersey: Pearson Education Inc., 2012), p.88.

[16] Morteza Kaleghi,Ph.D. with Constance Loizos,2008, *Free from Addiction*, New York:Palgrave Macmillan, 2008, p. 137

[17] "Drugs, Brains, and Behavior: The Science of Addiction," National Institute on Drug Abuse, July 2018, Accessed November 13, 2009, https://www.drugabuse.gov/publications/drugs-brains-behavior-science-addiction/treat-ment-recovery.

[18] Kaleghi, Ph.D. with Constance Loizos, *Free from Addiction*, p. 127

[19] "Total Alcohol Abstinence vs. Moderation: Which One Wins in the End?" American Addiction Centers, Accessed November 16, 2019, https://drugabuse.com/total-alcohol-abstinence-vs-moderation-which-one-wins-in-the-end.

Chapter Seven

1   May, *Addiction and Grace*, p. 133.

2   Mike Fabarez, *Lifelines for Tough Times*, (Oregon: Harvest House Publishers, 2014), p.16.

3   Wong Ding Mao, *A Stone Made Smooth*, (Singapore: Berean Publishers, 1981), p.51.

4   Gene Heyman, *Addiction: A Disorder of Choice*, (Cambridge: Harvard University Press, 2009), p.76.

5   Nancy Leigh DeMoss with Lawrence Kimbrough, *Choosing Gratitude*, (Chicago: Moody Publishers, 2009), p.183.

6   Alfred Tozer, *The Pursuit of God*, (Harrisburg, PA: Christian Publications Inc., 1948).

7   Epperly, *God's Touch*, p. 150.

Chapter Eight

1   Rachael Bletchly and Amanda Killelea, "Adolf Hitler's Drug Habit Revealed," Mirror, August 2013, Accessed October 11, 2019, https://www.mirror.co.uk/news/world-news/adolf-hitlers-drug-habit-revealed-2214040.

2   Barbara McCarthy, "A Brief History of War and Drugs," November 25 2016, Accessed February 18, 2020, https://www.aljazeera.com/indepth/features/2016/10/history-war-drugs-vikings-nazis-161005101505317.html.

3   Von Andreas Ulrich, "Hitler's Drugged Soldiers," Spiegel International, 2005, Accessed October 11, 2019, https://www.spiegel.de/international/the-nazi-death-machine-hitler-s-drugged-soldiers-a-354606.html.

4   Henry Murray, M.D., "Analysis of the Personality of Adolf Hitler," October 1943, Accessed October 9, 2019, https://www.cia.gov/library/readingroom/docs/CIA-RDP78-02646R000100030002-2.pdf.

5   C. S. Lewis, *Mere Christianity*, (New York: Collier/Macmillan, 1960), p. 121-122.

6   DeYoung, *Glittering Vices*, p. 18.

7   Anderson, *The Bondage Breaker*, p. 36.

8   Ringwald, *The Soul of Recovery*, p.33

9   "Researchers Identify Alcoholism Subtypes," National Institutes of Health, Accessed October 12, 2019, https://www.nih.gov/news-events/news-releases/researchers-identify-alcoholism-subtypes.

10   Donna Bush, Ph.D., F-ABFT and Rachel Lipari, Ph.D., "Substance Use and Substance Use Disorder by Industry," Substance Abuse and Mental Health

Services Administration, April 16, 2015, Accessed October 19, 2019, https://www.samhsa.gov/data/sites/default/files/report_1959/ShortReport-1959.html.

[11] "Opioid Overdose Crisis," National Institute on Drug Abuse, May 2020, Accessed July 9, 2020, https://www.drugabuse.gov/drugs-abuse/opioids/opioid-overdose-crisis.

[12] Martin Nicolaus, *Empowering your Sober Self,* (San Francisco: Jossey-Baas, a Wiley Imprint, 2009), pp.34-35

[13] Rupert Wingfield-Hayes, "Why Does Japan Have Such a High Suicide Rate?" BBC News - Tokyo, July 3, 2015, Accessed February 18, 2020, https://www.bbc.com/news/world-33362387.

[14] "Opioid Overdose," August 2020, World Health Organization, Accessed October 11, 2020, https://www.who.int/news-room/fact-sheets/detail/opioid-overdose.

Chapter Nine

[1] Kasl, *Many Roads, One Journey,* p.105

[2] Harold C. Urschell III, MD, *Healing the Addicted Brain,* (Illinois: Sourcebooks, Inc., 2009), pp.52-53.

[3] Anderson, *Bondage Breaker,* p. 22

[4] Manesh, Chavda, *The Hidden Power of Prayer and Fasting,* (Shippensburg, PA: Destiny Image Publishers, 1998), p.124.

Chapter Ten

[1] Heyman, *Addiction: A Disorder of Choice,* p. 67.

[2] Epperly, *God's Touch,* p. 38.

[3] *Ibid.,* p. 83.

[4] Kaleghi, *Free from Addiction,* pp.138-139.

[5] Ringwald, *The Soul of Recovery,* p.31.

[6] Rachel Lipari, Ph.D. and Struther Van Horn, "Children Living with Parents who have a Substance Use Disorder," The CBHSQ Report, August 2017, Accessed November 27, 2019, https://www.samhsa.gov/data/sites/default/files/report_3223/ShortReport-3223.html.

[7] Paul C. Vitz, "The Psychology of Atheism," Department of Psychology, New York University, Accessed December 25, 2019, http://www.leaderu.com/truth/1truth12.html.

8   "One Out of Five Pinoy Marriages is Annulled," GMA News Online, February 21, 2014, Accessed November 29, 2019, https://www.gmanetwork.com/news/lifestyle/content/349518/one-out-of-five-pinoy-marriages-is-annulled/story/.

9   Erika Joy Murcia, "'I Now Pronounce you: DIVORCED," Business World, January 22, 2019, Accessed February 18, 2020, https://www.bworldonline.com/i-now-pronounce-you-divorced/.

10   Jonathan Kaiman and Sunshine De Leon, "The Philippines has 1.8 Million Abandoned Children. Here's What Keeps Many from Adoption," Los Angeles Times, May 28, 2016, Accessed November 29, 2019, https://www.latimes.com/world/asia/la-fg-philippines-orphans-adv-snap-story.html.

11   Steve Doughty, "Nation of Broken Families," Mail Online, June 25, 2010, Accessed February 18, 2020, https://www.dailymail.co.uk/news/article-1289399/Nation-broken-families-One-children-lives-single-parent-stepmum-dad.html.

12   "Total Number of OFWs Estimated at 2.3 Million," Philippine Statistics Authority, April 30, 2019. Accessed February 18, 2020, https://psa.gov.ph/statistics/survey/labor-and-employment/survey-overseas-filipinos.

13   Kalehgi, *Free from Addiction*, p. 152.

14   John Vawter (Ed.), *Hit by a Ton of Bricks*, (Arkansas: Life Publishing, 2003), p.206.

15   "The Global Religious Landscape," Pew Research Center, December 18, 2012, Accessed December 2, 2019, https://www.pewforum.org/2012/12/18/global-religious-landscape-exec/.

16   Joseph A. Califano, Jr., "Religion, Science and Substance Abuse," February, 2002, Accessed October 12, 2020, https://www.americamagazine.org/issue/360/article/religion-science-and-substance-abuse.

17   Ibid.

18   Levin, *God, Faith, and Health*, p. 3.

19   May, *Addiction and Grace*, p. 146.

Chapter Eleven

1   Julian Ryall, "Japan to introduce internet 'fasting camps' for addicted kids," *The Telegraph*, August 27, 2013, Accessed February 19, 2020, https://www.telegraph.co.uk/news/worldnews/asia/japan/10267303/Japan-to-introduce-internet-fasting-camps-for-addicted-kids.html.

2   Arthur Wallis, *God's Chosen Fast,* (Fort Washington PA: CLC Publications, 1968), p.77.

[3]   Lindy Lowry, "Open doors Calls for 24-hour Prayer, Fasting," Open Doors, June 6, 2018, Accessed January 10, 2020, https://www.opendoorsusa.org/christian-persecution/stories/leading-up-to-u-s-north-korea-summit-open-doors-calls-for-24-hour-prayer-fasting-on-june-11/.

[4]   Wallis, *God's Chosen Fast*, p.14.

[5]   Elmer L. Towns, *Fasting for Spiritual Breakthrough*, (California: Regal Books, 1996), p.46.

[6]   Chavda, *The Hidden Power of Prayer and Fasting*, p. 36.

[7]   Denise Winterman, "Breakfast, Lunch, and Dinner: Have We always Eaten them?" BBC News Magazine, November 15, 2012, Accessed January 15, 2020, https://www.bbc.com/news/magazine-20243692.

[8]   John Piper, *A Hunger for God*, (Illinois: Crossway Books, 1997),p.14.

[9]   Towns, *Fasting for Spiritual Breakthrough*, pp.27- 28.

[10]   Cherill Hicks, "Why Fasting is now Back in Fashion," The Telegraph, April 2015, Accessed February 19, 2020, https://www.telegraph.co.uk/lifestyle/11524808/The-history-of-fasting.html.

[11]   Beach Combing, "Fasting Against God in Medieval Ireland," August 23, 2010, Accessed January 10, 2020, http://www.strangehistory.net/2010/08/23/fasting-against-god-in-medieval-ireland.

[12]   Gordon Cove, "Fasting Strengthens the Intensity of Prayer," Accessed January 14, 2020, https://heraldofhiscoming.org/index.php/152-past-issues/2010/may10/1882-fasting-strengthens-the-intensity-of-prayer-5-10.

[13]   *Ibid*.

[14]   Mischler, Ælfwine, "Fasting, an Introduction," Why Islam, July 2, 2014, Accessed January 14, 2020, https://www.whyislam.org/on-faith/introduction-to-fasting/.

[15]   "Martin Luther's Spiritual Practice was Key to Reformation," The Conversation, October 25, 2017, Accessed January 14, 2020, https://theconversation.com/martin-luthers-spiritual-practice-was-key-to-the-success-of-the-reformation-83340.

[16]   Cove, *Fasting Strengthens the Intensity of Prayer*.

[17]   *Ibid*.

[18]   "Prayer and Fasting," Campus Crusade for Christ, Accessed January 14, 2020, https://www.cru.org/us/en/train-and-grow/spiritual-growth/fasting/prayer-and-fasting.html.

[19]   Audrey H. Ensminger, N. E. Ensminger, James E. Konlande, and John R. K. Robson, *Food and Nutrition Encyclopedia 2nd Edition*, (Florida: CRC Press, 1994), p.683.

[20-]   Chavda, *The Hidden Power of Prayer and Fasting*, p. 132.

[21]   Wallis, *God's Chosen Fast*, p. 21.

22 Herbert T. Shelton, *The Science and Fine Art of Fasting*, The Hygienic System: Volume III, (Florida: Natural Hygiene Press, 1978), p.173.

23 Joel Fuhrman, M.D., *Fasting and Eating for Health,* (New York: St. Martin's Press, 1995), p. 128.

24 "Fasting for Health and Longevity," Blue Zones, Accessed January 16, 2020, https://www.bluezones.com/2018/10/fasting-for-health-and-longevity-nobel-prize-winning-research-on-cell-aging/.

25 Shelton, *The Science and Fine Art of Fasting*, p. 251.

26 Towns, *Fasting for Spiritual Breakthrough*, p.131.

27 Shelton, *The Science and Fine Art of Fasting*, p.173

28 Wallis, *God's Chosen Fast*, p. 32.

29 Fuhrman, *Fasting and Eating for Health*, p.145.

30 *Ibid.*, p. 21.

31 Shelton, *The Science and Fine Art of Fasting*, p. 363.

32 Mrs. Howard Taylor, *Pastor Hsi: Confucian Scholar and Christian,* (London: China Inland Mission, 1900), p.47.

33 *Ibid.*, p. 51

34 *Ibid.*, p. 69

35 *Ibid.*, p. 240

36 Alan D.C. Goldmayer, "The Benefits of Fasting," T. Colin Campbell Center for Nutrition Studies, December 24, 2018, Accessed January 15, 2020, https://nutritionstudies.org/benefits-fasting/#.

37 Chavda, *The Hidden Power of Prayer and Fasting*, p. 44.

38 Shelton, *The Science and Fine Art of Fasting*, p. 234.

39 Towns, *Fasting for Spiritual Breakthrough*, p. 193.

Chapter Twelve

1 May, *Addiction and Grace*, p. 137.

2 Welch, *Addictions: A Banquet in the Grave*, p. 47.

3 DeYoung, *Glittering Vices*, p. 184.

4 May, *Addiction and Grace*, p. 133.

5 Becky Dvorak, *Dare to Believe,* (PA: Destiny Image Publishers, 2012), p.89.

6 Allen Ross, "The Authority to Forgive Sins," Bible.Org, March 22, 2006, Accessed May 24, 2017, bible.org/seriespage/12-authority-forgive-sins-matthew-91-8.

Made in the USA
Monee, IL
20 August 2023